# PATHS

## I HAVE TRAVELED

# PATHS

## I HAVE TRAVELED

### What if?Expanded

RICHARD E. BUERY

| Library of Congress Control Number: | | 2019919683 |
|---|---|---|
| ISBN: | Hardcover | 978-1-7960-7331-7 |
| | Softcover | 978-1-7960-7330-0 |
| | eBook | 978-1-7960-7329-4 |

Print information available on the last page.

Rev. date: 12/04/2019

**To order additional copies of this book, contact:**
Xlibris
1-888-795-4274
www.Xlibris.com
Orders@Xlibris.com
805886

# CONTENTS

# 50<sup>th</sup> Wedding Anniversary Celebration

*Held at St. Gabriel's Episcopal Church.*
*Saturday April 26<sup>th</sup>, 2014*
*Renewal of Vows*
*Richard E & Olivia J Buery*

The celebrant was The Very Rev. Eddie Alleyne, with whom we were so very pleased and impressed with the solemnness of the service. The addition of the altar attendants contributed immensely to the service of "Renewal of Vows". Allow me to continue in this vain and note the participants:    Escorts- Ethan Buery, Noah Joyner, Sydney Lawson
Piano selections- Zoe Joyner and Charles Joyner
Readers- Jordan Lawson, Ellis Buery and Taylor Lawson
Organists- Roy Prescod, Quincy Dover and Karen Cox
Choir- The Roy Prescod Chorale
Closing remarks- Richard R. Buery

Most of all, the attendance of our family and friends. This includes those guests physically present and those present only in our hearts and mind.


======


Following, is my thank you address at the reception held immediately after the service in the Golden Hall.

*The blessings of a person is highlighted by the number of persons present at a celebration or occasion in their honor or on their behalf.*

*Having said that, we are therefore duly blessed, as indicated by your presence to celebrate with us this auspicious occasion. Olivia and I are very grateful for your presence.*

*Please allow me to read an excerpt from my book titled What If? Which is fitting for this occasion.*

*"The year 1964 was a monumental one. Throughout my life I have reflected on these seven (7) occurrences that are most important to me (Not counting my first car, a 1964 Ford Falcon)*

1. *John F. Kennedy, born May 29, 1917, at 43 years of age became the youngest man elected as president of the U.S.A. He will be remembered as a champion of Civil Rights. The governor of Alabama initially blocked the registration of 2 black students at the University of Alabama but was forced to step aside when confronted by the National Guard. Although President Kennedy was assassinated 11/22/1963, his speeches regarding this incident has been referred to as the defining moment towards the enactment of the Civil Rights Laws of 1964.*

2. *Nelson Mandela, born July 18, 1918, became a political activist during his early career as a lawyer and a member of the banned African National Congress (ANC). In 1964, he was arrested and sentenced to life in prison charged with plotting a violent revolution.*

3. *Shirley Chisolm, born 1924 in Brooklyn N.Y. to immigrants from the West Indies, she was the oldest of four girls. In 1964, she won a seat in the New York State Assembly as the first black congresswoman.*

4. *Malcom X was born on May 19th 1925 as Malcolm Little. His father was a Baptist Minister. Malcolm later became a Muslim minister and human rights activist. His 1964 visit to Mecca, Islam's holiest city, changed his approach to race. Malcolm X then believed in the possibility of brotherhood between black and white.*

5. *Dr. Martin Luther King Jr., was born January 15th 1929 in Atlanta, Georgia. His was also the son of a Baptist minister. Dr. King latter became a Baptist preacher and Civil Rights activist. Among other things, he is known for his famous speech during the March on Washington in 1963 "I have a dream" which is credited for the mobilization of supporters of desegregation and prompted the 1964 Civil Rights Acts. 1964 was also the year he was awarded the Nobel Peace Prize.*

6. *January 9th 1964 was one of the darkest moments between my native Panama and the USA. Panamanian students, in an effort to express*

*national pride, raised their nation's flag on a street light in the Panama Canal Zone. They were met with the force of the American military. There was rioting and several Panamanian's were killed. This event precipitated the eventual cessation of diplomatic relationship between the 2 countries.*

7. *I did mention 7 moments. Well this was the most personal moment. 50 years ago April 26th 1964 Olivia and I were joined in marriage at Holy Rosary Roman Catholic Church, Brooklyn. N.Y."*

This message was delivered after several speeches. I preempted it with some comments regarding the presence of so many friends, fellow members of the church, and participation of the Roy Prescod Chorale, who contributed to the Service by their rendition of choral selections, Also the master of ceremonies, Mr. Carlos Prescod, for the reception held immediately after, downstairs in the Golden Hall (aptly named, considering this is our Golden ceremony celebration).

My brother Roger toasted as the best man of our wedding 50 years ago, this was well delivered and received.

Rev. Lencia Garceran, Niece of the maid of honor Alicia Best (deceased) toast delivered in her absence. Also my Sister Yvonne Walcott who also toasted as an original member of the wedding party 50 years ago.

My thoughts at this moment, were on those members of the original wedding party who have gone on to a better place, Mr. Fernando Archibald. Ms. (Lelia) Alicia Best and Olivia's aunt Mrs. Gerdel Grant (R.I.P.)

Followed by Remarks from Ernesto Palache, Brother-in-law, on behalf of his family.

Who also served as photographer of this occasion?

Speech from the first born Samantha, who spoke on behalf of the three children, Sherena and Richard, on their involvement in planning this celebration. I expressed our gratitude to them and thanked all speakers who preceded me.

After delivering the message alluded to above, I threatened to read passage from my recently published book "What If?" Jokingly, of course, and to the delight of the audience, I instead proceeded to sing a serenade "Somewhere" from (west Side Story), to my wife with the able accompaniment on the piano by Mrs. Karen Cox.

At the beginning of this narration, I mentioned the 7 monumental occasions the year 1964 meant to me at which point I precluded my first car a 1964 Ford Falcon. Well at this time I will mention this car, I purchased it June 1966 from Hertz rent a car. I truly loved that car, it was a light green 4 door 6 cylinder and a very large trunk. I still have the registration the fee was $18.00. I used this car to take my driving lesson and am very proud to say that I passed the very first time I had a friend drive me to the testing location.

I had the shop manual and was able to keep it running very well, considering I was able to do most minor repairs and as the saying went, "take care of it and it would take care of you" we travelled to Ft Lauderdale, Florida several times, also to Ontario, Canada since we had a Time Share (Caribbean Beach Club) which has served us well, fortunately we were able to transfer to another Time Share and maintained 2 memberships until the original Co. went out of business.

As mentioned, this car had a rather large Trunk, which permitted us to accommodate all the lug gages plus a couple pillows, which was used at times when we pulled over at a rest station for a snooze. This was not always possible since Olivia became restless at the sound of other cars going and comings. Usually what I did was to start out early evenings, and drive until late and when possible, we will check into a motel/hotel with the kids, for overnight stay, and then get an early start continuing on and stopping for breakfast. This way we were on the road early in the day and made good travelling time, usually arriving at the resort at an appropriate check in time. Those were the days when Gas was affordable, so was food and lodging at the various rest stops. To be sure, we packed some lunch etc. to keep the energy up while travelling.

Since I mentioned Time Share. It was a very good thing for us as family travelling together, the children were young enough and able to share the same quarters. Also when traveling overseas, plane fare was affordable, this allowed us to visit faraway places such as Las Vegas, Hawaii, Mexico, Caribbean island and some. I was able to prepare our yearly Income Tax and usually from the returns, it was a boost in the Vacation travel expense. It was great while it lasted.

Gone are the days when food was served on the Plane flight, remember when we were able to pack some sandwiches and drinks to partake of on the plane, imagine, now even a bottle of water becomes a problem to take on an airplane. Air Travel used to be such a pleasure, now less than a pleasure, now more so a problem to be overcome, and a sigh of relief when arrived at destination.

# WHAT IF? CONTINUED/
## expanded (a fly on the wall)

Today Monday 4/28/14 after attending Sunday services and remaining at the church, attending to planning for our yearly Red Top dance sponsored by the Panamanian group, {as mentioned in book *What if?*} then, remaining for a conference held in the parish hall, a long Sunday afternoon. We rested for the remaining day. Monday it is up and try to make some order of previous chaos, and now here I am trying to record some instances, before the thought escape me.

I did make some parallel to the life of Malcolm X, where, his visit to *mecca* in 1964 was, shall we say? His" What *if?* Moment" which determined the re- direction of his thoughts, regarding brotherhood between white and black people. Compared to the moment where one's life take a turn for the better, in some specific situation. (+++) i.e. "when told not to be a follower, but instead be a leader" and there is an obvious indication where good things begin to happen with a positive direction.

Now that my book *what if? The Question or a Statement.* Has been published, I have set the date for the book signing for January 26th, 2014 (sounds familiar?) It was held at St. Gabriel's Church, and I would like to take this opportunity to thank The Very Rev Eddie Alleyne for his wonderful support in promoting the book signing, and actually purchasing some of the books for eventual distribution to special visitors on occasions, also to the Vestry and congregation for allowing me to have this presentation.

In addition to the book signing, I had prepared some of my photographs, including some of which were on display years ago at the Brooklyn Public library, where I had an individual photography showing, displaying places of interest I have visited throughout the years of travel, which was an added attraction, there was quite a good response from members of the church, family, relatives and friends who attended, I extend my gratitude.

Refreshments were prepared and served and I must thank Olivia for coordinating this effort also those persons who prepared and helped with the distribution. This made the occasion an enjoyable and memorable one.

Before going any further. There were a few omissions and errors which I must mention at this time. Firstly: The Photograph of myself used for the back cover and promotional pieces, was actually taken by my Daughter Sherena Lawson with her cell phone, at a ceremony held at the church. I have chided her (jokingly) at times, that the phone is not a camera, it was meant for communication (speaking).

Well, I stand corrected, since it was such a great photo of myself that I decided to use it for this project, and am therefore giving her deserved credit for it at this time.

Secondly: The spelling of the name of Mr. Euclid Jordon, which should be Jordan. I noticed after printing and apologized to him, but being the gentleman that he is, he said it was not a big deal, but since I have this occasion to refer to the book *What if?* Why not make it right huh? Thanks Euclid for your understanding.

I was truly overwhelmed with this undertaking and was mostly concerned with the reaction to this book, and what it really meant to me having taken this path, hence the title of the next endeavor, if I decide to follow up.

I would like to mention some of the reactions received regarding the book. The one which mostly "threw me for a loop" was while speaking to a very close family friend and telling them of the book (which I carried with me wherever I went) their 6 year son said to me, "you are an author". I was momentarily speechless, my mental thought was, (how about that, I really am)

After thanking him, I asked, where he knew about such things, His mother responded that he was learning about books etc. in school. Good for him I thought. This was a personal satisfaction to me.

Continuing in this vain, Ricardo (Rico) a high school classmate to whom I had mailed a copy of the book, e-mailed me telling of his reaction after reading it, he wrote "you now are on record with the library of congress." Wow, this further consolidated the previous thought. This is so satisfying to me (mentally) to know that my efforts were rewarded in some manner.

The following is an excerpt for an e-mail received from my friend CY (Euclid) mentioned above.

He picked up a news wire post fulfillment report by the book publisher, and this is his take on it.

(Quote) For (especially) those of us, of West Indian-Panamanian Heritage. Who were fully spiritually nurtured by our saintly ancestors through our formative/pre-adult life in the varied religious denominations in Panama- a critical key to character-building; though many of us were not aware at the time of its importance, there is a book recently penned by a staunch "church-rat"...up to this day, as I write, by the name of Richard Buery, prime mover of the St. Gabriel Episcopal Church crown heights, Brooklyn. Few people know of the story behind the successful erection/ongoing life of this church; which has had to overcome daunting challenges that have destroyed so many other churches which lack "spiritual intestinal fortitude" I implore you to get/read this book...for it reminds us of the way of life in these United States;....(end quote)

Yours- in –Christ.

Euclid C. Jordan

This was a very moving narrative by CY, asking my approval to transmit his entire message.

My response was.

Brother CY this is a wonderful compilation of thoughts, I am indeed grateful, please do. Thanks

Rich

Further reactions,

This from my friend Huge Winfield to whom I had mailed a copy of the book while he and family were traveling. I was anxious to know if he had reached the destination to which I had mailed the book especially since I ask for his unbiased reaction on reading it. Thankfully, I finally received a response by e-mail which reads in part as follows.

"Hey Rich,

First of all congratulation on the book. It brought back many memories for me. You also asked for comments on the script. Well I can tell you that the story presentation and the way it was written was pure Richard. We who grew up with you know this. Outside of our community group, however, I am not sure how the script would be received. People who do not know Richard, how Richard is and his personality will need, I think, to know you first before they will understand how you wrote this book. I think you have enough material about you, your family, etc. and your work, involvement in the construction of the Church to separate the two into two books. My take."

This is exactly what I needed to hear from a good friend. My response was as follows.

Hi Win.

Thank you so much for your response. Do you know? That was my initial thought. After getting into the book, I decided not to get too involved in my personal side, this is why I used excerpts of some of the personal situations, since it was not all about me. As you so aptly stated, there is enough information for separate covers. I had decided to do as you suggested, and have been gathering my thoughts for this very idea, but was not sure about my first attempt. I appreciate your candid observation, and will keep you informed with my progress.

Rich.

Overview from publisher. This from a good friend of mine Silvia Y Lavalas

"What I read thus far is interesting and makes me eager to obtain a copy of this autobiographical account of Richard's life growing up in Colon, rep of Panama, expanding his experiences in Brooklyn New York and being able to compare the shared similarities each of our lives has taken --especially that of being born in the great city of Colon, attending the same school, parents knowing each other and working together for most of our lives, our children growing up under similar circumstances and excelling as well, the great influence of the church lives ALWAYS. The Question asked by many of us but never taking the time to seek the answer, "WHAT IF?" gives us reason to pause and as "What if" at this time, What if we had stayed in Colon, Panama? What if we had said "yes" or "No" to the many challenges we have faced.

What if we had seized the opportunities presented to us without hesitation? I look forward to reading what I believe is going to be an inspirational autobiographical account of my brother in Christ, Richard's story.

Thank you for having the fortitude and courage to put your story to pen and paper. Many of us, I am certain, will live our lives in reading your account."

I take this opportunity to thank Silvia who I have known for most of my life, for her very kind thoughts, and trust that the book met some of her expectations.

As mentioned before, I always took some books with me wherever I went, at parties, gatherings, bus rides etc. When meeting friends and acquaintances I would tell about the book and from time to time I was able to sell a book. I would offer a book as a prize etc.

An example, while traveling to Chez B (Poconos) more about that later) It was a rainy day and on the highway I experienced a flat. That is a predicament since I was driving a loaded Jeep and did not have the heavy-duty jack required to remove the tire. We called the emergency service, and was not able to give an exact location, I did say it was raining, it was also foggy. Well to the best of our abilities, given the present situation, I tried to remove some of the lugs from the tire covered by a poncho which I luckily had in the truck. While trying in this endeavor, I saw a tow truck pull up behind us, what a relief, I asked the driver if he was sent by the service, he replied "no" he just saw that I was having a problem and therefore decided to help. Well you no doubt know that there is definitely a God. The tow truck operator was also having a hard time removing the tire, considering I had to drive on the flat a ways to get off the road onto the shoulder. Here is a *"what if?"* moment. Well after all is said and done, the spare connected and the stuff replace in the truck. I was so pleased that this was done. I offered to pay the operator for this yeoman job and coming to our aid. He would not accept payment. I then remembered that I had copies of my book, and asked his name and wrote it in the book with a message and signed it and offered it to him. He had to take it and was happy to receive it. The message I wrote was, ***there are good people in this world.***

There are times when visitors are in attendance to Service at St. Gabriel's Church, and I was asked to present a copy of the book. On such an occasion I made a presentation to the Ambassador of Grenada to the United Nations.

A published article about the appointment of my son Richard Buery as Deputy Mayor for Strategic Policy Initiatives by Mayor Bill de Blasio of New York, was sent him by Warden Stella.

I subsequently received an e-mail which reads in part, as follows:

"Please extend congratulations from the permanent Mission of Grenada to the United Nations to the extended family of Mr. Buery. It is in the spirit of values inculcated from the roots that has manifested such outcome. This prestigious appointment speaks well for the contributions which immigrants make toward the prosperity of the great USA...."

I expressed my gratitude to Stella for forwarding this information.


Further reactions:

This from another childhood friend Glenda "... I enjoyed reading your book though I wondered if you had had it edited. Some things were a bit unclear as far as what you meant to say"

*(As mentioned by Hugh Winfield --Further reactions --mentioned above, to understand me is to know me)*

Continuing, "in any case it's interesting to learn about someone else life experiences especially someone that you've known most of your life. It just shows that even though you may know someone under certain circumstances, you don't really know about them since you're not spending 24 hours a day with them. Even with someone of your own family, their experiences are often very different from yours.

It was also interesting to read about some of the struggles involved in such an undertaking, as constructing a new church building. I am sure you had to have a lot of patience and perseverance to see it through.

God always gives us the strength and the wherewith all to carry through the tasks that he puts before us. The best part is seeing the finished product.

Best wishes, Glenda"

Thank you Glenda, for your keen observations, and very kind words and wishes, I am grateful for your response.

Rich.

**I am not a writer, but yet I write. By writing my book *"what if? (The question or a Statement)"* and having it published, I suppose that makes me an author.**

I mentioned Chez B. Above, before going any further. Allow me to mention it at this time before it slips my thoughts. It was always my desire to build my own home, and made a promise to myself to accomplish this.

After my first job in this country, which was short, since the company was a victim of labor strike and as mentioned in the book What if? (Last in- first out) luckily the time I was told of this situation, and was notified on Monday that Friday will be my last day because of this situation, I therefore requested to be paid at this point, to which they agreed. Upon receipt of the check, I gathered my belongings and said my goodbyes. When reaching home, I was told by Olivia that someone called and left a number for me to call, which I immediately did. {Out one and right into another}

It was a job offer which without a doubt, I accepted. When I met the personnel manager, my first question was about a saving plan, he mentioned that it was available by payroll deduction, I consequently requested the maximum deduction, and it was implemented.

I mention this to explain how I came about, and was able to eventually purchase a home therefore, fulfilling my promise to be able to have a home to bring my children into. After some years I purchased a parcel of land in the Poconos area and eventually drew a plan based on my idea of a house, and consulted a builder with whom I maintained contact via frequent visits, phone calls and photos, where he would appraise me of each phase of the building progress.

I must mention at this point, before going on, architecture was one of my favorite subjects. *"Dibujos arte mecanic as"* roughly translated, "Mechanical drawings" Which is self-explanatory.

Unfortunately, this required extended scholastic preparation, consequently additional financial outlay and ultimately, more years in school, neither of which I was in a position to address.

I did the next best thing, always read books on the subject, which helped me to better understand and interpret the building plans as presented by the architect for ST. Gabriel's Church. It also gave me a working knowledge in developing plans for our own (vacation) home **Chez B.** The plan drawings as presented to the builder was followed, with the exception that while excavation was in progress, the area presented some problems, the abundance of stones required blasting, I therefore suggested the he flipped the plan over which resulted in the present format, where The entrance was reversed (Not a great problem) through the living room as opposed to the kitchen area.

My acquired savings were not much, but it enabled me to get things going, also keep financial investments at a minimum whereby the builder would finish only the basic living area, and I would finish the basement area. Some weekends I was able to have my son Richie with me to help get the major part of finishing done, such as hanging doors and some painting and floor tiling building partitions etc.

From time to time as I go up there, I would do a project such as laying tiles finishing closets etc. and eventually it became something to be proud of. This is the place I call **Chez-B** it is a place to have family and friends visit and spend some togetherness time.

With that, let me get back to where I left off. With my book completed and published, I am now faced with the task of getting it exposed and distributed to readers, other than my friends some of which I have mentioned above and am very grateful for their response.

I am quite aware that the audience, readership, is very limited due to the fact that the subject is related to the building of a new church in Brooklyn, NY. Something I am told, was not possible. But we have overcame the arduous task of making this happen in spite of all the negative situations we had to overcome as outlined in the book *"What if?"*.

There is still more to come, we found it necessary to replace the (lift) with an elevator, since it was not adequate for the actual predicament we have found ourselves in, as a result of our outreach program which includes an active and ever increasing Senior center, also increased activities, we now find ourselves in a situation where there is not enough space to put anything, we now have materials, office & household supplies stored in hallways, stairways, under stairs, sheds built in the patio. Anywhere we can find some place to put things.

We have put into place a proposed second floor over the lobby, plans have been drawn up, bids have been set into motion and loans have been applied for, Banks have denied our loan (nothing new here) We are now looking for a Church Building fund Loan for the past 3 years, and are very hopeful this will be forthcoming shortly.

In preparation, we prevailed on the elevator Co. To actually install a 3 stop elevator which extends to the area over the lobby in anticipation of the proposed expansion, and the area is presently enclosed with a matching brick enclosure until such time, and they will then unlock the elevator exit to this additional space when completed. Hopefully this would have been a fact when this book is published (hope this is not wishful thinking) as time proceed I will go into details of this project. (*Hasta entonces*) Until then.

# New business

At this point it is very obvious to me that my book *"What if? The Question or a Statement"*,

It is a forerunner or should I say a prelude to the things I really wanted to write about.

There are quite a lot of things that I would have liked to mention but because of the original project there were some self-imposed limits such as emphasis on my personal life growing up in Colon, Panama. As previously mentioned it would have highlighted the *Path I had taken*.

When I hear of or see photos of Colon, it leaves quite a void, to say the least. For what has become of where I came from. Therefore it is one of my primordial reason to try and relive the moments each time I am in the company of friends and acquaintances and always take the occasion to talk about the "old days", since it is all in our memories, especially since it is no longer there.

Those 16 streets and an equal amount of avenues were my world and a really, really wonderful world we lived in. This is why old photos and times spent, meant so much. At any given moment, someone may say to you "Do you remember...?" And your thoughts goes back to said time and place and a flood of good feelings begins to manifest itself in your memory. Those were the good old days, you would say. (Not to mention, some not so good days.)

*Friends are like possessions (working or not). As long as I keep them,*
*they are mine.*

This is a statement printed somewhere in my book I wonder who might
have seen it, however this is what I truly believe.

As a lad growing up with my Mom and sister living at Theater building
7th. Street. My playground used to be from our room outside the balcony,
to the end of the building, we used to play games, from that balcony down
into the yard, I used to shoot my Daisy rifle (b.b). Targets were placed on
Garbage cans or at times a stray Cats in the yard. Became targets. At other
times I made a target with a bar of soap in a cardboard box and placed it
at the end of the balcony on evenings when everyone was in their rooms.
I did this until one evening while shooting at the cats or cans, I noticed
a man standing in the stair case of the building beside ours.

Well the next time I saw a cat crossing, I could not resist the impulse to
fire at it. After that I heard someone running up our steps and realized
it was the man I previously noticed, so I grabbed my rifle and tried
to run past him into our room, he tried to take my rifle and I was a
small chap but a bit feisty so he could not get it from me, with this
commotion, my mother came out to see what was happening, the man
said I was shooting into his window across the patio. I said that was
not the case, after he explained where he lived, I then realized that the
b.b's were at times, ricocheting off the zinc platforms into his window,
well I apologized but still refused to let him take my rifle. Well my
mom interceded and said to him, she would take it away from me, this
placated him somewhat.

That was the end of my nighttime target shooting. My mom hid the
rifle from me temporarily, but as mentioned, my sister and I always re-
decorated the room for a new look from time to time, consequently, I
found the rifle but due to respect for Mom and the others in the area, I
only took the rifle in a case which I made out of heavy material, with
me when going to Camp or outings. Along with my handmade Bow
& Arrow. Oh yes I had one of those which I made, it was quite good
since during my weekends at the trade shop (cabinet making) where

my Godfather worked, I had a pick for the right kind of wood, and made the Bow.

Allow me to tell about a typical evening in Colon.

Let's start with Sunday:

Mom would get up early to attend the early morning service at Christ Church and she would be gone until about 7:30–8:00 then change into uniform for work, it was white and the "cool" thing about it was that the buttons were large studs with a Lupe which was connected with metal clip. These were removed for washing and ironing, remember the starch? These uniforms were always bleached and starched. After ironing we had to replace the buttons for her.

This is a good time to talk about washing, most of these buildings had an inner court yard, where a number of corrugated zinc was placed on platforms each person had theirs, or a group would have joint ownership. The white clothes were washed and left soaking to be spread out on these zinc platform, to be sunned (bleached) after Mom would ask us to go get the clothes, then she would wash them again then rinse. Then came another phase, usually between buildings, we would string rope and pulleys, which you shared with the person on the opposite building. There was the bag of clothes pins which you used to hang your clothes out to dry. Washing whites was about a two day project. Then the ironing.

Now that this is out of the way, I remember there was an old lady and her daughter we called Mina, We never see the mother Dada out of her room, anyway one evening the lady (Mina) said to me, "You don't know this, but your father watches over you when your mother is gone, {Mind you, my father died when I was 1 year old} I always see him sitting outside the door, until it's time for your mother's return". This was a strange thing for Mina to tell me. I used to sit by myself seemingly in a trance at times. This used to cause my mother some concern but Mina would tell her it was not a problem that it was my way to concentrate. Her words were (day dreaming).

Continuing with Sunday: Mother would go to the early morning service. After her return, we would get breakfast and ready for church, she went off to work and we off to church, on the way we would each get an *empanada* cornmeal patty with meat which we ate on the way to Christ Church, as part of our breakfast, since it was going to be a long day. That's a walk of approximately 6 blocks (From7th Street to 1st street}

Church at 9:00 a.m. Followed by Sunday school. Back home for lunch and possible change of clothing since we had another Sunday school at the Methodist church. I think that was 3:oo p.m. At times when we got a little older I would meet my friend and go to an early movie to be out in time to walk home and then some dinner then it's off to Christ Church by-the-sea for 7:00 P.m. service. I sang in the Choir. After service I along with others of our group, would walk down the park on central Ave which runs the length of the city. Noticed I said "I" since my sister went her own way with her girlfriends. Our group would continue on to one of the night clubs called Esquire, hence the term *"from choir to Esquire"*. When returning home. Sister and I would meet at a pre- determined place and go home together. That's how it was on Sunday.

Monday starts the school week;

I usually meet friends on the corner and walk to school (high School) it's a long walk and mostly sunny, so I usually have my Parasol. (*Interpretation.* For sun).There is usually a lot going on in school but on Monday we had to be on time before the gate closes since there is an assembly in the yard where we salute the flag and sing the national and the school anthems. If you are late and left outside, you would try to get it by some means even if it meant scaling the back fence, because all late comers are marched to the dean's office (Director) and issued some sort of punishment (late notice) We tried to avoid this embarrassment.

The students uniforms were as follows, in the first cycle (1–3 year) girls: blue pleated skirts with white short sleeved sailor collar blouse. Boys: Blue trousers white short sleeved shirt and blue tie.

Second cycle (4-6year) Girl's same thing except long sleeved. Boys: same thing except long sleeved shirts: always buttoned and white.

We were well dressed and always sharp looking in our uniforms. Most of us were very conscious of this, especially on Mondays, we went home half day and it was not unusual that we took our shirts off to air it and keep fresh (remember it is hot at midday) and replaced in time to get back to school on time, You must know that absence and tardiness is part of your overall score in your report card, which detract from your final notes.

That was Monday to Thursday. Friday being the last day of school, things got a little relaxed, some of the older girls would take a blouse in their bags and some of the boys would wear an undershirt and after school, sometimes a short day they would replace their blouses, since it was a very distinct one-of-a-kind blouse. There has been occasions, on a short day the director would go into the movies and have the lights turned on and pick out all the *Abelistas* (girls from Abel Bravo (Colegio Abel Bravo) the shirts had a patch CAB) on the pockets this is the reason they had to cover or change blouses.

Do you remember...? On one of such encounters. We had a short day and the Math. professor before the last class was absent (he usually is) our last class was English, most of us, the English speaking students, decided to cut the last two classes and we went into the back woods to get mangoes, well on the way home it started to rain and we eventually got to where we could get a bus. Most of us did not have fare. So we decided to con the driver into giving us rides 2 for the price of one, he allowed it, but speaking about *"it take a village to raise a child"*, someone in the bus knew my mother, so offered to pay for me, this was good but not good. Good: because I had a ride. Not good: because my mother will hear about this episode.

Besides having the riot act read to me by mother, on Monday when we had English class, the professor also read us the riot act about a *Golpe de Estado* "Government coup". When the class was assembled, he said to us." *La pequena republica Del 6o comercio se ha declarado Viernes el dia libre"*

(*Translation*) "The little republic of the 6ᵗʰ year commerce division has declared Friday a free day". After we tried to explain the situation at the time, he was not having any of this.

That was a typical week, so let's go on to Saturday:

Saturday we were able to get things ready for Monday since we had no time on Sunday to do this. My day usually started early in the morning, I would put on my bathing suit and a pair of old shorts and sneakers along with my inner tube (Given me by my Grandfather) and its off to the beach. I was living at 8ᵗʰ and central Ave. A short walk along this street to the beach. After disrobing and finding a big rock and wrapping my clothes in a bundle and placing the rock on it in the event of rain and also to keep from blowing away and in a safe visual area.

Sometimes I met some friends and spent a lot of time in the water. Our beach was not sandy where you could sit on the sand with snacks etc. But we had areas in the water where we could rest on "Big Iron" a platform built over a submerged engine which could not be removed therefore it was decided to build a concrete platform over it, it was great for diving off into my inner tube (carefully) or to take off swimming towards "Long Iron" Which is parallel with Big Iron.

"Long Iron" is part of a pier footing with part of the metal pylon standing tall. When swimming long distance from Big iron, this is a stop off resting place, on the way to 9ᵗʰ street beach, this was a little more like a beach since there was more level grounds where you could sit on the beach per Se. Even though I rather liked to enter the beach from the 7ᵗʰ street side with all its stones since, sitting on the beach was not my thing (9ᵗʰ street). Furthermore there are places to hide your clothes among the rocks. (7ᵗʰ street). There was always water coconut to get from the area. Water and the Jelly (Soft coconut) kept us nourished for the day.

So far I mentioned 7ᵗʰ and 9ᵗʰ street areas of the beach. You see, the 8ᵗʰ street area in not really a beach, this is the area where the remains of a pier is located submerged below waterline the surface in not graduated as is 7ᵗʰ & 9ᵗʰ. This is the area I mentioned in my book *What If?*

To elucidate. On one occasion while I was swimming long distance accompanied by a friend with my inner tube, we departed from "Big iron" past "Long iron" since the inner tube was within reach with my friend on it, so I continued swimming past 8th street area towards 9th beach, when reaching there, we decided to rest a bit.

It was on our return trip that after swimming a bit, on passing the 8th street area. Before going on with this narrative, let me make one thing clear. This was not your ordinary car tire inner tube. It was a rather large one, perhaps from a truck, which my grandfather had acquired. As I started to say, as I was swimming, I insisted that my friend Lali keep the tube going at a steady pace in order for me to maintain a comfortable stride, at one point as I reached for the touch of the tube in my stride, it was not there so I looked up to assure that the tube was still within reach while swimming.

Well Lali tapped me on the head to say that there is a shark in that area, on looking to the shore I realized the we both were to only ones in the otherwise filled beach, in the water, without even seeing a shark it was the wisest thing to get to hell out of the water so I joined him on the tube by resting my upper body on one edge, and he sitting on the other edge of the inner tube we both became one person he the hands and I the feet, so we propelled that tube as if were a motorboat. Even though the calls from shore were to come in, but since we both knew that there is an underwater structure at that point, we continued on to the 7th street beach. After been safe on land, my legs began to swell from the exertion, therefore I decided to take a quick short swim to loosen out my leg muscles.

After standing on shore for a while we suddenly saw the size of the shark which was trapped among the submerged remains of the pier. It became beached and a fisherman tried to harpoon it but missed his target, and the shark was able to wiggle away and got into the deep area and swam away. This was a reality check, and indeed a *What if?* Moment.

In retrospect, I wonder at what point was this shark sighted, since, when we both departed from the 9th street landing, everyone was in the water as usual. The sighting of the shark obviously prompted all to get out of the water, except us, since obviously we were unaware of its presence. Was the shark in the area all the time submerged? Or did it come in towards the shore passing us on the way in? (That's an ironic and troubling thought, now that I can speak of it).

While recounting this experience, and narrative from the book to some friends, one said it was just made up by me, well I started to say "no it really happened", but decided not to, since it was a fact and was not worth me trying to justify it to him. Anyway, I am here to tell the tale. (Pun intended) Normally on Saturdays after beach, we went to our separate homes, I would take a shower, wash the sand and salt clothes and hang them out to dry, and store my tube on top of our outdoor room (kitchen). In the afternoon after some lunch, and out to the park for long walks, meetings with friends or attend to any other things such as visits or meetings which were not scheduled during the week. Sometimes I had to go to the tailor where I apprenticed. Some other Saturdays when not going to the beach I also went to a trade with my godfather (cabinet making as was recently alluded to.

Further on I will mention some of the things which occupied my evenings and Saturdays

Ciao for now.

Hold the press.

Today August 27th 2015 I received a mail from a relative of Olivia who presently resides in Baltimore Md. We were puzzled who was it meant for, since it was addressed to me and not her. Well since it was obviously for me, proceeded to open it. Seemed to be a book of some sort, and lo and behold, it was a copy of my book *What if* accompanied with a note. Seemed he purchased it on line.

The note reads in part. Dated August 17, 2015 "Dear Richard,

Hope this little note finds you and Cousin Olivia doing well, I want to let you know I have read your book *What if?* I enjoyed the contents... Life in Panama was strikingly interesting.

A friend of mine just returned from Panama, now wants to retire there. Any chance that's what you and Olivia have planned? For me, reading the book has confirmed my desire to visit my mother's homeland, my roots. I'm hoping to make that a reality by 2018. From your escapades, looks like I would need at least 2 weeks. Thanks for the tour... Colon here I come/ Are there any relatives still there? Or are they all now in the USA?

I like to commend you on the part you played with the building of your church to its present status. I'm doing OK....here in Baltimore city.

Can you please autograph my book and return it I would greatly appreciate it. Hugs and kisses to my Cousin Olivia.

BOBO." (His nickname)"

I will say that I immediately autographed the book along with detailed note and some maps of Colon, with points of interest outlined including the beach I spoke of in the book. Mailed it back to him the very next day.

It is such a good feeling that I was able to inspire someone to some extent. Thanks Bobo Blessings to you.

Sorry, I had to interrupt my narrative, but this was so special to me that I had to include it.

As can be noted from time line, this is not an ongoing narrative, anyway, let me continue. I will enclose at some point, a map of (My world), to further explain the city of Colon and the beach area (Scene of the shark encounter)

Continuing with Saturday. As age continues, this routine differs, Friday evenings to the tailor, then Saturday mornings continuing in this endeavor, learning to sew my own as well of others clothes. I was able to make some pocket change doing this. There is a bit of history I will tell here.

The reason I mentioned Friday (a method to my madness) here it is. After school I went to the shop where there was always some work for me, the tailor would have customers for measurements etc. He would have some kind of clean-up work for me to complete namely, Button holes or edging the inseam of pants or tying off all loose ends on the work piece, then ironing the seams flat after which the Pants are ready for final pressing for eventual pick- up by customer. While I am doing this, he is measuring new customers and marking their pants cut, he will then fold each with their respective names etc., and neatly stack them for eventual cutting. The reason I go on Fridays is that I knew he did this on Fridays, therefore I was interested in learning to cut the work. Well after doing what I did I will then sweep up and he will close shop.

So on Saturdays I supposed he will open the individual work and mark and cut the pieces for the next job. Somehow however, regardless of how early I got there, all the work is already cut and ready for processing. How is this I wondered? After all, I cleaned up and he locked the shop.

Well, there were times I will meet my friends or going somewhere, I would pass the shop, and realized that there is a light in there even though the shop is closed. It dawned on me this is when he actually cut the work, a definite effort on his part, to keep me in the dark (so to speak).

You see, I was a quick learner so making a pair of pants was becoming second nature to me, the crux of the matter is, and I had to learn to measure and apply the measurement to the piece of cloth and then cut it for the eventual manufacturing of the garment. It became a cat and mouse game even when I got there earlier, the work was already cut. I was now convinced this was his way of keeping me out of this phase.

As the saying goes, "Story came to question". We were approaching the (*Fiestas Patrias*) National holidays, this is when most tailor shops are quite busy making uniforms therefore lots of pants to be made. I too had to have mine made therefor gave him my material earlier with the hopes that he would at least make mine before the rush. Not a chance, I therefore became anxious, and asked Mom her assessment to this situation. One of her dear friend's husband was a tailor Mr. George Hibbert.

My course of action was to withdraw my material from Mr. Clark and Mr. Hibbert was kind enough to cut my work, -a sigh of relief- I then asked my Mom to get me some of the heavy brown wrapping paper used in the commissary, you know the kind that was on a roll and used to wrap the produce as it is dispensed.

Armed with the paper, I placed in on a board and with the Iron, was able to press it flat and then pinned the material on it which allowed me to mark and cut the pieces, using my measurements I was then able to prorate the width and length for each piece for further references.

Bingo> Now I am able to sew for others by taking their measurements, compared it to mine, add or reduced as necessary. As mentioned before I knew how but did not know how to cut so there was no stopping me now (smile) to my Friend George, Your Dad got me started Thanks.

After a time, the patterns was no longer necessary since **REPITITION IS A GREAT TEACHER**.

My grandfather got me a priceless book on the art of measure ring and cutting pants and Jackets which I was able to do after a time. This is the way I was able to increase my pocket change, since I was now in the market during the *fiestas Patrias.(holidays)* I don't know what ever became of the book but be assured I used it assiduously.

*Pants cut.*

There were a few stores dedicated to tailors and those persons who wanted to buy a pants cut.

The stores had on display all types of materials from English tweed etc. The *pants cut* comprised of pre-cut cloth approximately 36 inches wide and a yard and a half long folded in half or you can have the store keeper cut this from a selected bolt. The tailor get his thread to match, required buttons, marking chalk, a wad of bees wax, used to fortify the thread for sewing buttons, a poplin material for pockets, also silk for jacket lining and all other necessary materials.

His tools, beside a good sewing machine, also comprised of several cutting shears, thimble, needles and chalk, not to omit the ever present measuring tape which is unique in that it has a 3inch metal tip (first three inches) this allows him to properly measure the inseam of a client. Know what I mean? It gives you sort of a tip to place the tape without getting personal.

A bit of levity here, as mentioned above, when measuring a male for a pair of pants, first you take a waist measurement, then a measurement around the hips, next their outer seam then the proverbial inseam. The difference will be the crotch accommodation.

I also used to make trousers/slacks for girls, as can be noted, the sequence is quite different, after the waist and hips for obvious reasons, usually we forgo the inseam, we take an outer length measurement from waist to ankle and calculate the difference in order to have a proper fit (know what I mean?) This does not always work, therefore when necessary, I will then ask the girl to place her skirt between legs in order to have a visual idea of where the inseam should be, if she is wearing slacks at time of measurement, this step is obviously omitted. It's a delicate situation if I do say so myself, I usually make allowances for ultimate correction on pre-fitting this usually work out in the long run. I guess you will have to use your imagination in this instance.

Like the doctor who is readily identified by the ever present stethoscope around their neck, the Tailor usually has his measuring tape around his neck, and sometime a few pins in his lapel or collar, also a trusted yard stick which is used when marking the pants cut. I have outlined all this to acquaint you with what it takes to get started, well as mentioned above, I have my pattern which have been outlined on the brown paper. Now with my *pants cut,* I also needed a flat piece of cardboard to lay on a table in order to spread out the material on which I will place the required pattern and use pins to secure it, after making the necessary adjustment (depending on individual measurements) i.e. If my waist is 40 inches, and the measurements of the new customer is more or less,

I will make the necessary calculations and make the chalk marks, after verifying (check twice) once the material is cut there is no going back.

As mentioned, I have to use pins since most cuts are doubled (back/front)-(left/right) this brings to mind. Why the term (A pair of pants)? Go figure. Anyway, once the cut is made, the manufacturing begins. Bear in mind, this was before we had all the new improvements in sewing machines, such as fancy stitches to self-edge the pants seams. All this was done manually, needle and thread with your thimble to protect your middle finger which is used to push the needles, or as I became more proficient with the machine I will manually zig-zag the edges as I stitch the length of the material. There were times that the machine needle catches my finger, which is quite painful as you can imagine, I have some lingering marks to attest to this fact.

After finishing the product, sometimes, if requested, I would have the customer come for a fitting, to verify form (we are not all formed the same) and length. Once satisfied, I will clean up the work i.e. Taking out all basing threads, tying off excess thread, I forgot to mention that it was also necessary to have a bar of bees wax which is used to wax the thread when manually sewing on the buttons (pants/Jacket) Then take it to the shop for pressing, and ultimate delivery or pick-up.

So that's it in a nutshell.

While on this, My Grandfather also taught me the art of caning rattan chairs (know those steam-bent chairs- sitting, armchairs, rocking chairs and settees.) I was able to increase my pocket change during the Christmas holidays, when households were sprucing up their homes, I would then take my gear to their homes and repair holes in their chairs or completely make it over. I was able to determine cost based on the size of the chairs, and the amount of material necessary to complete the particular job, as an example, there was more time spent on the rocking chairs since there was the seat and the back rest. Then the settee which was longer and the arm chair a bit larger than the sitting chair.

Before going any further, my "gear" consisted of a pocket knife to fashion pegs from a strip of wood, which are used to anchor the ends of caning strips in the holes as the process begins, also the cane material and separate the approximate amount for a specific job and after stripping the loose sides, I would soak it in water overnight, this process allows the cane to be flexible and pliable to work with. Once the job is completed and cleaned up, with the new cane, and when necessary, some stain on the wooden frame, we have a practically new piece of furniture for the holiday season.

There is an addition to my change can. Usually I am able to cover my holiday expenditures, know what I mean? With these additional sources of income, including odd and ends, painting and helping to run errands, also my weekend Jobs selling "Club" I spoke of in my book *What If?* For good order sake, I will briefly outline what this entailed. With my trusted bike, I used to take around a catalog supplied by a furniture store owned by Mr. Markland, to show prospective customers, who would select from jewelry, household items, furniture etc. And would make a specified deposit.

The selected items are then ordered and reserved for the client, and eventually delivered after a short period of time depending on cost. the catch was that this deposit is paid weekly based on the National Lottery for every week until the chosen number plays, at which time the client has ownership. This was a good thing since the payment is made until the number plays it could be the first, second third, tenth etc. Week. And the selection is yours. (No more payments)

The deposit is proportioned according to the value of the item and usually until the total cost is achieved. As an example, I personally purchased a "Laguna "wrist Watch, and selected my number. My weekly payment was $1:00 which was deducted from my weekly commission. Unfortunately my number did not play for the year so the watch cost me the total $52.00, the good thing was at least I had the use of the watch all the time. Mind you, that was in the 1950's, it is now the year 2016 and I still have that watch, working I might add, I only had the crystal changed and a new watch band from time to time. $52.00 well spent. Won't you say?

As I started to say, the commissions earned was added to my cash can. I mention all this to further indicate that even though my mother did all she could to see that we were always able to do the things we needed to, this was my way to make sure that her burden was somewhat lightened, since when there is a Dance, Outing, Picnic, trip etc. I always try to be able to have my share of the cost covered.

Along with what my Mom was able to accumulate, and help from my friend, I was able to contribute to my travel expense to the United States (remember my *cash can?)* it's in the book.

Another apology to be addressed, in the book I mentioned the group of girls my sister Yvonne hung out with. Inadvertently I called them *"Las Industriosas"* (The industrious girls) these were another set of girls mostly from The Methodist church. My Sister's group was actually called *"Las Corazones" (the hearts),* these were mostly from Christ Church, there was sort of a friendly rivalry among them, So sorry for this, however, this was an honest mix-up on my part, since I was actually friends with all of them From Christ Church and as mentioned, I also attended the Methodist church so there you are. *Perdoname.* (Forgive me).

Growing up we hear quite a number of sayings by our elders, especially regarding animals and

Insects, to name a few.

| | |
|---|---|
| ANIMALS= | Bulls or Oxen --strong as a bull--Ox |
| | Mules--Stubborn as a mule |
| | Fox-- Sly as a fox |
| INSECTS= | Ants-- fidgety as if he had ants in his pants |
| | Bees -- busy as a bee |
| | Flies-- I wish I was a fly on the wall |
| | Bugs-- bug the line--snug as a bug. |
| | Butterfly--float like a butterfly |
| | Drone-- (a male honey bee) *old dictionary* - you go on and on. |
| | *(*New dictionary*) also a* -A radio controlled airplane |
| | Mouse--(small rodent) -- quiet as a mouse |
| | (New *dictionary)*--an app for use with a computing. |
| | Ticks-- like a tick in my skin. |

These are a few of the common ones I used to hear as a lad, so for the purpose of this story, I choose to use the Fly which is an interesting insect as outlined on pages that follows.

When a person is interested in the action of another and is curious of what that person is about behind closed doors, you would hear this phrase. "I wish I was a fly on their wall", in order to see what goes on.

### THE FLY ON THE WALL

The head of the fly contains the eyes, antennae and mouth parts.

The Antennae provide flies with their primary source of smell.

The eyes are some of the most complex of the insect world, they are compound organs that are comprised of thousands of individual lenses, which are capable of detecting both the polarization of light and Color spectrum unseen by human eyes, allowing them to detect and react to movements at a quicker pace.

This allows the fly to see a significant radius around their body, this makes flies difficult to surprise, flick or swat.

### "I WISH I WAS A FLY ON THE WALL"

When wanting to see ones surroundings without been detected also to know what's going on the other side.

With this in mind, there is a story told me some time ago which I would narrate at a later time, since at this time in my life I have had some experiences which I must address. It has been some time since I have written anything. The date is now January 28th 2016. Therefore here goes.

On the Sunday of our yearly parish meeting I was scheduled to address the parishioners of the progress of negotiations in order to obtain Building permit. This was to be done after the service where everyone was to go downstairs to the "Golden hall" where the meeting was to be held. Much to my surprise, while the sermon was been delivered by Fr. Alleyne it also included the enactment of an interview I had with one of the oldest member of the Original church for inclusion in my Book *What if?* To say the least, this was flattering for me, especially after noticing the "actors" coming on the Altar, each with a copy of the book.

I was then asked to deliver my report at that time. I did not have my notes since, as mentioned above, this was to be done later. I took this opportunity to thank him for the inclusion, then proceeded to deliver my report, off the cuff. I then promised that on the coming Monday I will be on the phone, doing my very best to get the ball rolling.

As promised. I spent the day on the Phone and desk top with the Architect, Expediters, Title Insurance Co, City Register and others, in order to have all pertinent documents and drawings approved by the city and issuance of building permit. Before the week's end I was happy to hear from the responsible parties that all papers were properly prepared and recorded by the City Register, and also that the plans were approved and permit available to be picked up.

The next Sunday was a celebration of Martin Luther's Day, and the sermon delivered by Fr. Alleyne was primarily based on his life work and achievements. While listening to the sermon, I recognized some of the information which I had included in my Book *What if?* Another surprise for me. To add to this, I was able to address the congregation with the good news.

For good order sake and information, the building permit alluded to above, is for pending expansion of the Church Building in the form of the 2nd floor. We are on the way to getting this project started as soon as weather permits. I will report on this project as it progresses. It would be a great thing if this addition is completed in time for the celebration of our *Silver Jubilee.*

We are approaching 25 years since the new building was consecrated (1991) therefore the year 2016 will be called St. Gabriel's **SILVER JUBILEE** I will like to offer my view as an addition to the journal.

# St Gabriel's Episcopal Church

**Celebrating its silver jubilee.**

The original church located at 331 Hawthorne Street. Brooklyn N.Y was dedicated in 1905 and had served us well throughout these 86 years. It was not the most comfortable building as the years extended, but it was the place where we enjoyed worship and fellowship despite hardships.

As time continued and the need became more evident due to space and facilities were desperately required, we were faced with the thought of repairing and eventual expansion. After a few attempts were made by repairing the roof and flooring, it was obvious that continually trying to repair the boiler and pipes, which at time during the service, would begin to rumble and leaking, not to mention that during rain, the roof would leak. Another path had to be pursued.

Before going on with this, it is expedient that I start from the beginning as I knew it, and heard of, This Church with which we had become enamored.

The year 1905 was a bit before my time, therefore I will tell you what I have heard from predecessors. The parish house which is still standing and serves as our legacy, has a cross at the top with a legend In Memory of Anne Polk date 1872-1907on the front of the building. No one can determine what this means, therefore we can only assume that perhaps this person lived for 35 years and at some time later this was placed at the top of the building in her memory. Keep in mind that the church was consecrated year 1905 which is 2 years prior to her supposed demise.

It started out as a rather large property adjacent to it, which was used to park the conveyances of worshipers at St Paul's Church Flatbush, and other churches in that are (supposedly White) The workers would remain here and then return to pick up their employers after their service was over, to return them to their respective homes.

There was a need for a place of worship for the employees and consequently, the decision to provide such a place became necessary. The area next to the parish house (as we know it) a foundation was dug and cement walls were installed. Due to lack of finance, this project could not go forward. It was then decided to place a roof over this opening, and a church building was erected. This explains why in order to enter, one had to descend a few stairs. The roof line was located at the area now visible as a ledge where the windows of the house sits. From this explanation, it must be noted that the worship area was below street level. The present parking area of the new building is where the previous church was located.

1905 to 1960 I can recount from 1960 as was told to me by Mrs. Sheila Flawn who I had interviewed. She came to the US that year and visited St Gabriel's Church where Fr. Cowan and his mother were living at (331 Hawthorne St.). Eventually the 2nd floor was removed and converted into our parish house. During this time the church became a White people's church.

As Mrs. Flawn told it, when she visited the church there were only two other black persons as congregants there, who were actually caregivers. She continued to attend services there which were conducted daily. She became attached to St. Gabriel's church and Fr. Cohen was very good to her during his term. He was eventually transferred to St John's Episcopal Church.

Still a mission, the diocese started to send priests to be selected by the executive committee. During our conversations, she related an amusing story of one of the priest who was black with a white wife. One morning there were about twelve persons in church and he introduced his wife, who refused to shake their hands. And Sheila said to her "so what happen, you can't shake our hands? If you can't we don't want you".

Then came Fr Thompson who was selected by the executive committee. Well I can take it from here, since this is when I came to St. Gabriel's church as related in my book *What if?* The year was 1966. This is when the congregation began to increase and as mentioned above, after a series of priests and in the year 1979 came the appointment of Rev. Andries during which time St. Gabriel's continued to increase.

On Saturday February 20th 1982 at the 115th convention of the Diocese of Long Island St. Gabriel's Episcopal Church was made a **Parish** and enrolled as a member of the Diocese of L.I.

_=_=_=_=

### *The covenant of St Gabriel's Church*

**Thankful to God's abundant goodness and for his great gifts of salvation through Jesus Christ our Lord, I hereby covenant to seek, to know, to do his will, and to promote as far as I can, the interest of Christ's kingdom.**

**Heaven accepted the lord Jesus Christ as my personal savior. The Bible of God's revelation of himself and as my supreme standard of faith and practice, I seek fellowship with all who devoutly love the Lord Jesus Christ and accept His standard of teaching and conduct as set forth in the Testament.**

**Realizing that the success of the church depends upon the consecration of its individual members, I Covenant to uphold it by my prayers, to attend its services, to contribute to its support, to labor to maintain its peace and harmony, and as far as possible, in every way, to promote its temporal and spiritual welfare.**

_=_=_=_=

A decision was made to build a new edifice instead of spending each time to repair the frequent damages. A building fund was instituted and founded by various means too many to enumerate at this point. It was a joint effort by all persons, also contributions from many churches in the diocese of L.I, as well as other denominations in the city, which helped us to repay several loans, obtained from Banks, Episcopal Church Building Fund and from the General Loan Fund of the diocese. Thankfully, we were able to repay all our loans before maturity.

During the construction of the building, we were blessed to be offered a place to worship, by The Roman Catholic church St. Francis of Assisi located at 335 Maple Street between Nostrand and New York Avenues, Our neighbor. This enabled us to continue worshiping as a body.

This was not an easy effort, we had to approach two different architects. The first design was not compatible with our needs but we were finally satisfied with the outcome of the second and present design after few changes and revisions, contractors, sub- contractors, labor disputes which only delayed the project and increased the cost. But through it all, and by the extraordinary input of the congregation and personal friends other Churches, fraternal organizations etc. and most of all, the Grace of God; It was accomplished.

## The Silver Jubilee of ST. Gabriel's Episcopal Church Celebration

### Is

### Also the 34th year as a parish

Well here we are after much haggling, phone calls and e-communications, we are ready to start the expansion program, heavy machinery for excavation etc. has been brought in and the digging has started. Partitions has been erected around the site which has blocked off the driveway and around the perimeter of the area. In preparation for the demolition of the lobby roof area, the sanctuary doors had to be closed.

This is where things became problematic, I pointed out to the contractor that allowances had to be made for access to the restrooms, I suggested that a covered walkway be constructed, leading from one of the sanctuary doors direct to the entrance of the restroom, this will permit persons, especially the handicapped, to access the bathrooms during services. This was agreed to and was done to the satisfaction of all.

The excavation was quite more than expected, as pointed out by the contractor when questioned, it appears they had to dig to a solid base in order to build a sound footing for support of overhanging floor. In my report to the congregation, I mentioned this since there were questions regarding this increased mound of dirt. As I explained, out of this dirt there will rise a phoenix. (To their delight).

I have been recording photographically, the various steps during this endeavor each day as work progressed. After excavation then forms were constructed for the pouring of cement, after which, slowly but surely the steel decking, concrete flooring and brick laying started to take shape then the walls began to take on the shape of the projected addition.

At some point, I was able to put together a slide presentation with the help of the monitors' operator, (There are several sets on the walls of the sanctuary) which was a visual report of the progress, and as expected, the members of the congregation were encouraged and appreciated this. Once the project started, more interest and desire to see the outcome.

Some month later, I was able to update this presentation to the satisfaction of all. I promised that the next presentation would be at completion, hopefully in time of the **Silver jubilee celebration.**

We are at a standstill due to some glitch in the project which was presented, this had caused some consternation by parties concerned. It is now August 10, 2016, to date there seem to be some light in sight for the resumption of the project. To be continued...

At some point, a question was poised with the architect regarding the proposed enclosure of the internal stairways leading up to the 2$^{nd}$ floor his response was inconclusive therefore, the same question was asked of the D.O.B, which resulted in an audit by the dept. Of building which resulted in quit a delay in the progress of the project. After some negotiation, Is was noted that the reason for the audit which was the internal stairway being enclosed as opposed to our original intent and desire, which was to have an open stairway as a continuation of the stairway coming from the basement with the railings up to the second floor. On my objection relayed to the Architect on behalf of persons who expressed their concerns, the response was that this was due to fire code regulations.

Eventually we noted that the enclosure was done and the stairway was according to original plan, which was not fully noted in the plans by my untrained eyes, there were no specific notation to this effect. To continue from here however. There was some other reasons why we still are unable to obtain a permit for inspection for the plumbing in order to continue with the sheet rock enclosure and eventual painting of all open walls.

Considering the reason for the audit was the question of the enclosed stairway, and that was eventually done, the question is, apparently the audit was resolved to permit this, why are we still unable to have this inspection? We are told now that there were other issues in the architectural plans, causes us to wonder, *What if? The plans were not audited*? Would those additional issues come to light on completion and final inspection? That is the question.

Besides the above, we are also experiencing some tremendous delays by the Elevator co. To get the second floor addition. We have issued the required deposit, and provided the required color for the installation of the door frame and wall plate. To date Wednesday August 24, 2016

This is now promised for October 2016, this is quite a long time to deprive us of the use of the elevator service, especially for seniors accessing the Center. I requested that they send someone to conduct a maintenance service in order to resume use of the elevator from the basement to the first floor, until such time that they see fit to proceed with the installation of the 2nd. Floor. Elevator entrance. I was promised someone will be in attendance today.11/23/16 No show... This is where we are in this regard.

Good news, the technician came therefore I sent the following message to the elevator Co. "Greetings: Happy to notify you that today Friday 9/2/16 Tech. Attended to Elevator. Our parishioners are now able to access the senior center. Sunday which is going to be a really big day, Thank You...."

The next project delay was the outside exit from 2nd. Floor. Yesterday, 9/8/16 I visited the site and steel work was in progress. The walkway steel base was laid. There was no action today, therefore I have decided to write these few lines at least. *Hasta luego* (until later).

A change of pace here.

I was contacted by the founder of an organization called P.D.P.A.

PROGRESSIVE DEMOCRATIC POLITICAL ASSOCIATION.

I was asked to be one of the seven honorees to be presented on Sunday July 10 2016 celebrating CARIBBEAN HERITAGE MONTH. I was also told that *"no"* was not an answer, therefore I accepted. But questioned, why me? It was pointed out that beside other reasons, the involvement of time etc. in the building of the new St. Gabriel's church.

One of the requirements were that I had to submit a photograph also a Biography for the journal. Which I will attach to this. Also I had to invite Family and friends to "cheer me on"=

Biography: *Richard Evraud Buery* The son of Richard M. Buery and Winifred J. Jones Buery was born in Colon Republic of Panama. His formal education started at Christ Church Academy, then he was transferred to public schools Pablo Arosemena, (primary), and continued on to Colegio Abel Bravo, graduating with a (bachiller en comercio) Bachelor of Commerce with special interests in Mechanical Drawing and Musical Education. To this end, he enrolled in the school's Choir, and the School's drum and bugle core.

He attended church services at Christ Church by-the-sea Episcopal Church in Colon Republic of Panama where he served as an acolyte. After sometime, he was drafted by the rector Rev. Peterson, who was also the choir director, as a tenor (youngest) which he truly enjoyed.

Eventually, he went on to become a member of various singing ensembles, Four Notes (as a substitute in the absence of the leading tenor), also other mixed groups, choirs etc. He was also a member of the vocal quartet The Harmonizers. They appeared in numerous venues around the country, theaters, hotels, ballrooms...

After graduating from Abel Bravo, he worked for the U S Caribbean Command Post Exchange at Ft Kobe, C.Z. as a sales clerk, and he helped out in the Photo section.

After leaving Ft. Kobe, he worked for International Photo Co. In Panama City, as a stock control clerk, paymaster and part-time salesperson, Photography was dear to Richard. Therefore, subsequently he enrolled in a correspondence course with The School of Modern Photography and the grade received from this school were the source of his obtaining a visa to travel to the U.S.

In the U.S., he pursued PHOTOGRAPHY and was affiliated with 2 photo studios, Liberty Arts and Vogue studios as a wedding photographer, also served as the official photographer for the Black Athletes Hall of Fame in Las Vegas Nevada and for Miss Black America. In a New York City ballroom.

He was employed at Commander Steamship Co. as a bookkeeper, then to Bunge Corp as Import/Export Traffic Manager. He retired from Bunge Corp. after 23 years of service. He met and married his wife Olivia J Buery, a retired High School teacher. This marriage was rewarded with three children, Dr.Samantha D. Buery Joyner (Ob -Gyn.), Richard R. Buery Esq. Deputy mayor for strategic Policies and initiatives in NYC. And Sherena S. Buery Lawson Occupational Therapist, Dept. of Education. Together they are blessed with a total of eight sources of Joy. (Grandchildren)

Continuing on with his singing, he was a member of the Down town Glee Club for over 23 years and he served as President, among other position. He is also a member of the Roy Prescod Chorale. He became a member of. St. Gabriel's Episcopal Church and senior Choir. For over 40 years. He served as Sr. Warden for a number of terms and he was instrumental in the building of a new Episcopal church (after 100 years) in Brooklyn, N.Y. 25 years ago. St. Gabriel is now in the process of the expansion of a second floor, for which he has been asked to be the Project Manager.

End of biography. (To date)

During the presentation of awards, the call was in alphabetical order which, as it may be, I was the first one called, I therefore had a few thoughts to deliver, but was not permitted to do so since Una wanted me to sing instead of speak, I was not really prepared to do this, however I decides to Sing **Happy Birthday** to my sister Yvonne, who actually celebrated a birthday on July 10th. So we all sang for her, she was a bit surprised I think. I had planned to do this, therefore alerted the Disc Jockey to play the birthday record on my cue. That went according to plan. After I proceeded to sing one of my favorites and appropriate song "You'll Never Walk Alone" I think this went well, considering it was impromptu and there was no piano accompaniment. After this, I said a few words anyway.

It was a good thing that during the evening before the actual ceremony began, I made the rounds of the tables of family and friends who attended, and thanked them for attending.

This did not really allow me to really express how I felt regarding their presence, therefore I decided to write a few lines and presented copies to each of them at a later time. The complete audience was not privy to this, but those to whom it was intended got it.

# PROGRESSIVE DEMOCRATS
# POLITICAL ASSOCIATION

## In celebration of Caribbean Heritage month Celebration

## Sunday July 10 2016

## Richard Evraud Buery

As one of the honorees of this auspicious occasion, it is indeed my pleasure to be numbered among these distinguished gentlemen. This is something I have never imagined befalling me, but when the Hon. Dr. Una Clarke called to ask, correction, to tell me I was chosen to be one of the honorees she further stated that she will not accept *no* as an answer. I therefor agreed.

As a teenager, it was my habit to just sit and imagine ***What if?***

Hence the title of a book I wrote. I will speak of this later. My mother used to worry about this "Day dreaming". An elderly lady who lived on the building, always told her not to worry it was normal for one with an inquiring mind.

It was my habit to think about the reasons and why thing were the way they were, and would come up with a way to fix and repair them as well as I could, if a toy did not work, I would take it apart and fix it, I was called Mr. Fix it.

From my mini biography it would be noted that there were quite a few things that interested me while growing up, some of which I could do and some I wished I could, To name one, In High school I was quite interested in architecture and enjoyed and excelled in the subject of mechanical drawing, knowing that in order to pursue this line, it would be necessary to continue graduate studies "***What if?*** The question". If mother could, she would.

This interest did not completely go to waste, since it actually allowed me to develop the plans for my 2$^{nd}$ home (Chez B), which was presented to the builder for its completion. I mention this in order to justify my involvement with the building of the new St Gabriel's Church, my continued interest in architecture allowed me the ease of keeping up with the building plans as presented by an architect.

It has been 25 years of the new building, and we are now in the process of an expansion which became necessary due to the outreach program. I have been asked again to be the Project manager, and despite some immediate problems the work has been going forward.

Let's talk about the book" ***What if?*** The Question or a Statement"

I was prompted to write about the building of St. Gabriel's Church, the struggle and hard work in getting it done, even after we were told that there was no building of a new Episcopal church for over 100 years.

This was in my thoughts, since I had recorded and retained the paper trail etc. My premise in getting this started was to tell how I got here, it was necessary to tell from whence I came and especially to tell the story to our children and relatives of my life growing up in my little "world", Colon rep. Of Panama, which consisted of 16 streets and approximately 16 avenues.

In effect, the book is twofold: Autobiographical and historical of how we built the church and paid for it.

There is more to this story, it's in the book.

Thanks to My Wife. Who coordinated this by having my family and friends here to join me in celebration of this occasion?

*THANK YOU.*

Sunday September 11, 2016 was scheduled to be "Homecoming Sunday" at St. Gabriel's Church, traditionally the first Sunday after Labor Day is the day when parishioners of both

Insert#1services (9:00 and 11:00 a.m.) attend one service in order to meet each other and reunite in fellowship.

This was an exceptional service since it happens to be the day we commemorate {9/11} one of the saddest time in this country, the attack on the twin towers World Trade Center(New York) the Pentagon (Wash. D,C.) and Plane crash in an area of Philadelphia Pa., where so many lives were lost.

It was a day of reflection and the rector recalled some personal sentiments experienced by the loss of known firefighters of the station house near where he worshiped. It was a sad narrative and he was so moved that there was a long pause where we all personally reflected

During this time I reflected on where we were at the time of this tragedy which remains forever in my mind. The year 2001 fifteen years ago and I can still remember the details. We were enjoying a couple weeks of time share in Las Vegas, Nevada. And became known in the area by many of the folks who knew that we were from N.Y.

On the morning of the 11th. I was up and getting ready to take a ride on the Strip, while waiting for Olivia, I was watching the T.V and saw one of the towers exploded and on fire, my first thought was this is a movie, so I called out to Olivia to say that there is a movie on television about the New York World Trade Center, but as I continued to watch I actually saw a plane crash into the other tower and reality struck, so we knew this was real.

We went down to the lobby and then the street we were approached by some folks and all were reaching out to us expressing their sorrow. This is when one becomes aware that in time of tragedy we are one people. I remember writing the date in my note book, but in going to the reception desk and visiting other places, I lost the book. An unusual thing happened in Las Vegas at this time, all the attractive and festive lights were turned off on every one of the hotels, to be replaced with patriotic scenes and flags.

I went to the car rental to return the car. They were in demand since people who lived nearby, decided to rent cars to go home since all flights were canceled. So now we are without a car to return to the strip but as mentioned, people reached out and we were offered a ride back to town by a pair of workers of the hotel where the Sigfield & Roy show was appearing. We were able to see the white tigers used in their daily show.

Fortunately, since we were there for two weeks, we were able to fly back at a later day but New York airports were still off limits, therefore our flight landed at Newark Airport (New Jersey) and we were able to get a ride back in a Van which was a very long ride. But it was good to be back home, after experiencing a great vacation, marred by such a sad experience.

I have worked in the Wall Street area, One Chase Manhattan Plaza, Building since 1962, my window was on the 47th floor and I watched the Battery Park City been built from excavations of the World Trade center. A Dam was installed in the River and that total cite was created from the earth excavated to build that area, and watched the Towers and surrounding buildings go up. I supposed that it would have been more depressing for me to see them come down in person in 2011.

We have lost family relation, and I have missed a few persons who I am aware worked in the area who I have not seen but would not consider the worst. A friend of mine Chino was affected on both attempts, first when a truck exploded in the basement of one of the towers (years before) and the second time fortunately, by the Grace of the almighty he was hurt but survived.

It is now October 8th. 2016 and I have decided to take you back to the Expansion of the second floor of St. Gabriel's church, unfortunately the word is not encouraging, since after extensive delays in the construction I had to write an e-mail to the Builder requesting his whereabouts since I was unable to reach him by phone, this brought a response in which he stated that he was out of town but would be back by the week-end.

Time has elapsed and still no word, therefore I have followed up with a phone call and was promised that work would resume.

Earlier this week, Monday, Scaffolds were re-erected and some roof work was done, but that is it for now. Meanwhile I contacted the Elevator Co. regarding the necessary installation, since we were promised that October was the targeted date, but as usual, we have no positive word, only promises to return Phone calls, and this has been frustrating. I have reached out to other persons in the Co. And some more of the same. We have a saying in Colon, Panama in Spanish,

*"Paciencia piojo que la noche es larga")* Translation: (Bed bug, be patient because it's a long night.) So I will try to keep this in mind, and continue to keep pestering them as well as the builder, until something happens. Hopefully there would be some progress before the (*Silver Jubilee)* the 25th Anniversary Gala scheduled for the 28th of October, 2016. The reason for this anxiety is, if the work on the elevator starts soon, the Elevator will again be shut down to allow the construction, which will be a major disappointment, to say the least.

This is where we find ourselves now, All the work on the expansion has been in a static state, I have found some cracks in the flooring which should be addressed, the whole area, office, closets, conference room, storage room where a trap door is to be installed, Electrical work, doors ceiling walkway to internal, and external exits are all unfinished, the stairways are at a standstill to name a few. I know that work was stopped because of the objections placed, but the audit has been resolved and there is no reason for leaving things for such a long time, in limbo.

October 9th.2016 I was prompted to write another e-mail to Builder and team. Greetings all;

As was our initial agreement, we were to have periodic meetings to discuss the project which has not been the case for a long time. The audit by the D.O.B.(which resulted in a delay of construction), has been settled for quite some time, nevertheless we have come to a pause in the project and at times we are unable to keep in touch with each other. WE

ARE VERY CONCERNED about this long period of inactivity. The church (as owners) is at a loss why the construction has come to a pause.

Even though there was much work that could have been done on the exterior building while waiting for Audits to be resolved and permits to be granted. It is imperative that a meeting be called at a mutually agreed time, to resolve and explain the reason for these delays and lack of communication. Still there was no response, therefore a call was made to the builder and other members of the team, and for lack of agreed time by all involved, a conference call was planned for October 13th.

Matters arising out of the conference call involve questions regarding unfinished exit stairs, roof work to be completed in order to eventually close open area which would allow internal closing of ceiling, not to mention the fascia as well as the installation of gutters, repairing of the floors in the office and conference area which has developed cracks which has to be repaired prior to installation of finishing floors tiles, to name a few items.

Between Oct. 13th and Oct 24th there were only 2 days any work was done, such as some paneling and some carpentry (shelf installation) and that's it for now. Due to the absence of any workers at the site. I have left phone messages with the builder, noting the obvious (there were no response), the days are getting cooler.

The only work which was finally done was to clean up the Lobby and, as I called it, cosmetic work in order to make it presentable for the celebration of the ball, but no structural work which still remains undone. By this time of the year it was the expectation to have this project completed and occupied

# October 28 2016 (Silver Jubilee) 25th anniversary Gala

The following paragraph was takes from the Chair's message printed in the journal produced for the occasion.

"This year we are thrilled to incorporate into our festivities, a tribute to those members who have contributed selflessly over the past 25 years to the uplifting of our spiritual home. These individuals were truly deserving of this recognition and we applaud and salute them and their families for the blessing that they have been to the St Gabriel's community."

I was not present at this occasion since Olivia and I had to be at Chez–B. It was our understanding that it was truly a gala Affair. A good note was, that we were one of the recipients of a *25th anniversary award* issued for Olivia and myself. We are thankful for Sylvia Lavalas who accepted this award on our behalf. IT was in the form of an acrylic triangle on a base suitable for table or shelf with the emblem of the church with the following legend. "Distinguished Service Award. *Presented to* **Richard & Olivia Buery** with *appreciation for your years of unselfish service to God and Church.* ===**St. Gabriel's Episcopal Church.** *Celebrating 25 years in our Brooklyn, New York Sanctuary and Golden Hall. On October 28, 2016."* We will cherish and display this Award in a prominent place of our home.

There were 24 other persons who received awards, we were among good company. We have since expressed our appreciations to the Priest, wardens and committee.

In the meantime, the elevator Co. has set a target date of November 8th to start installation of the 2nd floor entrance, I have pointed out to them that is Election day, I have been assured that this is a working day for them, therefore work will start, I questioned the Rep. regarding the expected duration time for completion, I was told 2 weeks.

## APPRECIATION AWARD

Well to point out, the day came and went and no show. After inquiries, the next day is set for tomorrow 11/15/16 and was assured that confirmation has been obtained from the Co. So until then.

We are now faced with the D.O.B. required 2016 Annual Category Inspection Proposal for elevator testing. I have contacted the required third party elevator consulting Co. And explained the situation and they have agreed to place the works in motion as soon as we send the signed agreement form and check for $350.00 for filing fee to witness the inspection, (which we did), they will also contact the Elevator co. And on completion of installation of The Elevator extension, they will file the necessary papers with the D.O.B. whose Records indicate that November is the final date for testing. (Cutting the timing close), don't you think? I will report back when the time comes. Due to the change of time by the Elevator Co. This inspection has been re scheduled for Dec. 8th.2016.

Here we are, after spending the week of Thanksgiving (11/22–28/16) in Va. at the residence of our daughter. Samantha, Charles and children (Zoe, Chase and Noah) It was indeed a glorious time since the Family were in attendance, Richie, Deborah and children

(Ethan and Ellis), Sherena, Pete and children (Taylor, Jordan and Sydney) Also in attendance were Charles Mom and sister with her daughters (Imani and Nia) Also Olivia, my sisters Yasmina, Yolanda and Yvonne also Ernie.

It was a full house and a Happy Thanksgiving dinner. To top it all after some of the folks left, Olivia and I, along with Mrs. Joyner, Brothers Chase and Noah, Yvonne, Yasmina, Yolanda and Ernie attended a Cotillion-Beautillion celebrating, Zoe as one of the debutantes. It was a wonderful celebration. If I do say so she was beautifully made up and wonderfully attired and was escorted by her proud Mother and Father. The affair was sponsored by the Jack & Jill Reston Chapter 2016 Saturday Nov. 26, 2016. A week well spent.

Today, December 2, 2016 I have decided to continue this narrative, I am happy to report that yesterday 12/1/16 I decide to pay a visit to the construction site and was happy to find the workers were installing the 2nd floor elevator frame work and shoring up the walls, it is now beginning to look like something, also I was very happy to see three of the building workers on the job of clearing up the protective partitions and painting the lower area. Hopefully they will begin to address the 2nd floor area which needs much to be done. When the elevator workers are finished, they would not have any excuse to continue the process which is long overdue. I definitely cannot say "it's beginning to look a lot like Christmas"

I will therefore sign off for now, unless any further development, until next Year. 2017.

I have decided to continue with my narrative, since there is still much to be done. Eleven days later 12/13/16. The office area is practically made over, Doors have been installed Carpets have been laid, unfortunately before the ceiling tiles were completely installed, a cleanup had to done with the carpet, this step could have been avoided, if the opposite was done, first finish the ceiling tiles, then install the carpet. Anyway we have a saying where I come from, *"El orden de la factura no altera el producto"* translation, the order of the factors does not alter the results. Most importantly, it is beginning to take shape.

The promise to have a full staff of workers, as promised me the other day, was not a fact. So here we are, hopefully bit by bit the work is been done. The weather is getting colder and it does not look like the outside work is going to be accomplished in a timely manner. I am still hopeful that the elevator workers who have been in attendance, will get their part of the work done, it is my understanding that yesterday, Monday, they have worked on the inner workings of the system, I.e. the mechanical part which will allow the door to open on the second floor, as soon as the required program is completely installed. Who knows, perhaps this will enable us to get from the basement all the way to the second floor, this would be my Christmas present.

You see. I made the suggestion at the time when the original elevator was been installed, they should manufacture the system to eventually reach the second floor since it was our aim to accomplish this expansion, now that we are on our way to fulfill this reality, the anxiety to see this done is overwhelming, patience is the call for now. I will pause for now, and perhaps the next time, I might be able to say. EUREKA.

I have received a call from the church, that I should to prepare a report for "Gabriel's Horn", (the periodical publication) therefore I thought I would share it at this point.

# Progress report 2<sup>nd</sup> floor expansion

There has been quite some delays in the progress of this project and we were anxious to get things started again. After much effort, I am now happy to state that we were finally able to reach some agreement and decisions with the elevator co. And at this time the framework for the elevator has been installed, also upon contact with the mechanic, the final installation of the technical works has been promised, this will allow for the opening of the elevator door on the 2$^{nd}$ floor. At the time of this printing, hopefully, it would be functional.

In respect to the structure, there are some phase of the work still to be done, in the meantime, the cosmetic part has been addressed, such as the removal of temporary partitions and barriers, has been accomplished. The office space has been restored, the lobby is presentable, despite been reduced, due to the required covered access stairway to the second floor, we are now beginning to see the light at the end of the tunnel, so to speak. There are some exterior work left to done and the hope was to have that completed before the winter truly sets in.

Despite all this, *"It's beginning to look a lot like Christmas"*

***Greeting.*** We left for *Chez-B* on Monday Dec. 19$^{th}$ in order to make preparation to celebrate the Christmas season with family. We returned to Brooklyn on Monday Dec. 26$^{th.}$ I will tell you more about this later since today I went to the church in response to an Email from the elevator Co. regarding progress at the construction site. The workers were on the job and I am pleased to say that the outside has been much improved, the area has been cleared and paved under the steps. Inside the storage area has been sheet rocked and the access stairs is scheduled to be installed, also some finished carpentry has been done I n the office area.

The. Required inspection by the Building dept. was conducted, however there has been a glitch since an interior area has to be repaved, and this requires the return of the elevator sub-contractors in order to permit access to the elevator shaft. I immediately got on the horn to contact the rep. After a couple calls, we have received a reply stating that the visit is scheduled for next Wed. so here we go into the New Year. The inspection date by the Dept. Of Building will therefor take place after the year-end deadline, hopefully, there would be no pending fines since we did all that was possible to comply.

I will continue to visit the site to keep abreast of progress. Hopefully the construction workers would continue to address the remaining areas still to be done. Today Saturday 12/31/16. I have decided to visit in order to assess the progress, the Fascia (roof lining of the building) has been completely installed, this will eventually allow the scaffold to be removed which will add a visual improvement, there has been some platform cement work done to the external access stairs, which leaves the covering to be installed and some iron refining edges to the frame. Then painting. This is it for 2016 since tomorrow begins the New Year.

# Merry Christmas 2016

As I started to say before this interlude. We decided to travel to Pennsylvania to take care of preliminaries in getting the house ready and decorated. Unpacked the boxes with the tree and other items, set up and decorated the tree (7ft artificial) lights and trimmings, I really look forward to this therefore I hung some lights from the roof over the deck and around the perimeter of the house, also some interior decorations and the nativity scene, this gave some semblance of Christmas decorations.

In anticipation, we had to go shopping at Olivia's favorite Center. The task was that it was necessary to take all those packages off the car then load them on a cart then take them in and up the internal stairs to the kitchen. From experience and practice, what I had to do each time I go there, I had to take packages up a couple stairs at a time until reaching the top.

The thought came to me, why not install a pulley system? After giving it some careful thought. I proceeded to purchase the necessary items, pulleys, rope, hooks and fasteners, then installing them In stairwell with additional twine at each end, attached to center where pot hook is, which then enabled me to place the bags one at a time on the pot hook, (which I had), then Olivia taking the first light package up the stairs, will then use the upstairs twine to pull the rope and upon reaching the top, remove package, then I would use the twine installed downstairs to pull the rope back In order to place another package and repeat the process until all packages are upstairs.

After this process is completed, the end twine (UP & Downstairs) is then stored on the side out of the way until next use, a rather ingenious system, if I do say so myself. I will do some additional tweaking next time, by adding an extension to the hook area which will lower the packages placing them at waist level, instead having to reach up to install and retrieve. This became evident to me, since when we were leaving and I tried to load gift package for downward destination, and had to reach up to place bag on the hook, the bag ripped, therefore I had to abort. Notwithstanding, I should patent this system, what say ye?

There is the saying that "Christmas is for the children" but I do not entirely agree with this since I really enjoy spending the time with my children, grands, siblings and friends at Chez -B. there was a time that there were over 20 persons present and we will find somewhere for all to lay their heads overnight, this is evidenced by photos taken over the years. The numbers have been gradually reduced. This year we were grateful to have Yasmina, Yolanda and Roger present, Yvonne was not able to attend since she has been traveling quite a lot this year considering the distance from San Antonio, Texas.

The visit was quite enjoyable, considering the passing of Tony and Ernesto, who were sadly missed.(R.I.P.) I had to ask the Lord's blessing of the gathering and food, in the absence of Ernesto, who was very inspiring with the prayers at dinner time. We missed all those who were not able to attend due to individual obligations.

It was with this in mind that we built this home, a place to get away from the usual, and to have friends and family spend time together it was also intended to have the children use this place for a retreat at their will, each child was given a set of keys also instructions about the process of opening and preparing the place on arrival and departure.

# Happy New Year 2017

It has been a long time since we missed the midnight mass at church. Usually after this service we will attend a Ball held right there downstairs in the parish hall, the food is catered and the hall undergoes a transformation, to take on the atmosphere of a ballroom. This was convenient, which meant there was no need to go somewhere else and find parking, also the cost would be much higher. This is a fundraiser for the church to help defray the cost of operation, kind of "keeping it home".

This year the Old year Ball was canceled mostly because it was on a Saturday and as a practice, Saturday, events were discouraged since the hall should be prepared for Sunday and as you know, this is the day of worship. New Year's Day on Sunday worked out well, and the mass was a Lessons and carols service, followed by a New Year's Day People's Award Luncheon in the Golden hall at a nominal cost of $25.00 therefor there was not a total loss for our year's end fund raiser. 25 persons, (in keeping with our "silver Jubilee anniversary "), were presented with awards in recognition of their services to the parish.

Sunday, January 8th 2017 was our annual parish meeting. This is the time we render parish reports and vote for the new vestry, warden and delegates to the Diocesan convention also delegates to the deanery meeting. As project Supervisor, I was asked to present a report regarding the expansion Program. In the effort of time, the rector opted to render his pastoral report in place of his sermon and therefore surprised me by calling for my report at this time, I sensed that he was going to do this and as last year, my report was in the Choir room. Thanks to Stella, who had a copy of printed report on hand and brought it to me.

This allowed me to have a quick scan and I was able to ad lib it was fresh to me since it was written the night before. I will add the actual report which was printed in the report.

I have been experiencing a hard time getting my thoughts down, when it is not a matter of getting my desk top to cooperate, it is another thing. There was a snow situation and we were away for a while and on return I was trying to write and heard a dripping in the other room and then a thud, I got up to investigate this in the other room, and discovered that there was a leak. I had to go get a bucket and discovered that some of the books on a wall shelf which I had built for my movie tape cassettes, had fallen which accounted for the noise. Also some folded clothes on a stand under the shelf were soaked. They were there for an eventual time for pressing and storing in the proper place, I had to remove the other books also the clothes, those that were not soiled I hung them out to dry and others to be eventually re washed. Never a dull moment as the saying goes.

It must have been dripping for some time since the floor was extremely wet and when I decided to investigate further, I discovered that the damage was much more than imagined since the bedrooms ceilings on the lower floor were saturated, this makes it four rooms affected from this leak. I.e. adjoining rooms upstairs. First thing first. The roof had to be repaired, therefor we called a known roofer who did a good job by sealing the cracks In the roof paper and then sealed the entire roof in the silver colored compound (silver top) he suggested I wait for a time to ascertain that there are no further leaks before I take on the job of repairing the ceilings (it is my plan to do this myself).

Well today January 24th I have some good news. Let me start at the beginning, on Sunday 1/22/17 we went to church, as is the practice. I parked the car in the church lot. And noticed a stack of steel sheeting and decided to stay clear in order to allow the door to open. Well as that would be, as I exited the car, my left foot got caught by some of the binding lo and behold, I fell. Luckily the height of the stack prevented me from falling all the way to the ground, the worst situation was that there was a witness, beside my hurt pride, slight bruise to my hip and a slight gash to my thumb, no further harm.

On my return home in the evening, still offended due to the misplaced delivery, also the fact that a member of the staff notified me that he was not aware of this pending delivery by the contractor, I decided to send an e-mail to the rector, copy to the builder, warden and other member of the staff. Which reads in part, as follows: "This is to inform you of an existing situation. Today while attending Sunday's service and exiting my auto, I tripped and fell due to the delivered building material in the driveway. I asked an attendant about the delivery and was informed that they were not previously notified of this delivery, in as much of the inconvenience sustained by this fall, it is my hope that the use of this material will result in its removal post haste, it will be somewhat satisfying, Thank You, Richard Buery."

I received a reply from the rector, with c.c. to the recipients of my notice, also pointing out some unfinished work, also the dumpster which remains in the yard for some time. I responded to the rector, (c.c. to all) referencing to the sections of the construction plans (of which I have a set), pointing out the items which addressed his concerns, with the idea that the contractor, as a copy reader, can be advised, and react accordingly.

A call from the warden inquiring about the fall. And a call from the contractor, from whom I have not heard in some time, regarding the progress of work. I am sure that there was some concerns of liability on his mind regarding my sustained fall. There was some good results from my misfortune, since we agreed on a meeting face to face scheduled for today Monday 24th.at the site.

Today Monday was a very fulfilling day, for several reasons, firstly, I was able to meet the contractor and expressed my concerns, also to have a meeting of the minds, and noted that there was some work been done, and agree to keep in touch regarding scheduled work.

Also, I met the Elevator maintenance person who was there to make some final adjustments to the Elevator and I had the privilege to accompany him in the elevator up to the second floor, my "maiden" trip so to speak, this was a very refreshing moments to take this first trip.

Next I met the D.O.B.(department of building) city inspector who was there to check the Elevator (as required by law).after going over the aspects of the elevator, the three of us, also joined by the contractor, had a very pleasant chat about the building trade and other topics. I asked the inspector what were his conclusions and he said all was well and except for a minor patching by the contractor. It has met the inspection and passed. Great.

The elevator co. Rep. gave me his phone number to contact him when the builder is ready to make this patch and he would come and open the top to allow this. It is great to know that things are finally getting done.

2/1/17 to this date, I have not heard any further word from the contractor but have visited the site and there was some work been done by one of the worker, laying tiles in the bathroom floor and walls. Today he has laid the floor tiles in the conference room also the walkways into the office area. I noticed some work has been done with the steel beams I mentioned before, which caused my fall, at least they were removed from the driveway and some has been used.

Instead of going on regarding the day- to-day progress, to tell it all in a nutshell, there were still some ups and downs, but eventually all is well that ends well.

**CONSTRUCTION 2ND FLOOR**

# Project supervisor Report 2017

### St Gabriel's 2<sup>nd</sup> floor expansion program

Greetings: I would like to take this opportunity on behalf of my wife, to thank the Rector, Wardens, Vestry and committee of the 25<sup>th</sup> Anniversary Gala, celebrated October 28<sup>th</sup> 2016, for including us as one of the recipients of the 25<sup>th</sup> Anniversary award. This award will be prominently displayed I n our home.

Referring to the rector's report of January 2016, a Loan of $500.000 was obtained

Followed by a project supervisor report which was not printed but was delivered orally at that time. During the course of the subsequent year, I have presented a photographic report as well as updates from time to time. The building project started in January and was scheduled for completion in June.

Regretfully, due to a number of delays because of situations that needed some attention and clarifications regarding the architectural plans.There has been quite some delays in the progress of this project and we were anxious to get things started again. After much effort, I am now happy to state that we were finally able to reach some agreement and decisions with the elevator Co. At this time the framework for the elevator has been installed, also upon contact with the mechanic, the final installation of the technical works has been promised, this will allow for the opening of the elevator door on the 2<sup>nd</sup> floor.

Eventually, we got it together and the necessary work got under way and after some periodic delays, the inspection was denied due to some necessary internal work required by the construction workers, which is scheduled to be completed by this coming Monday, then the building inspector will be contacted, after which, baring other hiccups, the elevator will be ready for operation to the 2$^{nd}$ floor as soon as the rest of the interior construction is completed by the builders.

In respect to the structure, there are some phase of the work still to be done. In the meantime, the cosmetic part has been addressed, such as the removal of temporary partitions and barriers, has been accomplished. The office space has been restored, the lobby is presentable despite been reduced, due to the required access to the second floor and slowly, we are now beginning to see the light at the end of the tunnel. There are some exterior work left to done, namely, the exterior access stairs which needs to be refined and covered then painted. the hope was to have that completed before the winter truly sets in.

Respectfully submitted,
Richard E. Buery (1/6/17)

The promised report scheduled for the Annual Parish meeting which I was to present is printed above.

Permit me to get back to other pending item, namely the leaking roof in my primary home. We have had some rain also there was some snow, therefore I will assess the situation to verify that the leak has been repaired. I will continue to wait a bit more, and then would be convinced that all is ready then I will begin to get the necessary materials to get the internal job done.

I have made a list of the necessary items, and have taken some measurements and checked on the quantity and grade necessary, and then at the given time, I will get this show on the road.

After some waiting time I have decided to get to work. Olivia left for Virginia to visit with Samantha, therefore I was alone and was able to move things around to make room. I had to break out all the damaged portion of the roof and cut the size of sheetrock to fit. This was hard work and considering that I was not as young, therefore lots of efforts to secure this, lifting and drilling in place, I started with the bedroom, then proceeded with the Office (As Sydney calls it) since this is where I do my writing etc.

Next I went downstairs to face the next two rooms. I must say that three rooms were very hard. The total coverage needed a 4x8 sheetrock plus another partial 2x3. To cover the fourth room. After this, I had to plaster all seams and I must say that considering my naiveté I was able to accomplish a passable job, and one has to be an inspector to notice some slight imperfections.

Next step was priming then painting the ceilings and some walls. Then repairing and rebuilding

Water damaged furniture. That done. The pain is somewhat unbearable, however I could feel the body draining as I lay to sleep at nights, so not been a physician, I decided to lay still and let my body chill. Bit by bit the soreness and aches dissipated in time. The major work took approximately 4 days, by the time Olivia returned and I was able get some help in getting the last room sheet rocked. All left was the proverbial clean up. To date there is still some finishing painting left, but I will do that eventually. As I lay in bed at times I look at the ceiling and admire my handiwork, and if my hands could reach my back, I would pat it. (Smile)

I would like to add a communique regarding the Elevator situation at the church, which was quite a bother due to the constant back and forth. It was written on May 20th 2017 and forwarded to all parties concerned. I will try to copy and paste if

PROGRESS ELEVATOR.

Monday 7/17/2017

This past weekend was filled with disappointing news, I heard from Sisters Yvonne and Yasmina regarding the passing of our friend Rupert

Ranger who was quite ill and eventually passed away. We had a conference call with his wife Annett, and expressed our condolences and reminisced of times gone by, there was much to talk about since we all grew up in Colon, Panama each sharing personal experiences including Clausel who also shared in this exchange. Next I was informed of the passing of the husband of a good friend Anita that's (#2)

Next we spoke regarding the health condition of my cousin Herbert who was residing with a good Friend and acquaintance in Texas, only to receive a call early Sunday morning that he had passed away. That's (#3) we have heard that these sad news usually comes in three. We can only agree that the three persons who have gone *home* have suffered and are now in a better place, free from all sufferings, and we pray for their welcome in the presence of our savior and Lord. (R.I.P).

On Sunday during church service, I experienced a left shoulder discomfort and could hardly sustain holding the Hymnal and had to hold it with the aid of my right hand. For you who know, the correct way is to hold the book in your left hand just below your chin and sing looking forward in order to project your voice (Just thought I would mention this).

I mention this to further bring to mind, my way of treating these body pain as pointed out above.

I am not sure if this pain was developed because of sleeping position on Saturday night, however I did what I usually do, which is to find a comfortable position and support for my shoulder and remained motionless and let my body heal itself. I do not think doctors would agree with my principle, it is my feeling that in the case of minor aches, we should give the brains a chance to locate the area, and do its Job (This might sound strange to you) Try it. I can feel the area start to pulse and this is the action of the brain, I continue to remain motionless and then, in time I can sense that the pulsing is reduced. Don't know if this is because I am slowly drifting into sleep but it beats drugging myself with pain killers.

Today Monday I was able to get up and actually go outside with a push broom and cleaned the sidewalk and driveway, pushing the dirt into the curb before 11:00 am, and bringing my car into driveway in time for the street cleaner to pass by and clean the curb. That was done and so far no residual pain. So there you are another day, no discernable pain and no pain killing drug in my system.

Another thing, While sitting I actually rub my knee where there is always the presence of age related pain (Smile) If one feels and tries to rub the area of the pain carefully and ever so lightly, you are able to pin point the actual area, and there is a slight sense of a shock. Pay attention to the source of the pain and then treat it with slight massage and perhaps a salve or compress (hot or cold) it minimizes the need to take internal medication (pills etc.)

I must also tell you about my dentist. I have grown up with a bit of disdain of dentist. It all started with admission to the public School, one had to visit the school system appointed dentist, who I may say, had the need of bedside manners (to put it this way). As I got older, this became a necessary health requirement, therefor something to look forward to yearly, (or every 6 months)

At my most recent visit I was told that I had to visit a specialist because of some indication in the x-ray result, anyway there was nothing, I feel that there was a defect with the way their attendant took the pictures, since the report at this place only indicated that a molar had to be removed, which I was aware of, but as I mentioned before, extraction is not my favorite situation. On my return to the original office, a device was recommended, to reduce the grinding of teeth, which I did at times. An impression was taken and the dentist was prepared to do the extraction, but miraculously the tooth was no longer shaking (I had tried to keep it cleared and always tried to use mouthwash to keep it soaked timely) I told the attendant that this was not necessary, The dentist came to inspect the tooth and he realized this fact, but insisted that it should be removed. I declined and stated not at this time, his retort was "You will be coming back to me shortly with pain and begging me to take it out" Well. Thankfully, it has been approximately 6 months and I still can chew painlessly.

Be in tune with the symptoms of your body, remember the brains is the source of most of your bodily functions. I am sure that on television you have seen the way it is displayed with the electrical (simulated) charges. This explains to me the slight electric like shock I spoke of.

This is my medical advice for now, it is not my intention to deprive the medical dispensers of their livelihood, after all, my Daughter is a doctor and I know some friends who are also. Kudos.

Back to the task at hand, after painting all ceilings, and I have taken care of other things around the house. I have finally decided to paint the remaining room with some left over paint from Chez-B which I have brought to Brooklyn, 1 and ½ gallon along with brushes and rollers etc. I only used the ½ gallon since the wall was already primed. The job is done and the room cleaned up. Unfortunately, while moving a two-part dresser which I had already remade the damaged drawer, two legs were broken therefore I removed the other legs and placed the dresser flat on the floor and will eventually repair the bottom dresser and replace the legs, for the time being all looks well.

Now that the elevator problem at the church has been taken care of, let me tell you about that.

The elevator Co maintained that the problem was internal and not theirs. Anyway, Con Edison workers were outside doing some other work I therefor approached the supervisor to let him know about our problem, he then proceeded to check the feed into the church building and confirmed that there was no fault. I therefore invited him and crew to check the current as it entered the building and to determine where this fault was.

All was right at the point it enters the building, I therefore ask them to check the point where the current proceed to the junction box and the elevator's current emanates from, it was at this point we found some discrepancies therefore the conclusion was that between the point where the current travels to the junction box where the problem occurred, It was then necessary to have the Building electrician check this out, and the fault was located and eventually repaired, (contrary to the thought of others who advised me that the line from the main switch box to this distribution box should be replaced, to which I objected) This extra work and expense was averted. It appeared that as the cable exited the distribution box, a short occurred. This is what was repaired.

From that time to the Present all is well with the elevator, and by the grace of the Almighty God, it will continue. So as I was saying, I have no need to continue my daily visit to the church and I am able to remain at home, which leaves me this time to fill with deeds. As I look around I now find that the back yard need some attention therefore I started by cutting the growth which was tremendous, I rolled the cuttings into a stack and let nature take care of some of this by drying it up, then after a time I was able to use some plastic wrappings and tie it up into a bundle, I am now faced with the task of getting this out to the front for the sanitation pickup.

I have been able to gather all the dried up leaves and dirt into a large garbage bag which along with the bundle will have to be taken through the house to the front, since the last time I had this situation, I took the garbage through the neighbor's yard and caused a bit of an accident where the stalk caught the netting of their tent and tore it. I had to help repair it but I detected some unpleasantness. Because of this, considering our attached home is located in the middle and did not want an occurrence, I have discussed this with Olivia and at some time we will join efforts and get this out to the front as mentioned above, before the advent of winter, hopefully.

Now that this is done, there is another thought, some years ago, I built a lawn table and two benches each 8ft. long I saturated the wood with linseed oil prior to manufacturing them and they have lasted quite a long time but I have noted that the remaining bench is on it's last, therefore I have decided to scout the lumber yards for material, since I know what it was for, it was my thought if I could get some scrap instead of complete lengths wood, it would be a savings.

I wanted 1 piece of 1x6x8 which I could then cut into the required lengths to remanufacture the bench legs. I found a length which was a bit stained and therefor tried to barter a reduced cost, unsuccessfully, the owner wanted to charge me the actual cost, I pointed out the fact that the wood was stained and he should consider this, he was adamant therefore I decided to take the High road, why should I pay the actual cost for stained wood, I decided to get perfect wood for the job. Good luck for him getting the stained wood sold, since I found it on a table of stacked unsalable wood in his shop.

So I now have new perfect wood for my bench and have taken out my table saw and have measured and cut the wood, and have saturated it with the linseed Oil as before and after a day for seeping, I have built the new legs for the bench and have painted it along with the table which will now be around for some time.

Next project, I have one metal chair which was scheduled for the garbage but was around for the reason mentioned above, for disposal. I sat on it some time ago and it was so rusted that the rim bent. Well while I was out there doing the other repairs, a thought accrued to me, with the other piece of wood I was able to get from the shop, which was a small piece and the owner consented to give it to me along with my purchase. I designed a stand for this chair and was able to mount the top portion with the seat using the rest of the frame as aesthetics. It looked as it was intended except for the stand. After completing this, I then painted the metal with rust-oleum black and let stand for a few days to set and dry, then I painted that over with a bright yellow rust-oleum paint so now it stands out and is set to last for some time also. If I could, I will try to add photos for clarification. This could be a suggestion for Projects submitted to "this old house or D.I.Y". Magazines, just a thought.

In the meantime, I want to tell of the sale of my book. I have been taking some books with me whenever I attend some functions. The most recent was a celebration of life of a relative of a friend. I sat at the table with some persons and we were discussing all sort of things, including the topic of the day "Our president" One of the gentlemen ask what I did? This gave me an opportunity to mention that, among other things, I was an author so he mentioned that he would be interested in reading a copy of my book, I therefore sprang into action and said I have copies with me, he did not believe me so I excused myself and went to my bag and produced the book and another person wanted a copy also, and I had previously sold another copy to an acquaintance of my daughter Samantha. This was 3 copies at this gathering.

Next. I attended a barbeque and as usual I had my bag with copies with the hope of selling copies, it is a slow process but I will continue to do this.

Most recently we had a street fair at the church and I decided to print copies of my book cover to place it on the tables which eventually worked, someone saw the sheet and when she saw me with the book, she offered to purchase one, also I began to walk around with copies and was able to sell five copies. Bit by Bit as the saying goes.

There are times and situations when I have missed opportunities to plug the sale of my books, but I hesitate to do so because of restraints on my part, and how things might appear. I know that I am giving precedence to what others may think of this, but I guess this should not determine my actions as long as my actions does not offend others, which is truly not my intention. When I am attending a particular function I usually approach the host and ask if it is acceptable to talk about my book, I usually do this only in places where I am among friends who I am not usually in touch with.

Another missed opportunity. We attended a 50th.birthday party of a cousin of Olivia in Staten Island, after some well-wishers from friends of his and Family, I decided to offer a prayer and song, on behalf of this side of his family (The Lord is my light) I was in good voice, if I do say so myself. I was well received and compliments were extended me by folks in attendance.

I had copies of my book, as usual, but for reasons mentioned above, I did not have the courage to present it. Lost opportunity and an entirely new audience. Well "no use crying over spilled milk" as the saying goes.

Sherena (my daughter) contacted me with one of her co-workers who is also an author and he is planning to sponsor a book fair in the coming months and I hopefully, will be able to embrace this opportunity.

The next step I must plan for is the Church's international day. I hope to have some report of this occasion.

I recently mentioned my thoughts about the body healing itself to a point. We are faced daily with all the ads for Drugs, medications from Amlodipine to Zantax (A to Z) to treat all kinds of conditions, ailments, from Acne to Zit. The key word is **Treat** not heal. So to make my point, if the body is properly nourished and rested, there are conditions which would allow the brains to direct healing of the affected area. Something to think about.

Another instance to make my point. A week ago I was experiencing a tremendous head ache, you know the kind that you can actually feel the throbbing of the area. Well I was advised that if after I take a reading of the Blood pressure monitor, and depending on the results, we should go to the Doctor. I was not readily agreeable to this, I was also told to take a couple tablets.

I decided to use the monitor and the results were a normal reading. So no doctor. Instead I mentioned that I was hungry, got something to eat, after doing some strenuous work cleaning up the back yard and repairing the access door to the downstairs apartment, which allowed me to take the garbage through the lower floor to the front for eventual sanitation pick-up. Finally, mission accomplished.

After eating and resting a bit, I continued to have the throbbing sensation in my head, well I used some cold compresses and rubbed the area, anything to avoid taking the pills. As mentioned before, I decided to listen to my brains and let it do its work. Gently massaging and using the compress, bit by bit the sequence became less frequent, after that day, the next day there was quite a reduction in the intensity and frequency. So no pills.

I now try to relax and take a nap at times, and so far, all is just about normal. I was able to take the bag with the dirt and residue out one day, then the next day I took the rolled up dried stalks, the back-yard is now livable, so to speak. Labor day, the official end of the summer is here and even though we did not do the thing that this day instills such as barbeque etc., I was ready.

I have just received a call from a friend who has returned from Panama and we had quit an interesting and long conversation with him, He is quite knowledgeable and is able to tell me of the time growing up in Colon. It was enjoyable and informative of the incidents we have experienced growing up "Do you remember..?"

We spoke of the conditions in Colon and about the existing flooding's, we both agreed that one of the reasons is because the government has seen fit to remove the break water which existed while we were growing up, and we were thought in school that this was necessary to stem the tide of the Atlantic Ocean. When questioned, they stated that it was removed to allow the big ships to enter the area and dock in a newly installed port in Colon.

We are now experiencing these continued flooding and if nothing is done to reinstall those breakwaters, this situation will only continue and even get worse for the city. We learned this from children growing up in Colon. Allow me to explain "Break water" At the entrance of an area in the form of a lagoon, there existed a sort of stonewall which limited entrance of the Atlantic Ocean into this area. Hence, a "breakwater".

This time, I had quite a lot of information to share with him for a change. He mentioned that an attempt was made by him to access the newly renovated church we grew up in Christ Church by-the-sea. However he was able to meet with some folks in the rectory across the lane adjacent to the church, and he was able to inform them of what it was like at that time. I mentioned to him it must have been quite an experience been able to relate to those folks, it would have been nice to have his talk recorded for historical reasons. Especially to those who are new to the church.

I asked him about the bells, he was not aware of them, therefore I decided to enlighten him. Firstly regarding the renovation, I mentioned that when the contractors were about to commence, they wanted to have photos of how the interior of the church looked, I was able to send a set of photos of the interior showing the altar, lectern, Pulpit, etc. which helped them to retain the original look.

I described the bells for him, there are 8 bells of varying sizes in the tower which produces the musical scale which are activated by pulling attached rope to the clappers of each bell lined up in the below floor in order on tone. Do-re-mi-fa-sol-la-tee-do. Unfortunately, the one person George, who used to play them is no longer around. I remember this, since as kids, we used to sing the scale to the following;" bring your nickel- dimes- and quarters, bring –them- all- to- father- Packard." (These bells are stable it's the clappers which strikes the bell)

There were a number of tunes which were used to indicate the "angelus" usually at 6:00 P.M. and call to worship on Sunday mornings. I really used to like hearing these bells and I have somehow written the notes and assigned a number for each note corresponding to the bells for a couple songs, "Joy to the world" which is simple since it is almost like playing the scale, also to the tune of "Angel we have heard on high". I have sent these to Colon with Albertina, hopefully she did deliver them and somehow, someone would be able to get it going. Is this wishful thinking?

Then there was the huge bell used for toll, this one was attached to a wheel which was activated by pulling a rope which caused the bell to turn and make contact with the clapper. (Contrary to the other bells) We both remember Mr. Emil who used to pull the rope to ring this bell.

I then proceeded to tell him about the Pipe Organ which used to be an attraction to the church. Unfortunately there is no one available to repair it and all was lost. However I remember Handel K. Lawson who was the organist when I was inducted into the choir. There was a time when a note was stuck and the only time it would stop was if the organ was turned off. In order to explain this, I pointed out that in the acolyte room there was a concrete platform with a top. Which housed the compressor that produced the air that when the key on the organ was depressed, it open a stopper to the pipe pertaining to the required note and the release of air to this pipe produced the sound.

By way of furthering explaining this, you see, there were a series of pipes of varying sizes in sets attached to separate sources which we would call ranks. Not really sure how many there were since the area was quite full of these ranks with their pipes of all different sizes. I mention this in order to let you know how I was able to pinpoint the offending note. While the key on the organ was depressed I was able to see which stopper was not activated thus enabling me to actually manually remove the offending bit of object which was not allowing the stopper to close. I will never forget this incident since it was a personal sense of satisfaction which was never shared until this time. I was a small bodied person and was able to get into the side of the area to accomplish this.

Let's continue with the conversation with my friend Rupert who I consider to be an historian, speaking to him encourages me to sort of pick his brains, since he is a fountain of memories. Another thing came up while speaking about the renovation of the church I remembered when the deterioration of the roof began during the time where there was a need for the metal lead which was used in the manufacturing of bullets for the American army. As was the case at the time, the roof was lined with lead, and for some reason not known to me, the lead was stripped from the roof and we were aware that some of this metal was left in the yard and in time was overgrown with grass, consequently I was able to acquire some and was able to make some pocket change, Smithy's Garage located in third street. He paid you by the pound, I don't remember the going rate. Anyway, the church's roof was never the same from that time. Hopefully with this renovation this would be corrected.

We spoke of our days visiting the beach in Colon, I mentioned the episode with the shark. We spoke of other time spent there. At this time I asked him about a mutual friend Donald who has passed away. This brought to mind an incidence with Donald, who was swimming straight out to the 7th street entrance where we do not usually go, since as mentioned before, this is area where the fishermen comes in to sell their catch of the day. I was on the big iron and noticed that Donald suddenly start shouting and then continued swimming feverishly and as he emerged from the water he yelled *Jelly fish*, then he continued to run out to the street and all the way to the corner of central avenue where the pharmacy was located. At another time he told me that he went to have the pharmacist apply some salve to control the welt formed in the side of his face where he was stung.

We remember the area where the Colon Hospital was located in New Cristobal, there was a place we called Blue Hole. We never swam there since it was our understanding that waste from the hospital flowed into the ocean at that point. We could walk out on the walkway ad see all kinds of fish. Sat one point I noticed that a school of fishes were quickly swimming into the Chanel, after looking further I noticed a sting ray in pursuit, thankfully we were not swimming in that area.

Well that's it for now about Christ Church by-the-sea Colon Panama, which had been declared as a national monument by the Government of Panama.

We will now speak about St. Gabriel's Episcopal Church, Brooklyn N.Y. And my involvement in the construction of this building. I told him about the construction of a Church building which has certain requirements. First the Ares has to be cleared as usual. Then the required dimension of the proposed building is staked out. The length and direction is determined, in this case, north is the direction we face as entering. The length is determined then the width. A rope is staked from North to south then according to design, the distance from entrance is determined according to architectural drawings, rope is staked from east to west and at the point where the ropes intersect, and that point is where the center of the proposed altar will be situated.

The next idiosyncrasy is in the plumbing, the area behind the altar, the sacristy where the priests and other persons are robed etc., there is also a sink for washing the altar elements. The waste does not go into the ordinary sewer system, it goes into a well into the earth. After its completion, the edifice is consecrated after this, it can be really addressed as a Church. At the conclusion of our talk. I asked him to come visit the church, and I promised to take him around on a personal tour. The scheduled date is on international day which is celebrated the last Sunday is September. Will have to give him a call to confirm this.

Speaking of idiosyncrasies, I take this opportunity to note some changes that have occurred in today's church. First I have thought of the reason that during the preparation for communion, there is a part called the oblation where the officiating priest will have the servers approach the altar with vessels, one with water and the other with wine, and a receptacle. The priest extends his index finger and thumb of both hands over the receptacle and the server pours some water and wine, in effect, to wash them in order to handle the host (bread) when administering the communion.

Secondly, the practice of offering Communion to children, it was my understanding and teaching as an acolyte, children must first be prepared then confirmed by the Bishop, the next Sunday, they receive the First Communion, henceforth they are able to receive communion as offered.

Another item of note is the fact that only an ordained minister in the faith should administer the Host and chalice (wine) (…He took bread; and when he had given thanks, he brake it, and gave it to his disciples, saying, "Take, eat, this is my Body, which is given for you. Do this in remembrance of me") taken from The Book of Common Prayer *according to the use of* The Episcopal Church.

There was a time that all female were required to have their heads covered upon entering the sanctuary. This practice has been discontinued for quite some years now. Things have certainly changed. Remember it was the custom for men to remove their hats upon entering a home or indoors, now we are seeing men actually sitting at a table with their hats on. This was a definite no-no.

As promised, This coming Sunday September 24th 2017 is International day at ST Gabriel's, therefore I have called my friend Rupert and reminded him of his promised to visit the church, hopefully he will attend and I will be able to take him around to give him a tour of what was detailed to him during our talk.

I was talking about the finished clean-up of the back yard. Now I have decided to do some indoor work in the kitchen. While looking around

I have decided to replace the door/drawer pulls, since some were broken and I was unable to find replacements. Especially since they were dark Florentine style and 4/14 inches wide. Let me explain from the start.

When we bought this house, the kitchen cabinets were of the old style with rounded edges doors and a light colored stain, which began to reflect wear and tear. I decided to call Sears Co. to check the cost for re-surfing all the cabinets, the sales person came up with a price which was way more than I expected, I therefore told him that I did not want to replace them. He said that it was a big job and that was the cost. Well I mentioned to him that I was just toying with the idea and did not have any idea of the cost. At this point, I said to him that I could do the job myself in a timely manner, he said I did not have the necessary tools to do this job, what tools beside what I already have? He began to outline the necessary tools such as a belt sander, a router and the necessary bits the material to surface the area. I made a note of this and thanked him for his time.

On Monday during my lunch time I made the rounds of the tools supply area which existed at the time before the world trade center was built. This is what I did most time, therefore I was familiar with these stores. On lower Broadway. I entered the store and asked the clerk to tell me about a router, he was a bit curt and told me to look in the showcase outside. My reply to him was that if I knew what it was I would not have asked him. Off I went to visit another store and the clerk there was a bit more pleasant, I told him what I intended to do therefore I would appreciate his help.

He introduced me to my first router along with the necessary bits (never knew about this tool) then the belt sander and the required amount of sanding belts, hardware for the doors all of which I bought on the spot. Well on my next visit to the Broadway store I mentioned that I just purchased all the necessary tools to do the job for which I needed the router. He worked on commission and therefore lost that. Reminds me of the movie "Pretty Woman" where the girl tried to purchase an outfit in an upscale store and was shunned. Her rich boyfriend took her to another store and she was able to purchase a whole lot of expensive clothes. On her way back she went to the original store and remind the clerk. Tough, "this is what you lost in commission".

Now came the laminates for the covering, I selected a darker mahogany color, since the floor was ceramic tiles brown white pattern which I had done at an earlier time. I purchased 2 sheets 4x8 laminates and tied it to the top of my car. Unfortunately the wind caught it and one sheet was cracked. Not to worry, I was able to cut around the corners.

The first move was to take all the doors off and take them downstairs, this is where the router came into place, as mentioned before, the doors end drawers edges were rounded and with the laminates the edges had to be squared. I figured this out by using one of the bits in the router it was designed to make a 45 degree edge, after working all edges, I now had flat 45 degrees edges instead of rounded. The next step was to use ¼ round moldings and with the same router bit, I removed the round edges and the result was triangular, therefore by inverting the triangular mounding flat surface to the flat edges, voilà// squared edge. These were glued and tacked with a stapler designed to use small nails (brads).

After all this was done, then came the dirty/dusty work with the belt sander the surfaces were stripped to bear wood and the edges were paired perfectly squared, and ready to accept the laminate. This was delicate work since the laminate had to be carefully placed before coming into contact with the wood, since the glue used was quite effective once touched there is no going back. I learned a lesson therefore all the pieces of laminate were cut a bit larger than the intended surface. After all was set and secured, this is where the next bit for the router comes into place, this bit when used properly, evens the laminate with the surface. Then the exposed edges were stained to match the laminate. With the doors and drawers done and left to cure downstairs, I had to wait until the use of the kitchen was completed. This space became unusable for a couple days, eat out or take out.

Facing the frame of the cabinets was a bit tedious and delicate since each part had to be measured and cut to fit precisely, while this was done downstairs, I had previously sanded the framework and area to be covered, then wiped down to remove all trace of dust then the area had to be cleaned of all dust also. This allowed temporary use of the kitchen until all is cut and ready for gluing then routed to make all edges even.

Now all this was done and the framework covered with as usual, oversized in order to prevent any exposed area, then the router with the same straight edge bit, then clean up and next after placing the pullers on each door and drawer front. Now with some help, I had to re hang each door and replace each drawer. Bingo the job is done and I have saved a bundle, and am now in the possession of some useful tools.

It has been quite a few years now and eventually the ceramic floors after some replacement tiles and then eventually these have been replaced with laminated floor, since the cabinets are now dark, the floor is lighter and the maintenance is reversed. I was able to come up with a combination of floor upkeep along with the precise laminate, I had some remainder of floor care from a place I worked after retirement. Now the sheen has been renewed.

And the beat goes on, not finding the right size pullers, I went to Lows and found a modern steel color pullers 3-1/2" so now there is a predicament. No Problem after all, on the doors where the pullers were installed vertically therefore what I did was to hang one end in the upper established hole then by placing scotch tape in the area of the lower hole and made the mark accordingly then drilled the new hole then tightened both screws and the remaining hole, I was able to us toothpicks to fill the area then darken to match. The drawers presented a little complication since the pullers were mounted horizontally therefore I had to drill both holes, for esthetical reasons each puller had to be centered. My trick was to place a strip of tape over the both holes on the puller, mark the screw hole, then locate the puller in between then securing the tape and removing the puller, there remains the marks for the new puller, drill the both holes, stop the two old holes as above. Then install the pullers using the new holes. I must admit there were a couple misalignment but I just made up the discrepancies by making both holes a bit larger.

To make things even better, I have decided to renew the finish of the cabinets by using the same concoction I used on the floors. They look great and fit to go a long way. Now you can use this (*how to*) information to do your kitchen make over and not have to fork over a lump sum. This information is worth the price of this book, and some.

Good news, I called Rupert as promised, on Sunday morning on my was to church on international day to remind him, he was not at home, therefore I tried his cell phone number and there was no reply,. I could only surmise that he must be on his way and was not able to answer his cell phone. I was pleasantly surprised when he signaled me during the exchange of the "peace" in the service. As is the custom. For good order sake, let me explain. I was vested in my choral robe and in the stands on the altar. After service I accompanied him downstairs to the "Golden Hall".

The reception and international food was available and I was able to introduce him to some friends, some of which he knew from Colon, therefore, at some point I left him in their company and he was able to exchange some memories. It was quite an occasion and as he mentioned some days after the celebration I called and thanked him for coming to the service, and he expressed his enjoyment of the visit. The invitation for another visit was extended for November 5th 2018 when Panama celebrates its separation from Colombia.

The Panamanian group will host a lunch after service at St Gabriel's church service. It is the custom that at a determined part before service is concluded, the members of the group is scheduled to sing the National Anthem, also there is a plan to invite the Panamanian consul to attend this celebration, I know, since a letter of invitation was submitted to the rector for his confirmation and extending. I will hope to report this after. Since it promises to be quite a celebration.

I have checked with the church to determine if the letter was sent, considering I received a call inquiring of its existence. I went to the church and was able to obtain a copy of the text on the church's letterhead and took it over to Tony for forwarding to the consul. A subsequent call confirmed that the letter was received, so now we will await acceptance and confirmation.

As promised, I have called Rupert to remind him of the upcoming celebration, since November 5th is this coming Sunday. I have made arrangements with the monitor operator of the church to have the anthem and words of the National Anthem displayed and played in its entirety, on Sunday, we are scheduled to assemble in full force on the altar to pay tribute to our native land.

I am very happy to report that the service went well and before going any further, I called to ascertain if Rupert was coming, unfortunately he had a very pressing celebration of the birthday of his sister in New Jersey, which required his presence understandably.

We werwe surprised with the presence of a few very good friends who joined us for the service and I personally invited them to join us on the altar for the singing of the national anthem, including the consul representative along with the editor of a Panamanian magazine "La Pollera" who actually presented the rep. he in turn addressed the congregation conveying congratulations and good wishes, on behalf of the Consul. I presented him with a copy of my book, also the church presented them both with our tee-shirt and pin. After the service we retired to the Golden Hall for fellowship, food and exchange of pleasantry, they were seated at the head table along with Tony who was quite instrumental in getting this all together including invitation of friends mentioned above. Mr. Luis Vas also presented us with additional copies of the current edition of his magazine "La Pollera" Viva Panama.

Good news: Allow me to share this with you. I received a call from my daughter Sherena, informing that one of her co-workers has mentioned that he is getting ready to sponsor a book fair in October, she told him about my published book and gave me his contact information. We communicated and he was very kind to consider me part of the occasion. I expressed my gratitude to Sherena. This was a very satisfying contact.

October 6th-8th was the weekend scheduled for the 11th Hispanic/Latin Book Fair In New York, held at the Hispanic/Latino Cultural Center of New York celebrating Hispanic Heritage Month in Jackson Heights (Queens) N.Y. My presentation was scheduled for Sunday 8th. To be delivered in English. However, in an effort to have an idea of the process, I attended the Saturday festivities and I was able to personally meet the gentleman responsible for this opportunity. His name is Mr.

Juan Nicolas Tineo- Press & Literature Director also Book Director he is also an Educator Poet narrator and essayist. He recognized me from the Photo sent in advance for the publication in the program. On Sunday I was better prepared for my presentation. The time slot was 3:35-4:05 P.M. I prepared some Photographic display depicting Colon Rep. of Panama to acquaint the audience from where I hailed.

As the time approached for my presentation, Mr. Tineo mentioned to me that he would like me to start earlier since they were running a bit early, this presented a bit of a predicament since as I looked around, my daughter was not yet there, since she was aware of the time element, I mentioned that I will call to check on her. At which point my sister Yolanda and nephew Edgar arrived, He agreed to switch the lunch time (oh yes, there was food offered). As we were about to start eating, up came Sherena. So the gang is all here.

After eating, we were then ready for my presentation, Mr. Tineo asked Olivia to be the presenter, especially since she was able to do so in Spanish. Before starting I called Mr. Tineo to the stage and presented him with an autographed copy of my book *What if? The Question or a Statement* I then proceeded to sing the first two lines of Panama's national anthem in Spanish for sure. Naturally I remained standing. (*Alcanzamos por fin la Victoria en el campo feliz de la union*) the translation in effect reads "we have finally reached the victory in a happy camp of union"

At this point a standing microphone was brought, which I declined since the presentation is done seated at the table. I did not want to make a point, the only reason I remained standing was because I was singing the anthem. The thought was to signify that I have finally been able to have a victory book presentation, in this happy place where a person speaking English was among the Latinos. As a matter of fact I also interspersed this presentation with some Spanish (Which is my native language)

By explaining how I came about the title of the book, I sang a few verses of the song some of you may remember *"when I was just a little (lad) I asked my mother "what would I be?"*

Then I continued speaking of the meaning of the 7 circles on the cover 1-Camera (Photographer) 2-Book&pencil (Bookkeeper) 3-Solo Mike- (A soloist, choir) 4-console (apprentice A/C) 5- 4 Mikes-r/r group harmonizers) 6-Sewing machine (Tailor) 7- House (architect) after, I continued singing *"here's what she said to me, que sera, sera, whatever would be, would be the future's not ours to see, que sera, sera, what would be, would be"*. **What if?** For those of you who do not know this song, the ideal thing would be for me to print the music sheet, but this would be a bit much. Anyway, ask someone to hum the tune for you. (Smile).

Continuing, I spoke of instances in the book and answered a few questions one of which was "How old are you?" my reply was that I was born in the year (?) do the math, This drew some laughter, on a whole I was told by another person that the presentation was very entertaining, this made me happy that I was able to accomplish this, and thanked the speaker as well as the family (Olivia, Yolanda, Edgar) and the audience. I had over run my allotted time, however I asked their patience to mention the fact that there were a couple things not mentioned in the book, and as I see Sherena I mentioned the little jab I made to her about the fact that, "that is a Phone and not a camera" but after looking around for a suitable photo for my book cover, the best was the one taken by her phone, therefore I take that back and hereby gave her credit for this photo.

MUCHAS GRACIAS (Thank You Sherena)

I mentioned a couple things in the book, the other is the name of my friend Euclid Jordan (Not Jordon) I mentioned this to him and as a gentleman, he pardoned me. This brings to mind, I just recently received an application for a Journal been published for the pending retirement of his priest accompanied by a letter which with his permission, I quote in part "...As many of you know, my wife Daphne and I are members (49) years of St. David's Episcopal Church, Cambria Heights.

I was Senior Warden twice; primarily responsible for calling, a good shepherd, now Rev. Dr. Dean Mastine NIsbett in 1985 from Antigua, now close to retirement. We were deeply involved in getting our new church erected 25 years ago, along with St. Gabriel's Brooklyn in partnership with our compatriot Richard Buery. Just imagine two predominantly Black Episcopal Churches being built by predominantly Black Immigrants…"

We really shared like situations, I too was senior warden twice during that time and deeply involved in the building of our respective church. I started at St Gabriel 1966 which will add up to 51 years to date. Well done thou good and faithful servant, continued success in all your endeavors, present and future.

The past two Sundays, (October 22nd and 29th). I attended the evening services of St. Paul's Episcopal Church in the village of Flatbush to be part of the choir in the celebration of their 181st year of existence and I got to thinking, that as the present situation, and 69 years ago, there exist the same problem of parking. As a matter of fact, it's this problem which spawned the church I now attend, St Gabriel's which is located at 331 Hawthorne Street, Brooklyn, N.Y.

As history reveals, the workers who drove the carriages to transport the members of ST Paul's church, after dropping them off at service, they had to park at Hawthorne Street until service is over and then return to pick up their charges for return to their respective homes. After some time, there arose the situation where these workers needed a place to worship therefore, the decision was made to build a place of worship for them, well as that goes, the proverbial situation occurred, shortage of revenues/ financing, what to do? A foundation was set in place, and the only other alternative was to construct a roof over this, which resulted in a building below street level.

As can be noted, to enter the building, there were several steps down. Which explains why this church building was not readily visible while driving through Hawthorne Street when we were trying to locate it.

The formula I used to determine the 69 years difference. 181 years celebration. St Paul's church

112 years St. Gabriel's Church existence (including the new Building).

2017-181=1836 (St Paul's) 2017-1905= 112 (St Gabriel's) 181-112= 69 years difference.

Sometime earlier in this narrative, I mentioned my disdain with dentist which went back to earlier Public school in Colon Rep. of Panama, and about his lack of bedside manners. The reason for saying this is because he was not considerate of the pain I was feeling as he tried to drill the tooth, apparently he did not use enough pain killer. To make things worse, this was about the time that we were celebrating Yvonne's birthday, and mother had baked a cake which I could not partake of. You can well appreciate the depth of my disdain.

As time went by, this filling was still causing me problems, I therefore eventually picked the filling out. In those days, the practice was to use chewing tobacco to reduce the pain and be careful not to swallow. This tooth was eventually extracted while here in New York and the then dentist decided to build a bridge over the resulting space. When he was getting ready to do this, he mentioned that he would have to file down the two adjoining teeth in order to set the bridge. This further annoyed me, now I have two filed teeth with a bridge.

Well this brings me to this point, where we had a dental appointment for periodical checkup. It started with the usual x-rays and then inspection by the dentist, he took the opportunity to emphasize that this molar has to come out, while checking it, it is my belief that he exerted extra pressure at this point and, naturally I winced. He asked me "does that hurt?" I said "sure, if you placed extra pressure on it. I have been able to chew on this side while chewing without any inconvenience"

It is my conviction that he wants very badly to have my tooth extracted for the benefit of his assistances who were in attendance during this session, also to confirm his original diagnoses 6 months ago and I did not come back to him in pain as he predicted then. He had his nurse make an appointment with me to return Thursday in a couple weeks, hopefully, this would not be the time since its Thanksgiving Nov. 23rd. And we are scheduled to spend the week with Samantha in Virginia. I will report.

November 27th, 2017.

We had a very happy thanksgiving with the Joyner's (Samantha, Charles, Zoe, Chase and Noah) and had the occasion to be introduced to the newest member of the family, (Snoop Dog) a friendly and pleasant dog, not sure what the breed is. We left Brooklyn by taxi to Amtrak station in N.Y. Monday 20th. For a pleasant and comfortable train ride to VA Where we were picked up by Charles. We enjoyed a sumptuous meal on Thanksgiving Day and returned home on Friday 24th, only to be ready for Saturday morning trip to Long Island where we attended the birthday gathering of our Granddaughter Sydney who celebrated her 8th year.

We are happy to confirm our attendance to Sydney's party which was quite a gathering of family and friends. A good time was had by all, playing the video and electronic games, and a sit down to Pizza and cake and the works. I can attest that she had a great time and was genuinely happy to see all and interact with the several games with children as well as the young and old adults present. Including us (smile)

Fast forward to Sunday, December 10th 2017 this was a very happy and exhausting day, it started out on an early trip to Laurelton L.I. New York to visit the church where Sherina and Family attends. We were extended an invitation to celebrate the 21st anniversary of the pastor Rev. Dr. Charles C. Collymore, by one of his son. Who was also at the birthday party for Sydney with his family, as can be noted, there is a close friendship between the Collymore and Lawson family.

We arrived early and was able to settle in to await the arrival of all the guests (parishioners) also Sherena and Sydney. Service started at approximately 11:00 am with songs of praise and worship. It was quite enjoyable, then selections by the Jr youth group which Sydney joined, the older group which also rendered selections, followed by speeches and presentations and introduction of the main Speaker by min D. Collymore, The Rev. of another church, who is a fellow clergy and friend of Dr. Collymore.

His message was very informative and he recounted the growing up life of his friend and college, and in making his point, he allude to the fact that Dr. C previous years of pastoring was of such, Growing Up.

But now at 21 year he has finally gown up and "a man" now can make his own decisions and consider of age. This was all in good spirit and entertaining to the congregation.

At this point, the master of ceremonies, called the representatives of several groups of the church to make their respective presentations and remarks to the honoree and his wife, they were both moved and appreciative of this outpouring of love and appreciation by these gifts. It was at this point that I asked to speak on behalf of my family which was allowed. I started by singing the first line of one of my favorite hymns. "There is a sweet, sweet Spirit in this place, and I know it's the Spirit of the Lord". I continued by saying that this reminds me of the church where I grew up. I alluded to a comment made by his son David who mentioned that among the things he learned from his father was to keep good company. I therefore quoted a phrase I often remembered. "Show me your company and I can tell who you are". This makes me proud the say to my Daughter Sherena and directing myself to her, I said "Sherena you are in good company" at this point The Dr. asked her to stand and be acknowledge, and at the same time he asked Olivia and Sydney to stand, they were applauded by the congregation.

I made a presentation of a copy of my book to the Dr. which was signed and dedicated to him *"in recognition of his anniversary and 21 years in the service of the Lord. On behalf of Olivia and Richard. December 10th 2017"* I mentioned to him that on a previous visit he had invited me to attend a service to which I was unable, because of prior commitment to services at my church in Brooklyn but this time, since he has attained "manhood" (21yers) I had to make it.(smiles)

The time is now approaching 3:00 pm and I have to be in Brooklyn for a Christmas concert which a warm-up was scheduled for 3:30 pm. There was a reception after this service where food was been served, Sydney went up to the hall and asked for 2 takeout to be filled, Sherena was able to get them for us, we asked to be excused, and off we went after such and enjoyable and memorable occasion.

We reached the St. Augustine's Episcopal Church in Brooklyn just in time, and was fortunate to find a parking spot right around the corner from the site. Olivia was able to nosh on some food during the trip, luckily I had a sanitary fork in the glove box for her. Upon entering the church hall I was not as fortunate to find a fork therefore I washed my hands and used it for eating some of my food, so there, all is well I am fed, and ready to get started in time.

This concert titled "CHRISTMAS IN HIS PRESENCE" was presented by the Chancel Choir of St Mark's United Methodist Church. I was asked to be part of this group for this presentation, which required me to attend prior rehearsals, this was a bit of trying since parking space is not readily available, therefore at times I would travel around and around then on finally finding a spot to park my vehicle, had to find the place which was not so bad, but. It was after the session is over, I was not sure where I finally ended up parking (a senior moment). The next time I learned my lesson, when parking I write the address and location, after which I only had to follow my directions to the car. The last two times, I really left home 2 hours earlier which allowed me to get lost and eventually find the place with time to spare.

Despite inclement weather and a bit of a cold cough coming up, I was able to make it through and was happy to have been a part of this. The singing was quite extensive and demanding however, the music was partially familiar which allowed me to be comfortable in enjoying and participating in this concert. I got that old familiar feeling *it's beginning to look a lot like Christmas.*

The plan is to travel to Chez-B on Friday 15th this week-end to check out this old homestead. Will get back with this. Anticipating the drive to the Poconos, brings to mine the action of driving a car and riding a train. This is quite a difference experience one has to experience, endure or get through. Let me explain what I mean

At some point in my narratives I mentioned that my first experience riding on the train started the first day of my arrival in the U.S., I was able to board the train armed with a map which was giving me while in Colon, Panama which I memorized I was aware of the subway stops to get to Brooklyn, I even offered advice to a Young Lady who was anxious since it was her first time on the train. What I did not mention was the fact that after being here for a while, and relocated to the Flatbush area and finally had to take the trains to work.

Going was not a problem, since the directions were to take the train at the station Sterling Place and the stop in Manhattan was Wall Street. I was working in the financial district at the time. So there we are Start at Sterling Place, get off at Wall Street. Now after work, all I had to do was to board the train at Wall Street station and travel to Brooklyn and get off at Sterling place. Well after traveling for what seemed a long time, I did not see the sterling street stop. Panic sets in, therefore I decided to go back from the start to get on the train again hoping that, perhaps I passed the stop and did not see it. After doing this again, unsuccessfully, I realized I did not really know about the train system and decided to ask the attendant for directions, and was told that I had to board the # 3 train bound for Flatbush. So it's not only knowing the stops, but the right train to take. (**Frustration**)

After relocating to East New York I had to be aware of the right train, therefor I now had the train route down pat.

This was during the early 70's and as I travelled by train, which was elevated at some part I now I was aware of roof tops and all the antennas of varying sizes for television receptions, Those of you who were aware of this, know what I mean. As time goes by, slowly they began to disappear only to be replaced by Disks, some even on the sides of buildings. These are the changing times. (**Amazement**)

Now I will refer to driving a car, which can evoke quite myriad experiences, Road Rage, anxiety to mention a few. When travelling to a destination, it was necessary to have exact locations, Street, local, number of establishment, between which two streets. Etc. this entails getting familiar with the area, route to travel etc. In order to minimize these distractions, first there were maps to guide you. As time advances, we are now provided with MapQuest or the now popular aide, the GPS. (Global Position System).Before starting is advisable to have a sense of where you are heading. (**Bon Voyage)**

There are different ways to travel to a destination based on starting location, weather conditions, traffic congestions or your state of mind to name a few. As an example, it is convenient for me to take the Jackie Robinson (Inter borough parkway) towards the G.W.B. in order to travel via interstate 80 W. which is convenient, it is at the top of Pennsylvania Ave. 2 streets from where I now reside.

**(Sensation)**

A location in New Jersey to which I have travelled from time to time I have decided to go down town Brooklyn to take the Brooklyn Bridge this was during the time that extensive repairs were in effect and the trip was not easy, trying to get by the various road blocks etc. Then the actual bridge was covered or may a say, enclosed on both sides, not a pleasant trip.

The construction has been completed and the approach area is now made over and so pleasing to the sight and ease of accessing, followed by the trip to the Lincoln Tunnel, this is another sensation since the approach is somewhat trying, Ahead is the entrance and attempt to get in a lane and slowly trying to avoid slipping out of lane by interruptions of other vehicles, as I slowly approached I finally am in a path directly to the entrance and finally I am there and slowly advancing as the traffic is stop and go and continuing on this pace for a while, then things begin to slowly speed up therefor I try to keep up the pace and gradually the pace begin to accelerate to a steady pace and the end of the tunnel is in sight and oh what a feeling of exhilaration as I exit into the Ave. and now I am on the way to my destination.

We were able to enjoy the holiday season after all, we attended the 11: 00 am mass on Sunday 24th at St. Gabriel's church which was quite enjoyable. We spent the evening at home, in the evening we wrapped some gifts for the usual receptions then as the night progressed, lo and behold the time was after midnight, so technical it was now the dawn of the new day i.e. Christmas morn therefore I decided to look up some appropriate season music c.d. and I proceeded to crank up my component and blasted the night with my music.

I guess I made up for summertime when my neighbor would play loud music into the night so loud that the wall of my bedroom would vibrate.

I then logged on to my computer and sent Christmas wishes to family and friends.

An invitation was extended to us and also to the family of Sherena by Richie, to have dinner with his family at their home in the afternoon of Christmas day. Therefore 11 of us had a sumptuous dinned prepared by Debora with some help from the children and hubby. I asked her jokingly, if there were other gusts expected, since there was enough food. We were able to have some take home, which precluded any cooking for the next day. The rest of the evening was spent with games.

As if that was not a lot of vittles intake on the 25th. Sherena and Richie decided to invite Olivia and myself to have dinner at a local restaurant to enjoy some Mexican food to celebrate Olivia's birthday therefore the 11 of us met and spent another enjoyable day of eating and fellowship. Olivia made out well since this was her second birthday dinner, she and I had dinner on her birthday. We returned from Chez-B on the 20th in time to celebrate the day.

The rest of the week did not go so well, we had a setback since the Heat in the house was nonexistent, we called the home service and after several tries they finally sent someone to check the heating system out and it was determined that the Pilot light in the boiler was out, the repairman lighted it and the system was up and running again, I asked him to ascertain it was ok and he waited to make sure that water was heating and the pipes were getting hot. So we were good to go. A relative of Olivia visited in order to attend a 70th birthday party which we were all scheduled to attend, she will spend the night after. Well as fate would have it, the very next day I was washing my hands and realized that the water was not getting hot and after checking things out the boiler was again inoperative.

Several calls were made to the service again and because the weather was very cold and there was quite a demand therefore no serviceman was available to visit until the next day, this was not acceptable to us and we tried to convince them to consider this an emergency, which it was. They the offered to allow us $150, for a night's stay at a hotel, which we had no other choice but to accept, especially since we had a guest.

We got ready to attend the Birthday party and on the way, reserved a suite at the nearby hotel. The party was quite a spectacular one and very enjoyable, I must explain that in addition to this, there was some snow on the ground. To add to the aforementioned disaster after the party, as I approached the location where the car was parked, I spotted from the distance, an orange color missive on the windshield and as I neared the car, my worst fear was confirmed, there it was, a parking ticket. As it turned out I was a bit beyond the sign pole. $115.00 for parking in a bus stop.

We got to the Hotel at about 2:00 am. And spent the rest of the time and checked out about 11: am to be home in time for the service man who was scheduled to arrive between the hours of 12:00 noon to 4:00 p.m. a call was made to them at 2:00 am and they assured us that someone would be there at or before 4:00 P.m. The house was so cold that we remained cloaked and just before the stroke of 4: 00 P.m. the phone rang and it was the serviceman, I stood at the door to be sure he had the right place.

Well before he went to the basement, I mentioned that I had turned off the system to cover time while we were away, he said I should not have done that since any standing water could freeze, I started to inquire but he said first let him check the system, after looking at the thermostat, he proceeded downstairs and I accompanied him, my thoughts were, what if I had done some harm by turning off the system, I pointed out the switch to him, which he then turned on, and proceeded to disarm the flame gun and I was aware that this person knew what he was doing so I said to him "I will leave you to do your job"

After a while I decided to go down to explain my rational for turning off the system. "when I realized that the pilot flame was out, and to my understanding there should be the presence of a gas stream to keep the pilot flame on, since the flame is out I assume that the gas stream continues, and since we were not going to be there, it behooved me to turn it off" He agreed with me and said "You did right" (a sigh of relief from me) however, this system was adjusted to go out in the lack of a flame. I asked for further explanation of the procedure, if there is no flame, does the system shut down the stream of gas?, he confirmed this. Now I have a better understanding of how it works.

This disaster happened on the coldest time of the year, which brings to mind the year I first came to the U.S was December 15th 1962 and the temperature same date this year was 4 degrees below zero. It has never been this cold since that time. That time I had to sleep beside the radiator with army blankets and fully clothed, I was temporarily living in a basement apt. but as soon as the weather improved and I was able to get suitable lodging all was well.

In addition to the Traffic parking ticket $115.00 using Olivia's car, When going to my car to attend this morning's service, another orange missive was on my car, this time for alternate side parking, $45,00 =$160.00 in parking tickets is certainly not a good ending for the year. Hopefully the New Year will have a great start.

We received a call from the guest inquiring if all was well regarding the heating system, happily we were able to confirm that the heating system is presently working and hopefully the problem has been corrected, also to inform us that she had arrived back to Atlanta safe. That was good news. Things were not as it should have been but the heating was beyond our control and as the saying goes, "all is well that ends well"

It is now 10.29 p.m. 12/31/17 therefore in one hour and ½ it will be a new year, usually I would be at the midnight mass at church and at the bewitching hour each year, it would be my task to activate the electronic bells to chime welcoming the New Year, hopefully this year someone else will do this. We attended the 9:30 am mass which was a carol and lessons service, which was very well attended. After the midnight service there is a New Year's party in the Golden hall which we usually attend but we are skipping this year. I was listening to Ravel's Bolero and eventually I will try to watch the goings on in Times Square N.Y "dropping of the ball" on television.

**Happy and a prosperous New Year is my wish to all.**

We spent the New Year indoor relaxing and listening to some seasonal music going through all the cards and gifts, this is how it all starts. Now two days into the new year the temperature has been somewhat brutal to say the least, Thursday 1/4th It started to snow with a vengeance and this area has experienced 11inches of snow which has created a traffic dilemma, especially since word was received of the passing of a childhood friend and the "Going home" service was scheduled for Friday 1/5th. Despite the difficulty, thank goodness for 4wheel drive car (Jeep) I was able to navigate the snow mounds and was able to attend said service. It is on occasions such as these, friends and acquaintances get together and exchange experiences, about the good old times.

Continuing on the concept of a happy new year, so far not so good, since on the way to have my car checked, I received a phone call, I pulled over as anyone should, and took the call, which was from a member of the church's vestry inquiring where the gas meters are located, after telling him the location of the only gas meter I am aware of, I asked what about it? I was told that there was a Gas leak in the church and the Department of building ordered the building shut down and the National grid (Gas CO.) closed down the Gas feed to the building. I made several calls to get the lowdown, therefore after leaving the funeral service mentioned above. I decided to visit the Church to get a firsthand look on the situation. The worker was repairing the pipes in one area and they had already repaired some in another location.

The plan is to complete the repair and pressure test in order to ascertain the sealing of all leaks, at which point, the D.O.B will be called to inspect the work and on confirmation, the National grid will be called to restore the gas feed. Hopefully, if this is satisfactory, perhaps there will be a service on Sunday, and the senior center would be resumed on Monday. Speculation is the word, I will call the church office for an update. Apparently, repairs are ongoing and perhaps a temporary generator is to be expected in order to have service.

Regretfully, it was indeed speculation since on Sunday morning, services were held in the Golden hall, there were two portable heaters mounted at the top of the wall one at either end of the hall. A portable make shift altar was set up and chairs set up for the choir and altar personnel, the lectern served as the pulpit and a Piano brought into play. The order of services was conducted as usual.

On the following Monday, I went to the church to check on status, where I saw the ceiling open at various places and new 3"pipes lined up on the floor. The object was to replace all the pipes leading from the back where the gas entered the building. Therefore the complete line was replaced. My thoughts were that, there was no defect in the lengths of pipe, and a proper sealing of each joint to be addressed. Adding to the catastrophe. There was a water break in the water line at the north end of the floor where the senior center offices are located which resulted in water damage to Sunday school supply. Consequently the water pipe system network was also replaced.

As it turned out, there were gas leaks at each threaded joint, my thoughts were that instead of replacing the pipes with new ones, considering that there was no flaw in the body of each pipe and the fault was really in the joints. There is a saying my professor at school used to quote "A chain is as strong as its weakest link" so considering this analogy, each end could be rethreaded, reworked or cut if there were any cross thread. Then used of joint compound and reinstalled. If any cuts were made then an extension piece be added to make up the lost area. Granted there is additional time involved, but saving in cost of new material. I guess the difference in cost of time and cost of new hardware would have to be weighed.

Since this is only (after the deed), it also occurred to me, should there be some financial consideration made for the replaced pipes? Something to think of. Now it's Saturday January 13th. 2018 and I made a call to the church to check on the progress and I was told that all is connected and checked by the D.O.B. and National Grid has restored the Gas but there is another problem. ***And the beat goes on.*** The sprinkler system has erupted in the both offices of the senior center and extensive water damage sustained. And we say "a happy New Year?" this has to be looked into I wonder if at some point during work on the gas line, the water line that feeds the sprinkler system might have been damaged.

Sunday there was only one service since it was also our annual parish meeting all things considered, at least the sanctuary and the golden hall were habitable i.e. repairs were done and the ceiling of the hall was repaired and heat restored. It's a good thing, since the combined congregation would not have been properly accommodated if we had to repeat last week's situation. On entering the sanctuary, I detected a lingering odor of gas and brought it to the attention of a member of the vestry, he said they were aware of this and was told by one of the worker that this lingering odor would be eventually dissipated but they would be checking into it on Monday even thou it's a holiday (Martin Luther King day). I will check on Tuesday to ascertain the completion also the repair in the water damage.

After service which ran a bit longer, since we also celebrated Martin Luther King Day with musical selections by a Violinist which was quite well rendered. Also there was a farewell observance of our director of music and Organist who played his last service here, and would be going on to St. Mark's Episcopal Church where he will start next Sunday. We retired to the Golden hall downstairs, a lunch which was provided to all prior to the start of the meeting.

Nominations and presentations by nominated persons for various positions namely, Warden, Vestry members, Delegates to convention, Representatives to Deanery Consul. Followed by the Treasurer's report, which was quite detailed, followed by question and answers. At one point the treasurer mentioned that the golden hall was a source of great financial returns. I was very pleased to hear this and had to refrain from an outburst of a shout of Hallelujah.

In my records I have a cover letter dated February 12, 1989 to our lawyer R. Royce Esq. c.c. to Bishops Witcher and Orris Walker with attachments, indicating my requests to raise the height of the Church building in order to provide us with sufficient height to comply with building code in order to have a basement area suitable for a community center, receptions (wedding package) dances etc. where builder stated there would be additional costs to alter the drawings. Also added changes which also saved costs. It was eventually agreed that the additional costs would be justified. So with the Treasurer's comments regarding the hall being the second major source of income for the upkeep of the church, you can understand my elation.

This was alluded to on pages 82, 83 & 84 of my book *what if? The Question or a Statement*. Published 2013. In reflection, it has occurred to me that on this date January 14th, 2018 I too have a celebration to be observed, since it has been 52 years since I have become a member of this church. The only difference is that the organist have served 7 years as a staff member and is now moving on to increased rewards for his talent. My reward after these years was to hear justification for my insight in presenting my insistence in restructuring the plans for our new church at the increased cost. And now having this fact pointed out by the statement of the treasurer "the Golden Hall was the next best source of income in support of the church" that is my reward, there was justification in my insistence. Hallelujah, hallelujah. I will still be here.

It was my intent to address the congregation on the following Sunday, after meeting with the priest indicating my desires to do so, he suggested that because he would not be conducting the service himself, this would be a distraction, instead I should consider delivering my reflection during the upcoming Black history month celebrations. I pointed out that my reflections were not in regards to black history. I will give this some considerations and will amend some of my comments in order to comply, this way I can further generate some interest in my book.

I will make the following observations, ST. Gabriel's church has served as a training source for many persons who has gone on to further endeavors. Somewhat as (Basic training). Starting way back when one of our youths Rev Hickman Alexander who has gone on to be appointed rector to a parish, and as many other persons who have served internship (basic training) in this church, have gone on as "soldiers" to continue the "fight" to serve the Lord, each in his/her way to spread the Gospel, I refrain to mention their names at this time, for fear of omitting some of them. Presently we are blessed with our next "recruit" in the person of Leandra Lambert who will soon be ordained at this church and eventually will be on the march for her task in the "vineyard". We of ST. Gabriel's church ought to be proud of our accomplishments in this respect.

I will report on this next step. As promised, On Sunday February 4th 2018 I attended the 8: 00 am service and was able to set up with the monitor's attendant with the help of the parish admin. Who was able to scan photographs of the originals church and proposed architect drawings of the church from the office and e-mail to the monitor's station And have them include for display on monitors to enhance my presentation (the age of electronics is wonderful).

The service was running a bit long and I was anxious to infringe on the congregations time, therefor I apologized and abbreviated my presentation, (regretfully). But I made up for this at the 11:00 am service I was now composed and greeted the congregation in several languages (French, Jewish, Spanish and then English) "Good morning". Much to their delight. This eased the situation and now I was on a roll, so to speak. In order to link this presentation with Black History Month, I tweaked a bit and added the fact that ST, Gabriel's church was built despite the fact that we were admonished that there was no new Episcopal church built for the past 100+ years but we pursued and made it happen therefore, we should all applaud this fact. (They did)

I also told the story of on a recent trip to Norfolk Va. I met a person who was addressing a group of fellow graduates and indicated that he was in the process of getting a church building started, on hearing this and as usual, I reached into my bag which I carried at all times, and withdrew 2 copies of my book and presented it to him indicating that he should be guided from its contents to guide him on quest. And the other to be sold by him using the proceeds as a donation from me to get it started. His wife approached me after with tears in her eyes and thanked me for this gesture. I was later asked if he has started his building. I do not know since that was the last time seeing him, but can only hope that it was helpful.

I proceeded to read a passage found on page 81 of my book, and then mentioned that the facts are to be found in my book **What if? The question or a Statement.** Published 2013, and those who had a copy should read it and those persons who did not have a copy, I really have copies with me for those who wished to acquire it (a Plug on my part) which evokes some laughter. (*A re gato que sai mas*) phonetically written Japanese, meaning, thank you very much.

Happily, after the service I was asked to autograph three copies of the book to be presented to invited guests by Fr. Alleyne. I was able to sell another book therefore, the plug did reap some results.

I was genuinely surprised when I was called to the center of the altar along with the pastoral group, present and past wardens also Olivia and others, to join me I was presented with a beautiful acrylic Plaque which reads as follows:

"Longevity Award for Distinguished Service"

## LONGIVITY AWARD

Presented to
### *Richard E. Buery Snr.*
For 52 years of dedicated stewardship
to the church community
"Well done, good and faithful servant…"
Matthew 25:23
### *St. Gabriel's Episcopal Church*
331 Hawthorne Street Brooklyn NY 11225
Sunday, February 4, 2018

Fr. Alleyne preempted the presentation with some words of gratitude on behalf of the members of the church, which were encouraging and gratefully accepted. I thanked all of those persons who were part of the presentation. I will certainly place this plaque in a place of prominence in my home.

Despite the rocky start of the New Year, this has been a bright interlude. I refrain to say "a bright start", since there are some troubling occurrences which continues to plague us as a nation, which I will not get into, however, it brings to mind the historical readings of the (Rise and fall of the Roman Empire). Hopefully, history will be kind to us and we as a nation, will not suffer the same fate. **God bless America.**

2/25/18 Sunday. Today was a good day seems things are beginning to look up, we celebrated the closing of Black history month with a musical concert sponsored by the Gospel & Chancel choirs, which were part of a much varied program with spoken words, dances by the Dance ministries comprised by the youth of the church who choreographed their own presentation, the Mimes group (Male youths) who also did their own choreography, I Must say that the youth of our church are a source of pride, may they continue to grow in **HIS** grace. We were also favored with piano solos, also Vocal solos including yours truly, with one of my favorite "The holy city *(Arr. Stephen Adams)*" also elocutionary presentations. Quite entertaining, also interpretive dance, to mention some of the items on the program. I can safely say that everyone was rewarded with an entertaining evening. What's more, I was approached by a dear lady who requested a copy of my book, seems she was present at the last evening presentation, so I can truly say that it's beginning to look like a *happy new year.* I will have to stop here since there is some packing to do on our part, since tomorrow we are off to VA to spend the next week at the Joyner's.

During my visit, I have decided to update some previously recorded information on a flash drive I was able to use a laptop (hand me down from Olivia). After some trying and maneuvering to get acquainted with this different medium, I was able to get something written and will, at some time, add this information, which recorded the activities in VA, and the civic center of Washington D.C. we actually boarded one of the sightseeing busses. This information will be forthcoming.

(Add flash drive)

On Thursday 3/8/18 we celebrated the "home going" of one of our longtime parishioners, the service was quite impressive and her legacy was quite evidenced by the number in attendance, approximately 600 strong to see her off, she was quite a lady and was very much involved with the activities of the Church. May she rest in peace, sad to see her go but certainly the feelings and certainly the thoughts were truly indicated "well done thou good and faithful servant".

St. Gabriel's church was very active this past week and to top it off, on Sunday,11 March 2018 At 4:00 P.M., we celebrated the ordination of the "recruit" Leandra Thelma Lisa Lambert as mentioned previously, was conferred by the Bishop of the dioceses of Long Island The Right Reverend Lawrence C. Provenzano, to the Sacred order of Deacons. (Presider & Preacher). Others.

**Participants in the Liturgy: (**as printed in program)

The rev. Anthony Bowen, Deacon

Presenters: The Rev Eddie Alleyne (Rector of St. Gabriel's Church) also MS. Gifty Amposem, Dr. Dr.Kathy Bozzuti-Jones, Ms. Christina Bryza, The Rev. Barbara Cawthorne Crafton, Ms. Margaret N. Farrell, Canon Myra B. Garnes The Rev. Hershey Mallette Stephens, Mr. Wainright G.F. McKenzie, Ms. Summerlee, Ms. Laura F. Steele, The rev. Lawrence Womack.

*Vesting:*

Ms. Brianna Grazete, (stole) Ms. Amanda Davis, (Dalmatic) Mr. Kevin Howard, (dalmatic)
*Litanist:* Ms. Sarah Ittoop
*Lectors:* Mr. Jeremy Cox, Ms. Cynnia Semper
*Oblation Bearers:* Ms. Suzette Cumberbatch, Mr. Tre Laurence.

*Musicians:*

Mr. Davian D Alleyne. *Organ and Saxophone*
Mr. Tyler Cohen, *Steelpan*
Mr. Quincy J. Dover, *Organ*
Mr. Tony Goddard, *Drums*
Mr. Kurleigh Lowe, *Piano & Steelpan*

Combined Choirs of St. Gabriel's Episcopal Church Brooklyn & St. Augustin's Episcopal Church.

There were a number of clergy/ ministers present. All told, there were about 700 persons in attendance to witness this memorable and lively occasion, including our assisting bishop, the Right Rev. Daniel Alloy, the full staff of acolytes. And lay ministers.

Again we should extend a heartfelt appreciation to the neighboring Catholic church ST Francis of Assisi, who came to the rescue by providing parking for the numerous drivers in their facilities. Our church bus was provided for transporting to and from the celebration.

This is Sunday 2/25/18 we had a successful concert, celebrating Black History month. Monday we travelled via *(access a ride)*, to the Penn station train station in Manhattan N.Y. for our trip to Virginia where we will be spending a week at the home of Samantha, who will be travelling on behalf of her Job on a lecture tour. I will take the opportunity to learn about the workings and operation of the laptop I inherited from Olivia since she had to give it up for another one which was more compatible to her. I am having the task of my life trying to find my way around it, first I had to find the location of "Word"

The first thing I did was to find something written on this unit then I found the way to open a new document, then printed some text, then saved it as 'travel' now all I had to do was look in *documents* and open 'travel', an now thankfully, I on the way to explore. Since there is no mouse to use for navigation, I have to try the built in pad instead of hunting for the mouse, which I am used to on my P.C.

Wednesday 2/28/18 we decided to take a trip to the Capital (Washington D.C.). We called a yellow cab for transportation to Union Station in order to book a bus tour on the Big Bus double decker. There was a mix-up. Since the booking was made on the phone via a subsidiary agent. This definitely was not the best way to book reservations, since had we known, it could have been done on the spot when we arrived at the station.

Anyway, we had to go inside the terminal to the *Big Bus* Kiosk. We presented the downloaded ticket to the agent who was unable to accept it since the required bar code was no included in this print out, as far as I am concerned, I prefer to deal direct and in person. "The age of technology". As this fiasco continued, we had to call the booking agent and have them e-mail the bar code directly to the attending agent, which enabled them to issue a boarding pass to the bus. Frustration and time lost could have been better spent on the tour.

We are on the way and since this a Double Decker bus, it was conducive to have an unobstructed view for photography, to be sure I had my cameras (still and Movie) not my phone (hint). The top section was not full therefore this allowed me to place my camera bag next to me and allowed me the flexibility to twist and turn in order to capture the scenes as they materialized.

This is not where things ended, according to the ticket purchased, the stipulation was for all the stops included in this segment *Red loop* which comprised a total of 22 stops and a visit to the Madame Tussauds wax museum, also included in the cost of tickets. The published brochure showed this attraction as available, and clearly indicated it as a free add-on, also Olivia specifically asked about this on booking the trips, also when we were about to board the bus at Union station.

I mention this because as we approached stop #19, we debarked and indicated to the tour guide that we would be visiting the wax museum and he pointed out the location, well this was the highlights of the trip for Olivia, therefore we proceeded to the entrance and as we entered, the clerk asked to see our ticket, she said this ticket did not cover the entrance fee, well this is "the straw that broke the camel's back" I do not have to tell you what went on next, however after a bit of a tirade, the clerk indicated that we should go next door where the Big Bus had offices and there was another entrance to the museum, the clerk there was alerted of our arrival, therefore we were allowed to take the elevator entrance to the display. We were greeted by a believable likeness of Whoopi Goldberg.

On entering, there was a brief video about the museum, then we proceeded to visit the various halls, such as the hall of past presidents, Washington and others to name a few, Eisenhower, Nixon, Carter, Regan, Kennedy, Clinton, Bush & Bush, Obama. This area was enclosed by rope, and as we approached, we were invited in to be photographed with the likeness of President Barack Obama and first lady. Considering I had my camera, the Photographer offered to take photos with my camera also, Olivia offered her phone for photos. Continuing on, there were other statues, Snoop dog, Beyoncé, Rihanna and others. Unfortunately, we did not purchase the photos offered for sale taken by the photographer. On checking photos taken with my camera, they were more suitable, therefore I printed them and am now proud to display 8x10 photos of Olivia and myself with the Obamas.

The overall experience was enlightening and informative. On Sunday we were favored with the presence of Taylor, daughter of Sherena/Pete (our granddaughter) who attends Howard University. We attended Church services then a family dinner after which, Samantha took her back to school.

Our scheduled departure for home (Brooklyn) is on Monday. Things did not go as planned, since the Amtrak train was one and a half hour late, which caused us to miss the scheduled pick-up by the *'access-a-ride'* at the time of our arrival in Penn station, Manhattan. We could not re-schedule a pick-up therefore, we were obliged to hail a yellow cab. This was also a nightmare, since the driver was not familiar with traffic route to Brooklyn, and was using the G.P.S for the least travelled roads in order to avoid traffic congestion. As I always maintained, this is ok when one is have an idea where one is going, he obviously did not, and consequently we were unavoidable treated to a tour of the borough of queens, N.Y. I did not want to further upset him but finally I had to tell him that this is not what we bargained for, the charged fare was outlandish. The next day we called the system operator to complain and they agreed that we submit proof and documentation which we provided, and we were refunded for the excess charges. Despite all the unpleasantness experienced, we truly enjoyed a memorable week in Virginia with family.

= = = = = = =

I had a dream therefore decided to record it at this time for fear that it might escape my memory, and you know what they say about that, "better now than never" so here goes…. This dream includes my mother. It seems that we were living in a rather large house where most of us were residing. First dream. I was attending some sort of celebration, after which some of us went over to a get- together, which lasted some time into the night. Upon my return home, my mom said to me where were you? I said that after the celebration as usual, we visited the priest over to his place. Not even a call to let me know, was her reply.

It suddenly occurred to me that there was something on but I forgot, anyway I continued to get ready for whatever it was, in my mind I remembered that we had to go somewhere so I went to my car to get things started and I thought that perhaps we have to meet someone at the airport, while making room for passengers, I believe that if this was the case, then I would have to get started, while doing this Mom said she wanted to be included, I wondered, I would have to be sure to have room in the car to pick up whoever I had to, meanwhile a few persons passed me to say that they were going ahead. I still was in the fog about what it was that I had to do.

I returned inside and while sitting around, I overheard my mom talking on the phone, and after she said, "He is on his way and wanted to stay over and perhaps would be sleeping on my bed". I went along with this thought and therefore went about moving my bed to clean up behind making sure all was tidy, I must mention at this time that my bed was a converted Army cot and suddenly it reminded me of the bed I had as a young man while living in Panama, and in order to make it more comfortable, I actually made an extension by building an extension base attaching it to the cot then sewing and stuffing a width of material to be placed along the existing mattress therefore with the sheet over this, it gave the impression that it was wider. I knew this therefore it was ok for me. Mom asked for the fancy sheets I said there were no fancy sheets but she insisted, I therefore went to the place where sheets were kept, and withdrew a set which I had folded and put away, she said there should be 4 pillow cases, I said only two are included, since it was my practice to fold together, the fitted sheet with the top sheet and include the pillow cases. This way everything was always in one package, so to speak.

As I returned with the sheets, I noticed that my bed was removed and was been replaced by another real single bed, I was a bit moved and commented (Jokingly), after all this time me sleeping on this make-up bed, suddenly *He* will be offered this nice one. Well I still do not know who *He* was. I really was happy for this since *He* would not be aware of the bed I used to sleep on.

During all this, persons were leaving saying "we are going". I had to ask, where are we going? Someone mentioned the name of some town (I don't remember) then it suddenly occurred to me that at some earlier time, perhaps weeks, an invitation was issued, and I had to ask directions, it seemed that there was some celebration has been scheduled and those persons who left before, were car- pooling, which eased my conscience. No Airport pick- up. (Smile).

I imagine the party went well, also the guest who was expected, was comfortably rested on the bed which replaced mine. Not to say that mine was not comfortable, since over the years I can well remember the make-up of that bed which started out as an army cot, and me building an extension base, and the extended mattress. This brings to mind also, what ever happened to the rest of the furniture I made for my *"crib"* such as the chairs (stools) with the tapered legs and upholstered seats, also my record player.

Those were the days, I used to entertain my friends and all were accommodated, those who had no chair to sit on, well there was always the bed which served as a sofa (so to speak) we were able to listen to some music and engage in some lively conversations, also partake in some reserved libation, which I always had. Let me talk about this now, when I was employed in Panama City at Photo International, one of my charge was to retain the custody of a stack of Johnny Walker Black, and "Pinch" a bottle with dimples, remember that?. (Top Shelf) I suppose that is why it is called *"pinch"*.

From time to time, the boss would give me a bottle of scotch as a reward or an apology. When he got out of line and I would let him know it, he would call me in the office to ask for a bottle, when he is entertaining a major buyer or supplier. There were always reasons for me to get another bottle to take home. I used to be sure to have him sign it, (For Richard.) to protect myself from inquiring and roving eyes, such as other salespersons or his son.

This past week was very hectic at the church, especially, since it was the advent of holy week the choir was kept busy with rehearsals getting ready for services. It began with Palm Sunday service and I always wanted to sing for this service therefore I approached the new Choir master and presented him with a copy of the musical works especially for this occasion called "The Palms" which we rehearsed several times and was very happy we were able to present it during the service, as the offertory. (This come at a point in the service after the sermon) As I was told by some persons, the rendition was good, which pleased me very much, it was something I longed to do.

Next came the Holy week services, on Thursday **Maundy Thursday** there was the traditional service of foot washing in accordance with scripture, commemorating the time where Jesus washed the feet of **his** disciples. After this, the altar is stripped of all things including the sacrament, the altar table is stripped of its covering and then it is washed, after which service is concluded with the congregation quietly leaving.

As a young boy I remember this service which was celebrated in Christ Church By-the-sea, Colon Rep. of Panama when as an acolyte, we would take part in the stripping of the sacraments etc. and the church would remain open overnight to allow persons who wanted to pay penance of pray, we took turns, *watching* (Watch night) i.e. there was someone in attendance all night into morning.

Continuing with this reminiscence, there was a flowering tree in the church's yard which bore a very aromatic white flower, curiously once a year. (I do not know the name of this flower) however, we used to cut bunches to take home, and some folks along the way were willing to offer us some payment for a few of these flowers. It was placed in a vase with water in our homes and a pleasant aroma filled the home for the Easter season. The church officials did not mind us cutting the flowers, since after a period of time, all the petals will fall to the ground, which required cleaning, and in effect we were contributing to the décor of the yard.

Back to reality, then came **Good Friday**. There was the usual three hour service, commemorating the last seven last words of Christ during **his** crucifixion. This was presented by seven persons, each pontificating on one. (It could be stated as seven last *statements*, (something to consider) and the choir leading the singing during this service, which had exceeded the three hours. Three Hour is to reflect on the time **Jesus** hung on the cross.

Reminiscence: It was the custom in Colon, to have a parade from the cathedral around the city which was in commemoration of (Via Dolorosa) *translation* the painful way. Sponsored by the Roman Catholic Church. The three hour service was also the tradition of the Episcopal Church, of which I was a part.

Then came the grandest Celebration **Easter Sunday.** As was mentioned in the bulletin, a reflection by the Very Reverend Eddie Alleyne, The Pascal Triduum… of which this is the third of the most solemn celebration of all Christendom. (Holy Thursday, Good Friday and Easter).

This Sanctuary was spectacularly decorated with flowers, mainly Lilies, which were provided by persons in thanksgiving or in memorial. The persons who did the decorating were congratulated for a task of love, well done. The singing of the most appropriate hymns was robust, and an original composition by Davian Alleyne (no relation), Organist and choir director, was debuted as the offertory by the choir. The attendance was overwhelming and Easter was represented in all its glory.

After service was ended, we retired to the golden Hall and as usual our group of friends sat together to enjoy each other's company and the exchange of pleasantries, photographing each other with camera (mine) and phones (theirs) a little smile, to all who came by. I could not help but to recall the times we used to spend in our previous church, though small, after service we would spend the time on the lawn, (somehow the weather was more pleasant at that time of the year) want to talk about climate change?

At that time the lawn was big therefore we had time to spread out and have our own little Easter Parade, after which we would go our respective ways to meet with family, friends, parents, sibling for dinner or whatever. That is what friends are for. *Remember when?*

This year we, did have a reunion for dinner with Sherena, Pete, Jordan and Sydney. (Taylor is at college). Also with Richie, Deborah, Ellis and Ethan. The ten of us ate up a storm, it's always good to be with the children and grands whenever possible.

It is now the wee hour 2:45 am. I guess after such an exhilarating day and sumptuous meal, after checking out my messages (mostly spams) I decided to do this before the experience wears off. I will now clock out.

Today Monday 4/2/18 is what we used to call Easter Monday, which back in the day, we used to consider a day of relaxation, consequently there was an outing planned, either Bus or boat. We would meet early in the morning with our packed lunch and libation, this used to be quite a celebration, after a week of solemnity, fasting or restraining, and it was time for merrymaking. There was none of that, therefore, *now a days*, it is a day of relaxing which is what we did.

Tomorrow my plans include loading up the Jeep and we are going to check on *Chez-b* (that's the place in the Pocono which we have not visited since Christmas, I mentioned this scenario before, remember I mentioned that I was going on a strike, since all the children had their own family celebration, but Sisters Yolanda and Yasmina joined us for the season at Chez-b. I will try to finish a project started at that time, also check on things around the place, we have to give the appearance of a lived in place, especially; since I received a call from the security agent who indicated that there was approximately 6 break-ins in the Ares, which is quite strange, considering it is a mountain enclave (so-to-speak) I will call them while there to arrange some kind of phone monitoring adjustment.

150 miles drive each way, therefore I would hope to get an early start Tuesday for a planned return to Brooklyn on Friday or Saturday, depending on how things work out, with a stop off visit in N.J. as the saying goes, *God's willing.*

Unfortunately, after attending to what was necessary and making the visit to supermarket for the usual shopping both for Chez-B and for Brooklyn, I was not able to call the security therefore this will have to be done on another visit, things got prolonged and we were not able to leave until after 5: 00 P.M which was a bit late, considering the traffic flow, we would be late when arriving at the planned location for the visit. I definitely wanted to arrive in Brooklyn before dark. Saturday, the day set aside to attend to all scheduled appointments, were accomplished.

Sunday I had to inform the congregation of some sad news, before doing this, I wished all had enjoyed a Happy Easter. For those persons who were around in the early time of this church (old timers) that on the day of resurrection. One of our beloved pastors in the person of Canon Llewellyn Murray had "gone home to meet his maker" and the funeral service would be held at the Cathedral of The Incarnation on Monday 9th.

Fr. Murray was Ordained to the Sacred Order of Priest January 1, 1981 and he was assistant at St. Gabriel's church, and used to prepare the applicants for Confirmation, (including Olivia at that time) among his sacerdotal duties. He was later placed in charge of St. Lydia's church in East N.Y.

There was a yearly celebration of the patronal saint of Musicians "ST. Cecilia" at this church, most of the known Panamanian musician and Chorale who provided the service music, attended this service and after mass, we would enjoy music in its varied form, vocal and instrumental. Also there was a meal prepared by the members of St. Lydia's church and others. This used to be quite an enjoyable occasion. From the read obituary, we learned that Fr. Murray was quite a musician himself, which explains his interest in hosting this yearly event. We will surely miss him (R.I.P.)

Tuesday 4/10/18 while in a meeting with the editor of a popular magazine "La Pollera" at my home, I received a phone call from the warden inviting me on behalf of Fr. Alleyne, to attend a meeting on Thursday evening at 7:00 p.m. with the vestry, others and building Architects. I mentioned that this is the same time of Choir rehearsals, however considering the circumstance I will endeavor to attend.

On Thursday evening, I received a call from Fr. Alleyne asking if I had viewed the architectural plans, to which I replied I have not seen any. He mentioned that the Warden was asked to e-mail it to me. However he would send it to me at that time which was about 5:00, I immediately went to my P.C. and opened the attachment which was 5 pages of drawings. I sensed the importance and therefore proceeded to print the documents and proceeded to get dressed since I wanted very much to be there in time to listen to the proposal.

I only had time to glance at this impressive presentation, I therefore replied to the e-mail and informed Padre that I had received the document and will be in attendance. Then off I went not stopping to get any sustenance, (Food) not to worry, since I am aware that at these meetings, I am sure that some would be available. I arrived early and was able to have a look at the documents while awaiting the arrival of others and the start of the meeting.

During the presentation, it was pointed out that the proposal was based on the fact that the addition of the 2nd floor area would have to be demolished along with the present parish house, and this proposed building will encompass the entire area including the present driveway parking. As a matter-of-fact, it would occupy the entire area leaving the present walkway towards the present lobby which amounts to approx. 4ft. wide that would separate the two buildings. Again, St. Gabriel's will resort to the year 1905 when the original church building was consecrated. It was this little building tucked in besides the existing brown stone building, and one could drive through Hawthorne Street and not notice it. (This story is told in the book What if? telling how we found it).

Well by looking at the drawings layout, the new proposed building sitting on the very local where the original church building was located, (almost sacrilegious) it appears to be enfolding the new Church Building which appears as a second nature, since the newly proposed building takes precedence, This in retrospect causes one to wonder, which is more important? (The Cause or the reason).

I would also point out that the 2 floor building is basically part of the original foot print of the new church we only topped it with a 2nd floor. In this area (below) is located all the bathroom plumbing, elevator mechanical works, also main floor elevator, office space. Also please bear in mind that the good people of St. Gabriel's church have been contributing in addition to their usual pledge, to the construction of this 2nd floor, in order to provide much needed additional space. For which we are still paying off the loan. Granted, the space is not satisfactorily allocated.

A Thought aside, this brings to my mind, growing up, we were always made to believe that when we were hanging wall decorations, such as decorative items, pictures etc. we should always hang any religious items i.e. crucifixes, religious likeness of any kind should be placed in a higher plane. I am not sure is this a universal practice, all I do know this is how we were brought up to think.

I will try to contact the Architect in order to voice my thoughts, a phone call went unanswered, and I will try to e-mail this and hope to convey these thoughts to some of those persons in attendance of this presentation. In the meantime I have placed a call to the rector indicating my thoughts, I will have to express them to individual members to get a general consensus.

Flash- Flash Remember my encounter with the dentist who wanted to extract an upper molar to which I declined. Well so far that molar has repaired itself (mind 0ver matter), well sad to say, I now have experienced excruciating pain in the lower molar which is attached to a bridge which was installed by a dentist some years ago, to which I had some reservations, since in order to do this he had to file two healthy teeth next to the vacant area in order to locate the bridge, he insisted that was the way to go. I am now experiencing discomfort due to this.

As I have mentioned before, I have a bit of disdain (for lack of another word) towards dentist due to a boyhood experience. Last Tuesday 4/10/18 this pain started and I could not tolerate any contact to this tooth, consequently no chewing or solid food intake, went to bed without eating anything, I tried to self-medicate the tooth by using whatever I could find, medicated toothpaste, mouthwash etc. the next morning the pain was not so intense therefore I tried only liquid, soup.

That is enough about dentist. By this time I have conveyed my feelings toward dentist. Do not get me wrong, despite all there is a health need for good dental services and I do avail myself of regular visits to ensure that those that I have, are kept in the best condition, after all these are the instruments that enable you to thoroughly masticate the food that keeps you healthy

Anything to avoid going to the dentist, on Thursday I had a meeting at the church as mentioned above, there was food available therefore I tried to have some but the pain was still there only not as intense, I decided to take my potion home with the thought that with the application of some *Orajel* which is a temporary relief ointment. I was beginning to think that if this pain continues in the next morning, I might have to yield. Well, as that goes, *mind over matter* prevailed, since Friday morning was quite pleasant, I was able to chew a light breakfast, and I continue to treat the tooth with my usual self-medication. The reason I did not want to see the dentist, was that on Saturday evening there was a 25th Wedding anniversary I was scheduled to attend. Considering that I was the wedding photographer 25 years ago and it would have been a treat.

**God** is good all the time. By **His** grace, I was able to attend and enjoy a meal without any discomfort, Today Sunday, and as I write this, all seem to be moving along nicely. Allow me to tell you about this celebration. As we walked in, I saw a young lady who looked so much like the honoree, I even commented to Olivia, she probably is a sister to the honoree, but the thought was that perhaps this young lady might be part of the staff of the catering hall, only to find out later on that she was in fact a niece of the honoree. Upon learning this fact, from the host I pointed out the similarities, and she agreed that her niece is her younger version, which elicited a smile.

It seemed momentarily that I might have stepped into a time lapse machine, since it was at a wedding where I met the honoree some 3o years ago. As a photographer, I saw her just going back and forth, taking care of everything and finally she was called to render a song in honor of the wedded couple. (As it turned out, she was a relative). She so impressed me with her singing and me thinking she was somehow attached with the catering hall, as is the practice, as a photographer, it is the usual thing to contact the head waiter for a plate of food. I called her aside to ask for a plate of food, and also if she did not mind, I would like to talk to her about her singing to which she consented.

After introducing myself as the Photographer assigned by the studio to this wedding, I further notified her that I was a member of a Chorale which is quite good, and proceed to tout the laurels of the group, and pointed out that I would like to introduce her to said group for her consideration. She agreed and I therefore obtained her address and on that first Tuesday evening, after getting home from my job. I stopped be my Mother to spend some time until it was time to go get this Soprano to take her to rehearsals with me, she resided close by which was quite convenient. She came, she liked the group, and we liked her.

This routine continued for some time which worked out quite well, since it caused me to visit my mom each Tuesday, and she will always had a snack for me, stating that I am skinny and needed some nourishments, an excuse to make me eat (smile). After a while the Soprano got used to the group and travelled on her own, also our schedules were altered. We all continued this association with the Chorale which lasted for approximately another 25 years, for which she was one of the soloist.

At this point, even though The Chorale has been disbanded, due to retirement, most of us were invited to this 25th anniversary. Celebration, it was quite an occasion which also combined a congratulation on retirement (Husband). I had my camera, as usual, and therefore approached the couple at the bridal table and said to them that since I was their official photographer 25 years ago, it was only befitting that I be allowed to photograph them at this time., to which they agreed, I now have a table shot of them, I plan to print a copy for their memorabilia.

Today April 25th 2018 is Samantha's birthday (#50) how time has gone by? As I mentioned while congratulating her by phone, "Oh yes I remember the time quite well", which elicited a chuckle from her, it also served me as a yardstick to remember how long we are at this present location, December 1967 we moved into our new home (51 years) in keeping with the promise I made to bring my first newborn to our own home.

Goodness gracious, so far I can chew my food without any discomfort. Just thought I'd mention this if you are keeping score. Yesterday I attended a Parish council meeting and one of the topics discussed was brought up be the representative of the (E.C.W.) Episcopal Church Women, regarding their reaction towards the full schedule of the church which does not allow them to have fellowship after service, citing that they were displaced many times from their reunions due to pending activities by groups to whom the hall was rented which seemed to them every Sunday.

While voicing her displeasure, I asked her permission to also voice my opinion on this same topic which I have mentioned many times in the past, and agreed with her wholeheartedly. After a lively discussion by everyone present, the Chairman asked for a proposal to be presented, since no one would accept, he assigned me this task, however, I did not want to be the person to put this forward, since in the past, whenever I speak at meetings or to the priest or congregation regarding - *how things were, or how we did it in the past*- I was always rebuffed. The chairman assured me that he will take the responsibility to present my thoughts in his own way and time.

I was agreeable to this and in so doing, I have sent him via e-mail the following: As requested, a proposal to establish at least one Sunday of each month free of any other activity in the Golden hall after service to allow an evening of fellowship to congregants in order to meet and enjoy each other's company, especially for those persons who are usually alone and look forward to meeting with others.

As pointed out by other persons and even to revert to the origin of St. Gabriel's Church, it was the custom to meet after service each Sunday and extend fellowship and camaraderie to new comers, who from time to time are looking for a church to attend, and this is usually when they are approached and extended an informal welcome by individuals, also friends are invited to service, after which they are introduced to others, thus forming acquaintances.

This is the manner in which the previously unknown church became known to persons and they in turn passed the word along, expressing their ability to feel welcomed. There were times when the weather was good we would assemble in the yard and have our own Easter Parade (so to speak) and the children had some space to move around.

Please take note that during worship when the "peace" is passed, this is the time when conversations are held between persons who may have invited others to service and are using this opportunity to meet. In most cases, announcement has to be made to resume worship, perhaps if they were aware that there was fellowship after service in the Golden Hall, this laps during worship could be curtailed. Just my thoughts. R. Buery.

I have received a confirmation from the Chairman and he assured me that he will be assimilating this report for presentation to the vestry and Rector for their reaction. This now becomes a wait-n-see situation.

I have placed an advertisement in the magazine titled "La Pollera" published by an acquaintance in an effort to expand the reach of my book *"What if? The Question or a Statement"*. I will have to await any reaction to the circulation of the magazine.

5/1/18 the day before my birthday. I have been watching a television program PBS regarding the restoration of an historical sailing vessel, which had my undivided attention, especially since, as we were told by mother, this is the kind of work my father did, not exactly restoration but maintenance of sailing vessels, which required him going under water and working in the hot sun in this pursuit. And eventually caused his demise from over exposure. I have seen a photo of him working on the side of a docked vessel and can only imagine what life was like for him at that time.

May 11/2018 The Panamanians of ST Gabriel's church celebrated our 30th anniversary dance we choose to name it Red Top, all patrons are asked to wear a red top shirt/blouse. And it usually looks very nice to see everyone (few exceptions) dancing and merrymaking in their Red Top. Considering this was a milestone celebration, we had the hall decorated with the tri-color representing the colors of our national flag Red-White-Blue table coverings and balloons, it was quite festively decorated along with some posters depicting our National wear.

The program this year, included the presentation of a national dance group, performing the various folklore dances, accompanied by taped music. We were also graced by the presence of the Yearly elected queen from New York. As is the custom, she will represent the New York populace during the Carnivals in Panama. Also special guests D.J. which added to the enjoyment.

And, in addition to the dance celebrations, we also offer a smorgasbord and refreshments, to be sure that all who attends are delighted, danced, fed, entertained and satisfied.

This year, preparations were a bit more extensive and required more efforts and the reduced amount of volunteers, we were short staffed for various reasons, illness, and other personal reasons, which necessitated extra efforts by those who were present, especially since addend decorations were in place, such as the covering of the chairs and posting of other decorations. I.e. more work by less persons, despite it all we were able to rise to the occasion.

Something to be noted is the fact that the 29th. Red top (last Year 2017) we actually sold out the place and we were able to make a rather large presentation to the church, and as we tallied this year's return, it is much reduced.

If this is any indication of what's in store for the future, we might have to consider acquiring added help, which would reduce the financial outcome, adjustments in price charge increase, something to be considered will be as the age increase of our patrons, there will be less of the ability to meet this increased cost.

The smorgasbord is prepared and donated by the group for this occasion. The proceeds from this yearly endeavor is our way of contributing towards the general maintenance of the church. This is presented during a regular Sunday service to the treasurer, and a record is kept for verification.

We received a phone call from our son informing us that a request was made for couples who would be interested in a project spearheaded by The New York times, to which we agreed. The date was set for May 19th. The only drawback was the hour which was scheduled for 8:30 am, and we were to meet them at a location in downtown Brooklyn which means that we would have to be awake and set to leave home no later than 7:00 am. In order to meet them at the correct locale I decided to call for an address since this Photoshoot was to be on the street and not a set place. Mind you this is the day before (5/18) the address was noted as 80 Lafayette Ave. Brooklyn, which I entered in my GPS. We are now set and subsequently received an e- mail "Awesome Thank you we look forward to meeting you both tomorrow". On the morning we were eager to get this going and the time was approaching therefore all ready to go, a phone call informed us that there was a change in plans, our reaction was, is there a cancellation because of the rain? No, was the response, It is still a Go and they would contact us of time and change of locale.

After awaiting their call for some time, we were eventually notified that the locale was changed to China town in Manhattan and again I requested a specific address in order to note it in my G.P.S. on arrival, I decided to park temporarily in a side street and got out of my vehicle to take a walk to the intersection in order to locate any evidence of a Photo crew, no such luck, therefore we called the number provided, and were told that Parking was reserved for the day on that block.

Official papers issued by New York department of traffic was offered me to be placed on the dashboard of my vehicle. So we sat there along with the contact person's car. Imagine only two vehicles in that entire block which was lined up with traffic cones. Very impressive. Now we play the waiting game. At some point in time, I inquired from the contact person regarding the plan? His reply was that at some given time we would leave our car and be taken by another SUV. To chase a double-decker bus at some point, at which time we would board it to join the photographer team along with other couples.

Finally, by the use of cell phones etc. the bus was sighted, contact was made and we boarded the bus. At lease there was some snacks available. We had to sign releases, I was aware of this necessity considering that as a photographer myself, I realized that it was a necessary formality. Each couple was called to the top of the bus, where they were strapped in to provide security.

I still was not aware of the extent of our involvement, since as the bus travelled along the avenues, we could see people on the street looking up and waiving at the bus. At this point it appears that there were about 4-5 couples in addition to staff and photographers. When we were told that we were next, we had to climb the inner stairs to the top, and sure enough, a harness was placed around my waist to secure us while we stood, then instructions were given and we had to do what came naturally, at one point I heard tremendous applauds coming from the street, we were the attraction, well it was something else to realize that our actions evoked such a reaction.

After out turn in *the limelight*, it was time for us to *debark* from the bus and a taxi was called to take us back to where my SUV was parked. I could not miss it since it was the only vehicle on the block. This has certainly been an experience for us to remember and cherish, especially, while the Royalty was having their time across *the pond* (Royal wedding in London) we were having the time of our lives on a bus in the middle of New York City being photographed.

As it turned out, The New York Times Magazine ran this special issue to be recorded on this very day of Saturday May 19 2018 LOVE IN NEW YORK CITY A total of 24 couples shot on this day 24 hours of romance. Between 12 a.m. And 11:59 p.m. We finally received a number of copies of the magazines with our photo on the cover. There were 24 different magazines cover each portraying a couple. Which was distributed randomly

On June 10th 2018 the magazine was issued with the cover depicting each of the participating couples on 24 separate covers. As it turned out we were on cover 17 of 24. The publication was distributed randomly to subscribers, stores, newsstand, libraries and places of distribution. The cover which we actually saw at this point was cover #16. I am expecting to receive #17 cover with our likeness *to have and to hold.* We eventually received from the N.Y. times, 5 copies of the magazine # 17 with our likeness on the cover for our personal disposition.

On reading the article, describing the project by the staff, a call was made through social media and contacts, which resulted in approximately 1000 responses of which these 24 were selected, while checking the participants in the magazine, I have noted that we were the oldest couple, which would not be noticed nor determined if the ages were not published, know what I mean?

Also from reading the articles, it explains why there was such a span of waiting time since we were originally scheduled for the shoot, i.e. 8:30 AM then 9:30 AM then the long waiting time in order to change location and time from downtown Brooklyn to China town in the vicinity of the Manhattan Bridge then the delay which lasted until about midafternoon 3:00, when we were finally on board the bus, hungry, The problem as we understand it was the coordinating with the various couples also bus routing. Understandably a major fete of getting it all down in one day under the increment weather conditions.

We met and married in 1964. In 2014 (50 years later), we celebrated a renewal of vows. Now in 2018, (4 years later), we find ourselves on the front cover of the New York Times Magazine, expressing "**LOVE CITY**" 24 hours of romance in New York.

Who would have imagined this? I am now on the other side of the Camera lens. As a wedding photographer, it was required that I visit the home of the bride, helping and photographing her, which at times helping to locate garments, prepare and assist her in getting dressed then photographing her in the best light and pleasing surroundings, mainly in her bedroom. There were several situations which occurred during these photo shoot.

I will tell this very interesting occasion while in the completion of a photo-shoot, we discovered that the bedroom door was stuck, we both were a bit anxious, giving the situation, she therefore called through the shut door for her father to get us out of this room, it seems that it was a recent installation and he was unable to open the door from the outside, I also was a bit anxious, especially since this was a situation where She (a white girl) and I (a black man) was not a comfortable one. I asked the father to get a tool of some kind to pass it under the door since there was some space, he was able to get a flat tool and I was able to remove the pins from the hinges, thus removing the door, all of us breathed a sigh of relief. Next stop, I accompany the bride to the church.

When we arrived at the church, the news preceded us, (The bride was locked in the bedroom with the photographer) one can well imagine the thoughts of some of the invited guests, all went well since I conducted myself as usual, in a professional manner, I photographed the wedding ceremony without any further "hitch". After church we went to a location with the wedding party for group photos, then we proceed to the reception hall. Everyone was in good spirit and it seemed to me that in order to easy everyone's mind, the mother asked me to dance with her at the reception. // Whew\\. All was well since it ended well. I never forgot how tricky this could have been.

There were some good, great and happy times experienced by me behind the camera lens. This is one of the great and happy times for me on the other side of the Lens. We both expressed the same thought when this kissing photo-shoot was over "it's the most we have kissed in one setting" (smiles)… Just thought I would share this.

Back to the topic in question, we distributed copies to some family members, retaining a copy for ourselves, I made an 8x10 print of the front cover suitable for framing. On Tuesday 6/25th We decided to go to Chez-B (home in the Poconos) especially to install additional locks on the door which some time ago was not properly locked, and our neighbor called me in Brooklyn to advise me that the door was wide open, I thanked him profusely, and asked him to check if all was well and that he should try to lock the door, he said that the lock was not engaging, therefore I advised him to pull it as hard as possible until it was finally engaged.

The problem occurred due to my effort to properly seal the door with insulation, it resulted in preventing the proper engagement of the lock. I purchased a lock with deadbolt mechanisms, to be assured a locked door in the future, well as fate would have it, I had the proper tool, a hole-saw set, (circular blade of different dimensions) and while operating the drill with this saw, unfortunately, the tool broke. I had to make a trip to town and purchased a new set. For informational purposes, the door is steel clad and to my consternation, it was thicker than I imagined (it's a good thing) well with determination, I finally was able to cut the first hole, however, there was insulation between the inner and outer wall.

In view of this situation, I then decided to scuttle this ides and instead decided to install a steel patch over this partially open area and therefore decided to remove the existing lock and replace it with the deadbolt lock which was more secure, and made sure that the bolt was securely extended in to the area, by drilling the pit deep enough to accept the total extended bolt. Having done this, I decided to secure the upstairs door in the same manner. There is nothing better that peace of mind.

Having done this and other things, I decided to select from material on hand, and built a frame from 1"X2" stock, stained and finished it, to accept the 8x10 reproduction, mentioned above. We returned from Chez-b on Friday 29th since we had to attend a Funeral service on Saturday morning. Anyway, now the photo is properly framed and ready for a location where it will hang. Now I can truly say, _"To have and to hold"._ We are now in the possession of a printed framed copy of the magazine's cover, also our own copy of the published Time magazine.

This has been a very busy month, considering all the travels and family gathering, along with the other functions we had to attend, I must assure you that is has been a blessing to be able to enjoy and appreciate these occasions, there are times when a decision has to be made regarding which function to attend. At times this is very difficult since sometimes both occasions are very important to us and as we know, we can only be in one place at a time irrespective of modern technology. Which causes me to consider the Fairy tales we have read and heard of growing up. To name one in particular, the story of Red Riding hood, as can be remembered about the story, it is the damsel off in the woods to visit her Grandma, and not the reverse.

There is a new situation regarding the Church building. On Thursday 4/10/18 I received a call and was asked by the pastor if I had viewed the architectural drawings, my answer was that I did not receive any message to this effect, he promised to send it to me which I received on the next day, Friday at about 5;00 p.m. with the request that I attend the planned meeting on that evening at the church scheduled for 7:00 p.m. considering the importance to me, I downloaded a total of 5 pages and hurried to get dressed and left home. I arrived early and took the time to look over the document. Titled: **St.Gabriel's Episcopal Church Feasibility Study** dated 3/16/18

The first thing that caught my attention was that the project seemed to overpower the very reason it was created for, The Church Physical (Building). Next, on reading the next page (2) item G. **Development Scenario**.

This development scenario involves the demolition of the existing 2 story addition of the church facility and the construction of 27,825 gfs of multi-family residential space… and so on. This was a devastating situation to me since there was no 2 story addition, what actually exists is the original foot print of the church building (physical) with the recent addition of a second floor which is still being paid for. Next, to my understanding, the drawings was not in compliance with the word *Feasibility* in order to explain why I made this statement, I refer to *the American Heritage Dictionary; Feasible project. Capable of being utilized or dealt with successfully, suitable, logical; likely.*

Another interpretation; Feasibility: Feasibility quality 1. That can be done easily; possible without difficulty or damage.

The meeting was attended by several members of the Vestry, Rector, wardens, architect and a diocesan representative along with the person who is to make the presentation. On completion of this presentation, there were some questions asked, and I made my points as mentioned above. There were some verbal exchanges and continued statements that this was not "etched in stone" my point was, if it was not, then present us with an alternative plan which is really feasible.

I contacted the architectural firm and was able to make my point. Also to inform them of the fact that the proposed building was, in some of our estimation, over stated, also the fact that the proposed structural demolition of the (2 story building) was in fact part of the footprint of the existing building which included the bathroom plumbing, elevator, entrance to the lower floor, senior center, Golden hall. For this proposal to be even considered, it was not feasible.

The representative said that they were not aware of those points made, and the instructions received from contacting parties were, to present drawings maximizing the property. It seems to me that before this undertaking, there should have been a survey of existing plans in order to determine what situations should be considered. There were other points made, which I would not delve into, suffice to know that this has left quite a few persons uncomfortable with this proposal.

In order to comply with an alternative, I have taken it on myself to scope an actual construction in the area with just about the same size lot and conditions, and have photographed it from various angles, and have shown them to some persons in order to highlight the points which I tried to make when voicing my point of view at the various meetings.

Maximizing the proposed building, while minimizing the church building, for which the returns from such a proposal, is to help defray existing expenses, in the meantime, while this is been done, the existing church building would have to be closed down, since there would be devoid of sanitary conditions, use of Golden hall, (which was determined to be the major source of income for the church's maintenance). Think about this, where would the Plumbing be replaced in order to restore the functionality of the church building?

All this is left to the thoughts of persons, as this idea of this proposed project move forward, I have had my say, hope I have made a difference. **The church is one foundation.** This was to be the opening hymn at the June meeting of the Parish council, since I was nominated as the Chaplin, and due to travel out of town, I was unable to attend. Hopefully, I would be provided a copy of the report. Unfortunately, I have inquired from persons who I hoped would have attended the meeting, but no such luck, since they did not attend. After a recent service, I was able to make contact with one person, who have indicated to me that pressure was placed on them to try to influence my thoughts. We started a conversation and he was able to tell me some of the exchanges at the meeting, but we were interrupted, since a speaker was about to address the gathering in the Golden hall.

It has been a couple Sundays now (July 29ᵗʰ) and we had a special service, bidding farewell to our dear deacon, who has been assigned to a church on Long Island starting next Sunday, The Rector, wardens and vestry extended an invitation to the congregation to partake of a brunch in the Back yard of the church which has been paved and manicured for occasions such as this, I seized the opportunity to point out to some of the folks within earshot, to say that this is indeed an asset to the church to have this area for such outdoor occasions, instead of planning to build a monstrous apartment building which is in no way *feasible*. In this area. I guess you cannot blame me for this stab at their awareness.

While I was on my way to this area, I was approached by one of the officials to tell me that the rector required that I join a special meeting with the vestry and the chairman of the parish council in the conference room, well, I was a bit curious as to the reason for this seemingly, impromptu meeting, well while waiting, my thoughts were that perhaps this meeting might be about the proposal building, therefore I began to prepare my thoughts in this regards, therefor I should go to my car and get my bag containing documents which I am rarely without. Returning to the steps the rector saw me and indicated that the meeting would be a short one and is about to begin.

I was somewhat blindsided, since as he was speaking, I realized that this was not the case, instead he outlined his years spent with us as a parish, and the time for a change is upon us, and that contacts with the Bishop and other Parishes had been in progress, ad as of October 1ˢᵗ.this year, he would no longer be the rector of St. Gabriel's church, and by this means he and Family has chosen to tell this assembled group, and as soon as signatures are placed on the dotted lines, he will formally announce it to the congregation. There ensued a pregnant pause after this announcement, and no one spoke for a while, perhaps, stunned or for lack of words.

I spoke saying since no one spoke, "I will say that it has been quite an experience having you as the rector of this parish and despite the fact that at times when I dear to speak of the past, you were not receptive, however, when I do speak of the past I am in no way comparing you with others, since there is no comparison, each Priest has their ways of doing things. I have served this parish during several priests and each in an effort to express my sentiment for this church which I often refer to, and hold to be **my church,** as any person who has deep sentiments for, should be allowed to say. I hope you are aware that it is not personal. May I continue to say that we have always manage to get things done, and it is sad to be at this stage, however I would honestly hope that you will keep us in mind to help in steering the person you consider for a replacement, even though you cannot be replaced. Thank You ". After this, others began to speak, apparently, the *wind* which had been knocked out of us all had been replaced, at some point during the summation and reflections, I made some other comments which I might not have had the opportunity to express hereafter. Wishing Him and family the best in his future endeavors. Fr Alleyne assured us that he will still be associated with the diocese of L.I. considering that he had offers by churches in other states, to which he did not apply, surely we would be hearing and seeing him and family from time to time. (*Blessed Assurance.*)

Among the comments expressed, I recall one made by a previous rector, "the thing about Richard is that he always tell it like it is". My retort was that I do not mean to be disrespectful but if I have something constructive to say, I say it. Perhaps this is a trait that I can trace back to the days of my youth.

Do you remember the cartoon character, Linus and Lucy? There is a bench Linus sits on, well my sister and I each had our own bench, while growing up, I never complained or cried and for this I was usually ignored, therefore I decided if I am to be acknowledge, when I am hungry, I would take my bench and place it in the doorway, then lay across it and fall asleep. Surely, this way I cannot be ignored. The word was out, it was time to feed me. This reminds me of a saying in Spanish (*el bebe que no llora, no ama leche*) *literal translation*: "the baby who does not cry, does not get to drink milk". As I grew up, I no longer had my bench and considering that I was usually small and frail, I concluded that, if I am to be heard and acknowledged, it was necessary for me to be seen and to speak up.

Perhaps, this is why it becomes quite disconcerting to me when I am not allowed to respectfully speak my thoughts. I might have mentioned this some time ago. While in high school, I remember during a class in religion, the professor stated that the only true faith was the Catholic faith, well it was no secret among my class mates and this professor, that I was a member of the episcopal faith. I immediately stood up and first stated to the professor that "all due respect to you, but you are out of order to make such a statement, you are here to teach religion as a subject, and not a faith". I continued to state the facts as I knew them, regarding the history of the English reformation and the start of the episcopal faith, to thunderous applaud from my class mates. The professor threatened to have me expelled, but she could not follow through, because the statement I made was a fact, and she would the person subject to discipline. Mind you, I knew that I was walking on thin ice, therefore, I was duly respectful during my discourse.

Back to the original subject, it will be a loss to us at St.Gabriel's church, that after such a long and rewarding tenure of approximately twelve years, having the Pastor and his wife, and watching his children grow up to fine and outstanding young people, members of the acolyte staff and an integral part of our own church family. My family as well as many of those with whom I have been in touch, have certainly felt and expressed this sentiment.

New business: We were informed that a family trip to Panama with the plan to embark on a south American cruise comprised of the following persons, Yvonne, Ernest (Edgar, Eric, Yolette, her three children (Paisley, Peony & Pryns), also Yasmina and Yolanda to which we were happy to join, total of 12 persons. Plans began and we first start with the coordination of flight schedules. The task was for each party to be at the Tocumen airport in Panama about the same time, considering the fact Than Yvonne who was in contact with Panama regrading land transportation from and to the city, as well as from the Panama to Colon where this happy band of travelers would board the vessel for the impending cruise, which was also arraigned by Yvonne.

Travelling from San Antonio, Texas (Yvonne and Ernest) via United Airline with connection

Travelling from JFK. New York (Yolette and family) Via Copa Airline-Direct

Travelling from JFK. N.Y. Richard and Olivia via A/A With connection in Miami

At this point, I can explain the problems we had trying to get to Tocumen. After leaving home very early in the morning and awaiting the announcement of the flight, I noted that it was near departure time, consequently, I approached the desk attendant to inquire status of the flight schedule, since I noticed that there was no visible appearance of a plane at the appointed door only to be told that the plane was on its way from the hanger, my retort was, why was this not indicated on your announcement board for customers information? AT this point, the change of gate departure was posted on the board. It's a good thing I asked this question.

As can be readily noted, scheduling was of the utmost importance to us. After much effort, we were able to get started, and on arriving at Miami. For the connecting flight, we were ushered onto a waiting plane, as we entered the cabin (only the both of us), someone greeted me. As it turned out, that knew me. Apparently an announcement was made inquiring of our appearance. I was told by this person, that the plane was awaiting our arrival. It is certainly a small world, Good thing we made an issue at the departure from JFK, of the fact that we had to make a connection. As mentioned above, **speak out** when necessary.

Now we are on the way to the Tocumen airport, Panama. The hope is that we will be able to connect with the rest of the party. As it turned out, the others were somewhere in the airport, awaiting our arrival. As I exited the terminal with our Luggage, someone approached me asking if we were in the Walcott's party and I responded in the affirmative, I asked how he was able to identify me out of all these arriving persons? His response was, that he just hoped I was that person. This chance recognition occurred again while awaiting transportation to Colon. Must be *Karma* or something in the way I look.

After this encounter, we were all able to get together, Yasmina and Yolanda arrived on the 7th. Day before. The conveyer was quite comfortable to accommodate us and luggage, therefore after loading, we had a very pleasant and informative drive throughout the City, seeing the many changes and improvements to this city we called home. We made it to the Hotel Torres de Alba, located on the corner of 49A West Street and Eusebio A Morales Street. Located across from The Hotel Panama. This was a most comfortable and fully equipped place to be. Staff and personnel were very accommodating. All 12 of us were well fed and accommodated for 2 days, since we had to be on the way to Colon- Pier2000, early on the morning of the 10th, to board the ship check in time(09:00 -11:00) Monarch operated by the Pullmantur cruises line. All luggage were properly tagged and left on pier, where they were taken aboard by staff and located at the entrance of assigned cabins. Kudos to Yvonne's contact with the cruise line. This phase went quite well. Our cabin was # 6591.

Our first stop on the cruise was Cartagena Colombia Saturday 8/11th followed by a day at sea. Next Monday 13th. Curacao Tuesday 14th. Bonaire. Wednesday 15th. Aruba. Thursday 16th. At sea on the way back to Colon arriving morning of Friday 17th. This is where the next surprising approach to me occurred. Before going on, I must mention that at the point where we were about to board the vessel, we had the pleasure of meeting our cousin Joy McLaughlin which was one of the highlights of this trip.

Among the highlights of our visit to Aruba, this being Olivia and my second trip which we accomplished some years ago, at that time we were aware of some unique aspect of the trees called "divi-divi", where the trees growth always in the southern/eastern direction no other explanation for this. Except that it also serves as a directional guideline (i.e. pointing east) Well I took the opportunity this time to ask the bus driver if he could tell us about this, which he could not. I offered a suggestion that it had to do with the direction of the Sun light, therefore the branches tend to grow away towards the shade. (This is my personal plausible explanation).

There were good times on board the vessel, plenty food, and family togetherness, we had our own theme nights, Red top where we all wore red tops, then White nights where we all wore some white. We also celebrated the Birthday celebrations of Yvonne and Yolanda, a cake was provided and the waters staff along with those assigned to our table, sang the traditional birthday song also the Latin version which we taught them. Then there was the traditional Captain's night where we all were dressed in formal attire even Prynce was in his most formal attire. Photographs documented this.

I must mention that the services extended by waiter assigned to our table 142 and his assistant were superb, also the Lady who handled our cabin needs was very efficient and attentive, she kept the ever so small cabin, in a neat and presentable condition each day. They all were above and beyond required expectation.

Well as the saying goes, all is well that went well. Not really, there were some trying times where things were not up to par, such as the process for debarking the vessel for required cruises, there is much to be improved, as I mentioned to several of the cruise directors, "The attraction of a cruise voyage is the visitation of the various ports therefore this process should be executed as comfortably and as pleasant as possible, and not an ordeal of going up to the higher floors for assembly and returning to the pier level for debarking. Once on pier the loading of land conveyances should be reasonably effective, passengers should not be treated as kindergarten students.

This phase of a cruise should be the memorable highlight of the trip." I really wanted to respond to a survey questioner issued on boar prior to debarking, however this was another source of inconvenience and displeasure which I experienced, when approaching the tour desk attendant on vessel, to whom I expressed in no uncertain terms, my sentiments partially stated above. Enough said.

On debarkation, we were required to transit the required customs inspection, which was quite an operation, since, by selecting ones luggage etc. we were dispersed among all those approx. 2000 travelers. Fortunately for us, a family member of Ernesto works on the pier, and he was able to usher me to a comfortable waiting area, awaiting the assembly of the others in our party. Mind you, there were quite a number of persons in this area, while sitting there, someone approached me to ask if I am part of the group he is looking for. It has happened again as mentioned above, on my confirmation, he was extremely happy, and I was again perplexed, how did he pass all others and came to me? I must always be at my best behavior, since somehow, I am recognizable. (Smile).

Turns out that, the owner of the bus with whom Yvonne contracted, asked this driver to pick up this group at the pier in Colon for conveyance to the same Hotel Torres de Alba in Panama, where we spent the first two days on arrival to Panama. We are now scheduled to spend the rest of the week there. Good planning has paid off, along with the ability to identify persons.

The good thing is that now we are all together on the bus, it allowed me to see some familiar sights and the extent of the changes over these years, the only thing missing was a narration from the driver or an assigned guide, especially for those younger persons in our group.

It's now Friday 17th. While lounging in the lobby, a group of persons entered and sure enough, there were two who I readily recognized, one was a member of ST. Gabriel's Church and the other, a very good friend who I had not seen for a very long time, Grace was the leader of this group. I immediately offered to sell her a copy of my book, which I always carried. I also offered to sell a copy to my Church sister. That's #2, next, on a visit to another friend of Yvonne, I was able to sell another that #3. I will have to keep this up.

On Saturday, we assembled with this same bus, and did some sightseeing, included a visit to the visitor's center at the *Miraflores* locks which required an entrance fee, fortunately we who had a *Panamanian Cedula*, and enjoyed *(Tercera edad)* advanced age discount, the cost was $3.50. We witnessed the transit of a vessel which entailed said vessel been towed into the lock chamber, then the water raised the vessel to the next level, after which the door is opened and the vessel proceeds on its own power toward the next set of locks, *Pedro Miguel* depending on the direction of travel (towards the Pacific Ocean) F.Y.I Locks are located at Gatun, Pedro Miguel and Miraflores) the newly expanded lock system is located closer to the Atlantic side in *Agua Clara* and Cocoli but due to time restraints, we were not privileged to visit.

I mentioned Panamanian Cedula,(identification card) as it turned out, on Thursday 8/9/18 Yvonne, Yasmina, Olivia and myself, visited the *Cedulacion* (A government office which issues personal identification cards) to have ours renewed and updated, and we were promised these on the 18th. Just in time for this visit, consequently, we were able to take advantage of the reduced rate. The general rate was $15.00, quite a difference. This card (Cedula) is required for each citizen of adult age, and used for personal identification and any official participation and transaction.

In exchanging ideas with Yvonne, I wondered if the wider set of locks existed in Agua Clara, at what point does this parallel the existing canal at that point. We ascertained that it was the Gatun sets of locks. My next wonder is, there ought to be another place where these large vessels (Post max) transit another set of wide locks, upon checking, Yvonne called back to say that she was informed that there is an exit point to the Pacific ocean with wider set of locks at *Cocoli*. Which apparently would make logical sense as an answer to my inquiry, paralleling with MIraflores equaling the sea level of the Pacific Ocean. At some point perhaps I would be able to see these point in a map, outlining the configuration of the route these post max vessels take in transiting between Atlantic and Pacific oceans. I hope this was not too confusing to you the reader. Eventually, it will all be made clear.

This is the confirmation which I was able to extract from a magazine on Panama. The third set of amplified (*esclusas)* locks on the Atlantic side named "Agua Clara", was officially opened June 26, 2016 and the first "*mega*" ship transited was the grain ship "Andronikos" 300 meters long and a gross weight of 94,300 tons. The other set of locks is in Cocoli on the pacific side. As also indicated, there is an observation platform which is presently under construction, in Gatun on the same magnitude as the one in Miraflores on the pacific side. It will be very informative and interesting, to view the operation.

The system of operation has been improved, where the water used to fill the basins when the ship is enclosed, is recycled into adjourning reservoirs, the retaining gate is **retracted** into the area, instead of **swinging** along the side walls of the basin. This system minimizes the loss of water into the ocean.

After our mini tour, we dined at a fish diner (Mercado de Mariscos). We then got back on the bus and returned to the hotel. I reminded Yvonne to make the promised call to Cecilia and Carmen. While lounging in the lobby of the hotel, we had a visit from Mrs. Josiah, also Olivia's cousins, and eventually (Tooty) as we call her, and Carmen arrived, I was very happy to at last meeting these ladies with whom we grew up, after meeting all, introductions were made all around including Olivia's cousins, to who I mentioned that Cecilia was my lifesaver, really so, she look a bit perplexed, therefore I asked Ceci to tell her why I made that statement. Ceci told her the abbreviated story "we all as young people travelled yearly to a camp in Santa Clara and at one of these visits, Richard took very ill and was severely shaking and could not stop" (I interjected at this point that in spite of me been covered with an army blanket.) Ceci continued, "We all just laid on him and he eventually stopped the shaking" I continued the story to say that I contacted double pneumonia and was eventually taken to the hospital in Penonome where a Blood transfusion had to be administered, blood was donated by the accompanying Priest Fr. Farmer to whom I also was indebted.

From this narrative you can well appreciate my appreciation by finally meeting these ladies, it afforded me the privilege of actually embracing the person who, in my time of need, was there to add her body heat, thus stabilizing my trembling. They remained for a short time later, and I wished them both a safe travel to their respective homes.

Considering the fact that we were on limited time, my wish was to be able to have them join us in some fellowship time, recounting our experiences as young people growing up in Colón Rep of Panama also for the benefit of others present in this assembled group. This is something to look forward to, given the occasion and opportunity.

On Sunday, 8/19/18 we attended services at St. Paul's Episcopal Church in Panama City, we were familiar with this church since when we had exchange of Youth services, also this is where our Friend Bishop James

Ottley attended at some point, and especially where Yvonne attended while living in Panama City. Even though the services were in Spanish, we were somewhat comfortable, after service we met with the pastor also with the church staff with whom Yvonne was acquainted, we had coffee and met with some of the folks, and by the way, I presented the pastor with a copy of my book. (Can't omit this fact) We took separate taxis back to the hotel

On Monday we visited a family some of us knew, after a short visit there, it turned out that we were able to revive some past experiences and share personal impressions of our individual lives back then and now. (To accentuate my impressions, I took the opportunity to sell a copy of my book, (I told you I always try to have copies on hand) after this, the hosts who are quite prominent and known in the area, decided to visit a popular restaurant, and we had quite a time at it, good service, good food and good conversations, then we said our goodbyes and took taxis back to the hotel, our driver was able to take us via the scenic route which enabled us to see the old areas, some of which I recognized, also new improvements to areas, buildings and roads, this was quite an experience to see all the changes in Panama.

We arrived at the hotel, and the task at hand now is to retire to our separates suites and pack to get everything in place and ready for the trip to the airport. Early morning on Tuesday 21$^{st}$. most of us were on the way back to our separate homes, except Yasmin and Yolanda who are remaining in town for a few more days. I wish circumstance were of such, where we could remain a few more days also, to do and see more in Panama. In all it was a great and wonderful occasion to meet, enjoy and spend some time with family.

It is incumbent that I digress and tell the whole story which an abbreviated version was told by Ceci of the "encounter" at Santa Clara of how we got to this point. Well it all started while growing up at Christ church by-the-sea, Colon Republic of Panama. Our parents as they went to church, also took their children with them, these children grew up in Sunday school and as they grew, they became acquainted with each other, now becoming teenagers and having friends in their personal and separate circles, but never straying from the church. We then became members of the young people's fellowship (Y.P.F) as we grew, we then invited our friends to join us in this fellowship.

While this was going on at Christ church, it was the same in other parishes in the Anglican communion in Panama, and other towns of the Canal zone, to name a few, Gamboa, Paraiso, La Boca, Rainbow City etc. The name of some of the parishes as I remember them are as follows.

Christ Church by-the sea. ---- St. Christopher---- St Alban----St. Peter----St. Mary----St. Paul---- and. ---- St. Simon---- These are the ones I found photos of in my scrap book. We were able to get to know each other and have formed lifelong friendships, there were even some marriages resulting from these friendships.

The Panama dioceses acquired some property and built summer camps which were placed at the disposal of all the churches, and schedules were made for each parish to send contingences during the summer to spend weeks where retreats, lectures etc. which were conducted by a guest preacher or persons of some distinction. Each group would plan fund raisers during the year, in order to defray travel expenses for the trip to Santa Clara at our determined date.

Occasionally, there was a leaders training conference (L.T.C) scheduled where selected persons from each group would travel to Santa Clara, this allowed us to be in the company of Youth representatives from each parish. Another way we were able to accomplishes this, was to invite each group to spend a weekend at your parish, and we would have a member as guest in each family to entertain and feed and get to know each other, then in the evening, a program of entertainment is planned at a designated place, mostly in the Parish hall or, in our case, at the Christ church academy school hall.

It was during one of these trips to Santa Clara that the "encounter" alluded to by Ceci occurred. Our group which consisted of two churches, Christ Church (Colon) Pastored by Fr. Farmer, and St. Mary (Rainbow city) pastored by Fr. Spaulding. Both on the Atlantic side. After a long bus ride, on arrival, we were assigned separate houses Male-Females. There is a large house for dining and meetings also a bath house where all is required to wash the sand off prior to entering either place. There is also a chapel for worship.

My predicament perhaps, had its start from a very active schedule. In the morning as I remembered it, Both Lester and I used to have an early run on the beach prior to breakfast, on one of our runs, suddenly I noticed Lester was no longer running along with me, when I checked he was not readily in sight along the shoreline, but as the tide receded I saw him rolling on the sand, I ran towards him I also got knocked down by the next incoming wave, but recovered in time to help him to his feet.

It appears that he was running too much off the water line, it is what we did, since it's at this point, the sand is most compacted which allowed us to be on solid and not sandy ground. Easier on the stride. As required, we then proceeded to the back of the house and hosed off then proceeded to the "Mess hall" for breakfast, followed by some horseback riding and playing ball in the sun, in retrospect, too much exposure for me. As mentioned above, I was admitted to the Pheromone hospital in the next town, where I remained for some days after the rest of the group had gone home.

I wondered at this juncture, what happened to my gear (clothes, Camera and personal belongings) when the group went back to Colon, considering we did not take them with us to the hospital. I asked Yvonne who had accompanied me along with Fr. Farmer to the Hospital. She was not sure about this, anyway, on my discharge date mother was there with Fr. Farmer who was so kind to accompany her to take me back home to Colon, Panama. Perhaps we did make a stop at the camp to recover my belongings prior to continuing on the trip back home. I was charged by the other Priest, that I can no longer do the strenuous things I used to do without proper rest, and I had to report to the local doctor in Colon for further observation, which I did. To relate, this was surely a *"What if? The question" Moment.*

After Santa Clara. On subsequent years, The venue was changed to a closer place to Colon known to us as "The rubber farm", I do not know the actual name of the area where this farm was located, (perhaps on the Gatun Lake) but it was necessary to board a launch to get there, and we had to provide our sleeping accommodations (cot) this was different, instead of the ocean, we are now on a lake, we still had to provide for transportation and in addition, refreshment while on the launch, speaking of refreshments, we have now grown a bit in age, not much, and are now among older persons, young adults, therefore we decided to spike the Kool aid with some "levity" and it was discovered by some of the older ones and our cover was blown. It was refreshing while it lasted. In addition to the regular change of clothes, bathing suits towels etc. I also had my Daisy Air rifle along with a supply of ammo (B.B.) we each staked out our place in this house, younger ones apart from the others.

In retaliation to those who reported us to the supervisors, at night when all were settled in, someone took the shoes of one of them and threw it outside. In the morning, he was franticly searching for his shoes, the house was in an upstir until the shoes were discovered under the house. We would never forget the remarks from one of the supervisors. "...I will not associate myself with you anymore". This was not really meant to be sincere, since before long, we were all one group again.

The time spent there were quite varied (including horseback riding) and memorable. To tell the stories of some of the highlights. Prior to our departure, all were admonished not to take bathing suits is you do not know how to swim, since swimming in the lake is different from ocean, because of weed growth in the lake. One day as we were all on the pier ready to take a dive, mind you, as a rule, everyone on the pier had on bathing suits therefore, knows how to swim right? Not so, since one girl was pushed off the pier (horse playing) but we quickly realized that she was not doing well, therefore we dove into the lake to assist her back up on the pier, and in doing so, she also lost her bracelet, it's a good thing some of us were good swimmers, and were able to dive down and retrieve it, considering it did not sink to the bottom (which is quite deep) but it was caught on some weed growth.

Next episode was, one of the young adults, (who also did not know how to swim) was in a "*cayuca*" row boat, which overturned, and the swimmers among us, had to go to his rescue.

There were not many swimmers among the group since, most of us are used to swimming in the ocean and perhaps in rivers, opposed to Lake (with weed growth), the sensation of been entangled with seaweeds while swimming was not a comfortable one, in spite of this, the cool lake water was a counter to the heat and we managed to enjoy the daily refreshing swim.

Another episode: A few of us went bird hunting with my Air rifle and got carried away timewise, since there was a strict schedule imposed, when we eat, lunch, pray, dine, supper etc. to say the least, we were off schedule for supper, and on arrival, we were denied food which consisted of spaghetti and meatballs, and had to make do with snacks, and sequestered tid bits from the kitchen. In the morning upon waking, we saw a lot of discarded spaghetti under the building, which evoked much displeasure since the rules could have been slackened, considering the circumstances. This prompted us to create the thirteen commandment "THOU SHALL NOT WASTE SPAGETTI"

Another Episode: As an observation, it got very dark as the sun goes down, one evening a few of the boys who were adventurous wanted to go hiking, I had my trusted Daisy air rifle (much good that would be against an animal). We stipulated our intentions to the leaders, but one of the pastors refused to allow it, so we took our case to Fr. Farmer, who graciously agreed to accompany us. Armed with the Air rifle and the ever potent Man Of God, we were invincible.

On and on we went into the night, marching, singing, and whistling, it was now getting late therefore, "Padre" decided it was time to head back to camp. As we approached, we detected some uneasiness among those in camp, and one of the girls said, "See, they are afraid, see, they are whistling" as I relate this story, it still evokes a smile, for them to worry and to think we were in danger and lost. Remember a certain line of the Lord's Prayer "And lead us not into temptation, but deliver us from evil, for thine is the kingdom…"

All in all, we spent a lovely time at camp, getting to know each other likes and dislikes, also under very relaxed circumstances. In retrospect, I can truly say that some of the most lasting friendship has been sustained to this day. That is the story in a nutshell, of our time spent at Santa Clara and The Rubber Farm as young peoples and young Adults.

Back to the where we left off. We all left Panama to our various destinations and thankfully each group arrived safely. Tuesday August 21st. It was my desire to contact the Cruise line to complain of some of the problem we encountered during the voyage, which was specifically about the planning for the shore visits at the various ports of stop. My point was that the reason for a cruise was to permit the voyagers to visit each port of call, getting to know something about the places visited, therefore the arrangements should be smooth and comfortable as possible, for those persons going on shore.

To say the least, it was far from this, since each group was shuttled on board from floor to floor, to be assembled into specific group, then elevator trip to the lower level for debarkation, then

Having each groups together on shore into their separate conveyances, this was not a good, comfortable way to start a land tour. This was the specific complaint. Besides all, the voyage and accommodation on board the vessel was very pleasant, and we were able to meet other people from various part of the nation. It especially was a great way for our family to get together under one conveyance and enjoy each other. Let do it again and again under any circumstance.

Fortunately or unfortunately I was not able to get my thoughts conveyed to the cruise line since my attempt on board was thwarted, and from home my efforts on computer on line was not to be since the passage of time was too long. All is well that ended well.

On Sunday August 26th. After 2 weeks of vacation, as I entered the sanctuary for service fully robed in my choir vestment, to my astonishment and surprise, I was confronted with the placement of easels displaying the drawings of the proposed *feasibility study* on the altar.

Astonishment: that it should be on the altar platform prior and during the celebration of service

Surprised: that this has been the time scheduled to talk and make a pitch for this project, to the congregation.

At the conclusion of the service, a presentation was made to the congregation, taking them by surprise, and no questions were allowed, especially as known by myself, the information was not sufficiently disseminated, I tried to ask questions that I am sure were in the minds of some persons hearing this for the first time. But was told that there would be another presentation where a representative from Garden City would be on hand where questions would be allowed.

I was approached by a number of concerned persons asking if I was in favor of this proposal, to which my reply was at all time, was "**no, not in the form as it was presented.**" When able, I proceeded to show and explain my objections, since I usually have in my briefcase, copies of the drawings also photos of my alternate proposal, which consist of an actual building in progress which comprise of (a brownstone demolished and incorporated into this construction)

While showing some persons, my photos of the alternate suggestion, a person said that I should produce the alternate in the same manner of the original, well I was a bit incensed, but controlled my reply and therefor said to that person, I am not an architect, we have paid thousands of dollars for the present drawing which we are contesting, they are the ones who should produce an alternative drawing.

This is exactly what this proposal is intended to cover, which is the demolition of our actual parish house, including the present driveway up to the actual walkway to the side entrance of the present church building, accounting for the width of said proposed structure, then extended from the start of the facing sidewalk, all the way back and including the demolition of the actual lobby area including the newly constructed second floor on top of the lobby, extending to the back of the present building. Which would account for the length of this proposal.

This is where I strongly abject. When I was made aware of this proposal, I contacted the Architect who produced this drawing, and asked him what made him consider the demolition of the area of the actual Lobby area which includes all the plumbing and staircase to the basement and including elevator from basement to the second floor. His response was "I was told to maximize the space" my reply was. "Precisely/ **Space,** there was no space, it is an extension of the church building's footprint with a second floor and not a (2 story building) as indicated in the legend of your drawing." I further observed that if a **study** was actually made, as indicated on the drawing, a visit to the local (site) or a view of the blueprint of the present constructed building would have indicated that fact. **Feasibility** is another cause to question the feasibility of this proposal. From checking with the **American Heritage Dictionary**: Feasible: Capable of being utilized or dealt with successfully, suitable, logical. **Britannica World Language Dictionary:** feasible: That may be done practicably. Individual conclusions can be drawn from these definitions, we must ask ourselves, would this proposal be practical giving the present circumstances?

The facts are presently apparent that the plan as presented by those persons presenting it, is to **maximize** a structure (Apartment building) by **minimizing** the very structure which it was intended to assist in meeting operating expenses.(St. Gabriel's Church) This does not readily make any sense. Considering that the thought of this construction, would definitely shut the operation of the church since there would not be the presence of plumbing facilities, the income which is presently derived from the use of the Golden Hall would be none existent (Hall rental, Senior center, etc.) Which has been determined to be the 2nd. Highest source of income.

At each meeting or occasion where I have voiced my sentiments I have been barraged with the quote "it is not etched in stone", when I persist, "then if not, then show us an alternative" If a person continuously utter this quote then said person should offer an alternative. Some persons indicated that perhaps I do not understand the meaning of the quote. Be assured that I know precisely the meaning of *etch*. As a matter of fact the word *Etch* is from Dutch [*etsen*] from German [*atzen*] meaning to feed. A sample of an expressed phrase: "her face was etched in my memory" (this is after seeing her face over and over. Same as seeing something on & on)

A moment of pause or wonder. Perhaps the plan is to etch this proposal in our memory, since it's the only one been presented over and over. Do you think this is the plan?

According to Wikipedia:

Etching- The process of using strong acid or <u>mordant</u> to cut into the unprotected parts of a metal surface to create a design in <u>intaglio</u> (image is created by cutting, carving into a flat surface).

<u>Word meaning</u>-- Mordant: Any substance, such as tannic acid,,, forming an insoluble compound … To produce a fixed color. The corrosive used in etching

Intaglio: Incised carving to engrave with a sunken design.

The Britannica World Language dictionary:

Etch: To engrave by the means of acid or other corrosive fluid, especially for making a design on a plate, for printing.

Etching- A process of engraving in which lines are scratched with a needle on a plate covered with wax or other coating, and the parts exposed are subjected to the biting of an acid.

I have looked up this word in approximately 6 different dictionaries, in addition to those sources mentioned above, and in none of these, is there a mention of etching in stone, which leads me to conclude: etching is not necessarily referred to **stone**. On one occasion in the abstract, it was mentioned (etched in my *memory*,) so there you are. What I do know is that there are references made to, chisel, carved, written on stone, also, formed of, or sculptured. From stone. I will follow up on this situation as it progresses.

The following weekend, was spent at Chez-B, there was much to catch up on but I really did not stay as long to accomplish all, at least I was able to manufacture some frames for a couple "Molas" (native Panamanian handmade needlework depicting animals, floral etc.) very colorful and attractive, suitable for display. I was able to have mine set up beautifully in the frame, and now it is installed on a wall for all to see and appreciate.

The following weeks were full of all kinds of occasions, doctor visits, meetings and other things, then to top off the next weekend, there was the ordination of deacon Leandra at the Cathedral, where almost all the clergy of the diocese plus parishioners from the various churches, came together to witness the tradition of the laying on of hands, led by the Bishop, for the ordination of this wonderful lady who had spent her time as a deacon at St.Gabriel's church. This was quite a celebration, evidenced by the overwhelming presence of persons in attendance. I was able to meet Rev. Hickman Alexander who was the first postulant to the Holy order of priesthood from St.Gabriel's Church, also many of the priests who have served there.

The following Sunday September 16$^{th}$, we had the privilege of hosting Rev. Mother Leandra Thelma Lisa Lambert as the officiating priest, her very first service as newly ordained priest (her request).As a member of this parish, it was quite an honor, I am sure that was the sentiment experienced by most of the members of the congregation, as evidenced by the overwhelming attendance, which included visiting priests, family, friends and guests. There was a combined church choir (Chancel and Gospel) and one service scheduled for this occasion. We all wished her God's richest blessings on her future endeavor in the ministry.

September, 23$^{rd}$. As mentioned before, today is the promised visit by the diocesan rep. regarding the feasibility study, this service was dedicated to have him present their views regarding this study and rational for this proposal. After his presentation the floor was open to questions, while he was talking, I realized that the points I originally made, were not addressed, and as a matter of fact they had the drawings sighted on the monitors, which did not reflect the actual facts. At that point I decided to go to my car which was parked in the driveway, to retrieve my copy of the actual blueprints (Plans) of the original church building, produced by the architect who was in attendance for the building of the 2$^{nd}$ floor.

Several questions were asked by others, requesting clarification and reasons for the proposal, some of the concerns were regarding the necessity for such a large building towering over the existing church building, also containing large apartments which would demand large rental cost for tenants, which seems doubtful and beyond the reach of likely renters in this area.

I voiced my questions and proceeded to show him the page where it clearly shows, that is not a two story building, (as mentioned in their proposal), marked for demolition as an extension for the proposed building, but in fact, it is part of the actual "footprint" of the church building with a second floor added, in order to acquire space for Priest, conference room and storage, furthermore, the foundation of this area, contains the Plumbing and bathrooms, access to the lower floor where the Golden Hall is located, also the elevator.

The rep. indicated some doubt, but I assured him that in spite of me not been an architect, I do have some knowledge and understanding of the drawings, and that I was also involved in the plans (drawings) of the original church building. I further indicated to him that, if this proposal is considered, by demolishing this area, the Church building would be shut down, since there would be no sanitary facility available, the Golden Hall will cease to be the source of income of the church, since there would be no hall rental, no senior center, no services.

I found it necessary to repeat this since, this repetition was made for the benefit of the congregation who is hearing about this proposal for the first time, since the presenters have been repeating this one and only plan (etching it in the minds of those who hear it over and over).

The month of September was indeed a busy one. Sunday Sept. 30th INTERNATIONAL DAY. This is the fourth Sunday of September each year which has been dedicate to this endeavor, it is the day when groups from each participating country who worship in St. Gabriel's Church, would wear their national garment/ colors, tables are sectioned off in specific areas and duly decorated accordingly throughout the golden hall, each group provide their national food etc. for all.

This tradition was started from the time it was agreed that each group would sponsor individual activities in order to raise funds during the year toward the *"Building found"* (a friendly competition), and at the Mass on this 4th Sunday, there would be the reporting of each country's returns with the display of national flags end enjoyment. Some years after the new church building was a reality, prior to the mass, we would engage a steel band to lead the choir and parishioners in a march around the block, as the years went on we would have factions of the Panamanian marching band lead us in parade.

This year 2018 the service was quite longer since there were many facets addressed, first after the parade, the mass, this been especially important/ sad. The very Reverend Eddie Alleyne said some of the prayers of the mass in Spanish, much to the delight of all of the Panamanians & others, which evoked some polite applauds. He noted that Olivia was his tutor. We feel he did quite well, considering it was his first attempt. He have decided that after 12 years, October 1st 2018 would be his last day as rector of this parish.

He has taken this time to pay homage to those persons selected, to receive the Bishop's cross, among those were Olivia J. Buery also a number of persons were presented with certificates and awards. After this, a numbers of persons, groups and organizations presented him with gifts memorabilia, some folks were beginning to get uneasy and hungry, and considering there was food awaiting them.

Fr. had mentioned the intent for Olivia, but asked me to keep it quiet, therefore I said nothing, there was no indication that is was going to happen, on the Saturday, when we were at the church for preparation, I asked him if it was still on, he said yes, therefore I started to mention it to the family, Sherena was previously asked by Olivia to attend the International day celebration, as customarily, but she was unsure,

After I called and told her of the plan, and she was not to spill the beans she then decided to attend with Sydney, I saw her in church and approached her to whisper that, at my indication, she was to bring Olivia to the altar, At that point I was unaware of the extent of the number of those persons receiving awards, I had my camera to take photos, when it was clear the number of persons been called, I looked to Sherena and wondered where Olivia was. The surprise plot was foiled, since Olivia decided to go downstairs to prepare with the Panamanian group to serve food. When Olivia's name was called, CY, who was present, and I had also swore him to secrecy, went downstairs to the Golden Hall to get her on the pretext that she was needed upstairs. When she was ushered to the altar, there was still some concern on her face, at least some element of surprise, not the impact that was planned. I got the photos with her, daughter and her Granddaughter. I wished her well and welcomed her to the "club" I received mine in march1992 that's 26 years later. Better late than never.

October 21st. we went to Chez B to check on things, since it has been over a month, and we have been experiencing some problem with the Direct T.V. and I wanted to try and get this straighten out, seems that The monthly bill is paid, but we do not avail ourselves of this service. As I have pointed out to them, this place is where we go to relax and escape temporarily, stress of daily living, but on the contrary, each time we go there a night is spent getting the Television back ibn service which is very stressful, each time we leave there they turn off the service, my point to them is, if I continue to pay monthly, even thou the T.V is not in use why turn it off?

Most disconcertingly, I am always complaining to someone in the Philippines who does not seems to grasp the inconvenience we are enduring, therefore I demanded that they connect me to a supervisor which would alleviate the language difference. After trying several times, this situation was finally alleviated by them setting an appointment for a visit by a technician. This finally got us back to viewing T.V after a night of stress, however this does not address the financial part of this problem. We finally came to a solution, where it was agreed that I call each time I am leaving Chez B (I was sure to ask for direct number) the system will be on *Pause* but I would be charged a nominal fee of $5.00 for the month and service would be automatically resumed at the end of that month. This is somewhat satisfying, since hopefully, on my return on or after the determined date, there should be service, well this ls left to be determined on our next visit.

Friday, October 26th 2018, the total church sponsored our yearly Gala in the Golden Hall, which was transformed into *A Gatsby Night*, The gala and journal was dedicated to The Alleyne family, who were themselves, also dressed in the fashion of the era. Most of those attending this gala were dressed accordingly and it was certainly a night to remember, featuring a Jazz band who provided entertaining and dance music appropriate to the era of *Gatsby*, also a D.J playing music of all time, also catered meal including a cocktail hour of "Hor D'Oeuvers" followed by a well prepared and tasty meal served by waiters, which also featured a rolling bar. The whole shebang.

We are now in a situation where there is no rector assigned to our parish and the vestry will have to establish a search committee, fortunately, we are blessed to have a retired bishop as well as a retired Canon assigned to St Gabriel's Church, therefore we are not devoid of Pastoral care. The time is approaching where there is another reason for all to be alerted since by January, we will have to prepare for election of new members for the vestry, there is no time to vacillate, the work of the church continues.

The parish council of which I am a member, is scheduled to have our much delayed meeting caused by numerous cancellations. Hopefully, one has been scheduled for this Tuesday. Among the items on the agenda, are the reading of the last meeting, June 26th this gives you the reader of the delays mentioned. The much contested Land Use "Feasibility Study) also a search committee for an interim priest/rector and a report of the Parish Gala just observed. A lot to cover.

While speaking to one of the parishioner who has been very interested in the progress of the feasibility study, I mentioned to her that I too am very interested in hearing what is going on, but that a council meeting is scheduled for Tuesday and I certainly intend to inquire, and I will keep her informed, well she said that she was notified that there is going to be a funeral service on Tuesday, this caused me to wonder about the scheduled meeting, therefore on reaching home, I sent an e-mail to the director informing of the service, and alerted him to check with the booking clerk regarding a possible repast after the funeral service, which is the usual practice.

Well, on checking my e-messages on Monday, voila/, it was confirmed that there will be a repast after the service. Another cancellation, the meeting has been re-scheduled for November 13th. Hopefully, there will be no further development during this lapse in time, it is now a wait and see what happens in this regard. November promises to be a very busy month in the life of the church, I will suggest that the venue be changed from the Golden hall, to the conference room, Parish house or the pastor's office, which is large enough to accommodate the gathering. At this rate, we would not be able to meet before the end of the year.

A little on the lighter side: "Urinary session"

As we age, we are prone to get up sometime during bedtime to pay a visit to the water depository, well, most time it takes a dream to suddenly awake you to perform this task. Usually, when one dream, some of the facts are forgotten when we recall the dreams after we are wide awake, however not these dreams, since it require immediate awakening to address the *situation*.

Most recently: Dreamt that I was located at a rather fancy place and was experiencing the need to make a deposit, therefore I approached a bathroom which was quite unusual since the door was wide open and there sat, a fully clothed lady on a fancy commode actually reading a book. I proceed to go to another room this door was closed, therefore I knocked on the door as is the proper thing to do, in order to determine if it was unoccupied. Unfortunately I heard a voice of a lady in reply to the knock, she asked what I wanted, I said I wanted to avail myself of the toilet, she directed me to go to the other room, but I mentioned the unusual fact that it was occupied by this other lady actually reading.

She instructed me in no uncertain terms, to "go tell that lady to give the room up to you right away and if not I would go there myself to get her out". Well as can well be determined, time was of the essence therefore, as I hurriedly approached the other room, the seated lady saw me coming and she got up and was about to leave, I told her what the other lady said anyway, she left and I was allowed to enter the bathroom, before settling down, I tried unsuccessfully to push the door close, but the need was imminent therefor I sat and reached out to keep the door closed while attending to the *matter* on hand.

While attending to this *matter*, a man knocked on the door and before I could answer, he proceeded to push the door open, my thought was, why bother to knock since you came in anyway? Fortunately I had finished my *task*, and left the area, I saw this man later, and he asked me if I had an encounter with a lady prior to the use of the bathroom where we both met? I replied as a matter of fact I did, and asked him, why this question? He said that he heard her telling some people that she was "displaced from her seat by a Democrat." An interesting way to explain what really happened, don't you think?

That was a rather detailed and extensive dream to make a point. There have been some short, and precise dreams which required an instant reaction, such as, taking a dive into a pool fully clothed, which would result in a rather messy and wet situation. This would require one to hit the floor running (so to speak) and making a bee line to the bath room door and hoping that there are no obstructions, such as a lady occupying the room for other than what it was intended, upon finding the road to the destination unimpeded, //whew//, you can perform your *task*. Upon completion, after adjusting, flushing, washing and dressing, you can return to your slumber, and resume your relaxing and perhaps, a more pleasing topic and refreshing state of dreaming.

How did I ever get on this topic anyway? Well to explain, I almost had an uncomfortable situation while in the hotel in Panama on our recent sojourn, it was a rather large suite with strange surroundings. I must have experienced one of these dreams I spoke of before, which required me to visit the **room,** it was rather dark, and after walking into a wall, I had to try to find my way (in the dark) since the light switch was not readily locatable, Finally, I was able to find the door to exit the bedroom and consequently the door to the other **room.** After that, I made sure to know where the switch for the lights were located and orientation of said suite.

Now that I have mentioned our recent family reunion in Panama, there are a few things I must mention. While traveling to Colon to get to the pier where we were to board the ocean vessel for the ocean tours, had I known that the pier was locate at the entrance of the city, I would have asked the bus driver to take us on a run through the city in order to view some of the places where we grew up, and be able to point them out to the young members of the family, also to reminisce. Opportunity lost, however we were able to see the High school, what's left of it, this allow me to remember some of the good times spent there. As the saying goes. {One opportunity lost, another one gained}.

I would have liked to see the house we lived on with the Gordon's family which was located at 4th street and Hudson Lane, I mentioned this in my book What if? But I would like to describe this building at this point, it was a two storied building entirely of cement, and went through to the adjoining building that extended to Central Ave. we could walk right past a court yard, where we used to play stick ball, and cross the street into the park, on a Sunday afternoon we would sit on the benches, or walk up and down the park from 4th to 5th streets.

In the evenings we had the run of the entire length of the building. The Gordons had the balcony sectioned off and enclosed also extending to the next two rooms. The balcony area was what was considered as the sitting room, kitchen and dining area, the next room, was their bedroom, separated by a partition, the front of which, was a large standing radio where we would listen to programs from the British broadcasting stations and the army radio stations, next was an area where her son Vibert slept. Followed by the room where we slept. There was a door from the side veranda, therefore we could enter/ exit without having to go through the other rooms. The width of the building included wrap around veranda and rooms were side by side with a sound barrier cement wall in the center, dividing each side which extended the length of the space up to the back where there existed the stairs and a platform where all the tenants congregated at times. Then followed by the common kitchens and bathrooms for each side. I wish I was in a position to provide actual measurements at this point to further impress the expanse of what we enjoyed. If memory served me well, there were 4 families on each side, the 3 families' area was comprised of I room each, only the front families had the expanse areas as described on each side.

On the ground floor there were some shops, on one side a shoe repair, but I was never sure what was on the other side, I do know that the allocations of rooms were different, since there was no balcony, instead this area was the side walk, (street floor). This is all we knew of the tenants of the ground floor of this building, however, we were acquainted with the tenants of the upper floor of the building beside us, which was so close that one could cross over the balconies back and forth, we did not do this for very obvious reasons, our size and the danger which existed, some of the adults did. As mentioned in the book What If?

I used to visit with the gentleman whose room was directly opposite ours, we could look across the balcony into each other rooms when doors were open. He was a hunter and had shot guns and rifles which I was allowed to handle, unloaded I might add, as told previously, I was looking forward to a planned trip, where I would have been allowed to actually fire them, I purchased all my gear, from the Army & Navy store which consisted of pots and pans appropriate clothes etc. and was ready to go. On the appointed time, everything fell through and the trip was cancelled, I was never told of the reason.

We became friends with the children from this building, also attended the same schools and eventually in some cases, even class mates. I must point out that it was a small city and our various path has been crossed at some point, even though we travelled in different circles and interests.

Next. I would have cherished the opportunity to visit the church we attended while growing up in Colon, Christ Church by-the-sea, I wanted very much to be able to check out the bells which I mentioned previously, and with the hope of ringing them using the note chart I had written of 2 familiar tunes that were played on the bells back in those days, and forwarded by Tina, with the hope that someone would try to chime them.

Here we go again, and the dreams go on. On waking up on Thursday morning, I remembered having a dream that something was wrong, since there was a cloud of smoke around my car and I panicked and wondered if the car was on fire. That said, I went to the window to check on the car, all was well, and I relaxed, it was only a dream. I left the car there all day and went by taxi to Manhattan, since we were invited to a Gala Program at Lincoln center, sponsored by City Limits. org. Our son Richard, was one of three persons honored, he received from the exec. Editor, the Community Beacon award. It was quite a memorable and impressive evening, along with his family and parents we shared our table with the honorable mayor David Dinkins.

On Friday evening because of the alternate side parking rule, I had to find parking for my vehicle. At the end of Vermont St. at the very end, there was a spot, and I was very careful to park beyond the cross walk line, so much so, that I exited the car and realized that there was room to back up a bit more since the front bumper was just against the line, I did not want what happened some month earlier, where my back bumper was just against the line at the start of the street, and I was issued a summons by what I think, was an unscrupulous meter maid, not the right nomenclature since there was no meter, therefore let's call him a traffic enforcer, I had to pay that summons.

Saturday afternoon, I decided to go get my car and bring it up in front of our home. As I was about to enter the car, I noticed a summons stuck in the wiper (customary place) my immediate thought, It must be the same "traffic enforce" who got me the first time, I retrieve the summons and still fuming in thought, as I read the ticket, this time it was for an expired inspection (10/30/18) I guess this time with the hope of issuing me the summons for the same infraction and noticing that I was sufficiently clear of the line, he decided to check further and he had the last laugh (inspection violation).

This dream was not a **nightmare**, it was the start of a (**day mare**) considering this is an intensely distressing occurrence during the day. I decided to leave the summons on the dashboard plainly visible for any other *enforcer*. Since I would have to leave the car on the street for the rest of the Saturday. This continues, Sunday morning, all ready to go to church, I went to the car, got in and turned the key, no response. I opened the engine lid and removed the battery cover and discovered that there was some white corrosive on the battery posts, I scraped it off and place some oil and tried to tap the contacts, hopefully resuming some electrical contact to the battery, upon trying the key again, there was no response, which confirms that the battery is dead.

We decided to use Olivia's car to get us to the church on time. After returning home from church, I changed clothes and tried again, to no avail, therefore I did the next best thing, I called the Roadside assistance co. and after the usual delay, the young man arrived with a portable battery jump starter and gave it a boost and the car immediately started, he advised me to take the car to the auto store to have battery checked, he further stated that he was in the area earlier, I mentioned the fact that I went to church earlier. Anyway, I decided to drive the car for a bit in order for the battery to recharge itself, on further thought I decided to drive the car to the auto store, on checking, it was determined that the battery needed replacement, which I did.

With the new battery in place, the next move was to get the inspection done and car tagged. I mentioned that this was the start of a **day-mare**, it continues, since as the mechanic connected his scanner, he said the inspection failed and he showed me some configuration on the screen and uttered something about me having a full tank and getting on the highway and drive the car for 100 miles, I asked him to explain this, his reply was that car was not ready. Of all the years I have been owning and driving cars, I have never heard or experienced this dilemma.

IT was a rainy day however I drove the car to check on a sale at a department store which was quite a distance, after which I returned to the mechanic shop, after scanning he said the car was still not ready and I should make the run and maintain a fast speed, I mentioned that this encourages speeding on highways to which confirmed, and that I return the next day. I decided to go to a mechanic I was quite acquainted with, and ask him to explain what this was all about, he explained the situation in depth, also this was not an unusual situation, with the new cars.

As I now understand the situation, after the battery died, the on board computer sort of crashed, and by driving the car for a sustained period of time, it sort of reboot. On further question and answer, I further understood that each time the brakes is applied while driving, the cycle start over again, now this is quite understandable to me, this tells me that speed is not necessarily the thing, it's the continued pace without applying the brakes, this allows the cycle to continue rebooting without interruption.

Armed with this explanation and information, I started out this morning about 11:00 a.m. took Pennsylvania Av. towards the belt parkway east on to the Southern state parkway (same as I did the day before) only this time I was able to keep pace, and as the traffic starts to backup, I would slow down in order not to have to brake, the as the gaps between traffic starts to widen, I then would speed up in order to keep pace, as I approach curbs in road instead of breaking, I slow down to make the curbs without applying brake, this way I was able to travel over 50 miles without touching the brakes, upon reaching exit 40 and nearing 50 miles I was able to exit at some point without stopping and continuing on to hway27 westward which eventually becomes Sunrise Highway, I kept a look forward to see when the lights are on and will speed up, keeping within limits, as I neared the more populated areas the traffic lights were more and eventually I had to break at times.

Today I was more comfortable since I was aware of what I needed to accomplish, instead of trying to keep up speed and as the other mechanic said, I had to keep punching the car. This time when able, I would speed and then slow when necessary. At all times I kept in mind that I have a traffic summons on my dash in order to ward the overzealous traffic police off. The night before I switched with Olivia's car and parked in the driveway, thus keeping the truck off the street. Well today as I reached the mechanic shop, I was more confident and sure enough, the assistant who scanned the truck, tried to pretend that it was still not ready, but I knew that all was well since I knew that I did well.

I was tagged with the sticker and then parked on the street, when Olivia returned, she was able to park her car in the driveway and was then cognizant to the fact that the truck had passed inspection. It has been quite a **day-mare** but it is now over, thankfully, as we say in Spanish. *Gracias A Dios*. Thank God. Now I will have to attend to the payment of the summons, thus ending this **day-mare**.

Monday, Nov. 13th we finally had the Parish council meeting, after discussing the various items on the agenda, the last and most important topic was addressed, the proposed "Feasibility Study" referred to earlier in this narrative. I mentioned my objections for the benefit of the minutes of this meeting, pointing out that I feel very strongly that this proposal in neither "feasible", since it does not comply with the true meaning of the word. It is not suitable, logical or likely. It is not a "study" since thought were not made regarding the existence of a two storied building, which is in fact, the actual footprint of the church where the plumbing and bathrooms exist serving the entire church building, including the golden hall, and the proposed demolition of this area in order to extend the scope of the proposed building would necessitate the closing of the entire structure during construction.

During my presentation, someone mentioned the fact that it "was not etched…" I immediately stopped, and politely asked that person, not to ever mention this saying during this presentation, since the word "etch" is a process of using strong acid or other corrosive fluid, while engraving on metal plate, glass, etc., never on stone. I continued with my presentation and eventually asked the members to pass this on to their members, and to continue asking about this proposal, which is very important to the life and existence of this congregation, especially since, if this proposal is ever considered, it would be to the reason for the disintegration of this congregation since members wishing to worship, and seniors seeking a place to assemble, would have to attend different places, Also no source of income (hall rentals) considering this present church building will be out of service for the duration.

Contrary to the thoughts of those persons who continue to tell me that (It is not etched in stone) as if I do not understand that the proposal is not final, I say to them, if that's the case, then show me an alternative. I have mentioned this several times, and the proposers continues to present the same proposal, which tells me that in their minds it is actually "etched" (final)

I am aware that this saying is an **idiomatic** statement, as I mentioned previously, my search through 6 dictionaries also the internet, has not mentioned (etched in stone). Let's check this out. The American

Heritage Dictionary states. Idiomatic: 1. Peculiar to or characteristic of a given language. A further exploration of this word, **idio<u>ma</u>tic**. Eliminating the underlined letters,

M=mental…..A=ability…. without mental ability,

We are left with **idiotic.** I suppose this explains why this statement is not found in the dictionaries I perused. (Just my thoughts). The constant repetition of this analogical statement, "it's not edged in stone", (such a corrosive statement). A more acceptable analogy with the same thought, would be "It is not written in ink" more factual. Anyway, this brings to my mind, an age-old commercial for a hamburger company, whose catch phrase line was, "//where's the beef? \\" the idea being, was that they had more beef in their burger than their competition. Case in point. It became quite a popular statement, from the constant repetition, consumers were convinced that, that was a fact. So much alike from what is been instilled by the present feasibility study.

Another statement /question made at the council meeting was, that some folks might not know what I mean when I relate to the "footprint" of the church building in citing the fact that there was no (space) involved when the presented drawings proposed to demolish the 2 storied building, which was in fact, part of the "footprint" of the present structure, with a second floor added. (Not a two storied building)

I mention (Space) since when I asked the person who prepared the drawings, what prompted him to draw such an overwhelming structure? His reply was, that he was asked to maximize the available space, my retort to him was that there was no space, the area intended for demolition was actually part of the church building's ***footprint***

This is my reply as a clarification for the very few who might not understand the terminology. To begin, at some point we have come across a greeting card or during the religious scripture, where it was told of a certain person who while walking along the beach, noticed that on their trek it was noticed that at times there were two sets of footprints, but at times there was only one, therefore he asked the Lord about this,

The Lord responded that "I am always with you, the times where there was only one set of footprints, was when I bore you on my shoulders"

*Footprint:* as the word clearly implies, it is the print made by the foot. I.e. the area confined within the confines of the outline made by the foot. Therefore, as analogically inferred, when I refer to the ***Footprint*** of the Church building, it is the total floor space within the confines of the perimeter of said building. This is a term used in the architectural jargon when defining the area occupied by a structure

At the conclusion of the meeting and from reports presented by the Wardens of the church, the determination was that so far the project is temporarily on hold, since the pressing matter that's been addressed by the vestry of the church, is the acquisition of an interim, or supply priests until such time that the established search committee is able to meet with prospective applicants for consideration and approval.

The charge from the council leader was that the members should divulge this fact to their constituents, instead of them hearing different versions. As charged, I have been relating this fact to those persons who have been asking, some have asked the question, on hold by who, the church or the presenters? Therein lies the question, we will have to wait and see.

This past week has been quiet event and busy. To start, on Saturday there was a birthday celebration held in New Jersey, getting there was quite a challenge since the local was not familiar to us nor the GPS system since there were some diversions, as a matter of course, it is always good to have an idea of the intended destination in order to overcome some of these distractions. We managed to arrive at the location in good time, and as it turned out, we were not the only ones who had some trying times getting there. The party was attended by many friends of the birthday Lady, and it was an indication of how well liked she was, since this celebration was a means to bring together acquaintances from "way back when" It was a great party, and renewed friendships.

Sunday, was Church services, as usual, for those of us who attend in their separate place of worship.

Monday, was also a memorable occasion since we had the sad occasion to attend the "Going home service" of a very dear friend, Sonny, as we called him, he was the Husband of one of our childhood friend from Christ church by-the-sea, Colon Rep of Panama, and he lived on the front building in Colon where I lived. He attended the same primary school Pablo Arosemena. Jean is also a member of the church choir in Colon as well here in Brooklyn N.Y. and a member of the Choral, of which I am a member.

In Brooklyn, N.Y he and his wife Jean were inseparable, since they were always present at every concert, dance, outings, parties etc. (you get the gist). In other words, they were part of our circle of friends. The Funeral service was very well attended, which was an indication of the wonderful person that he was. There is so much which could be said in describing this day spent, even the weather was an indication, since the weekend before the weather was so uncomfortable with unpredicted snow accumulation. The description of this Monday was, "It was sunny for Sonny".

To get back to reality so to speak, I had received a package via UPS containing job order for lens drilling on Friday, considering the fact that I would not be able to work on this order for shipment on Saturday, for reasons mentioned. On Monday, I decided to open the package, which contained three spectacles for drilling, plus additional supply of loupes. For my stock.

I must have been both mentally a physically exhausted, two of the spectacles required one of the lenses blacken, therefore I removed the required lens from each of these spec. and prepared them by sanding the inside of each lens then sprayed them with black paint. And left them to dry, while proceeding to mark and commenced drilling each of the remaining lens. Remember there were two of three lens set for drying, which leaves one spec. with both lens.

The reason was that the third spec. only needed drilling in one lens the other to remain Plano (no blacken) for explanation purpose, Plano lenses are not for drilling since by doing this, the lens will crack. Polycarbonate lens are required for drilling, the residue while drilling is flakes of plastic. I mention this for the following reason. As I placed the marked lens on the drill press and started the drill going, I noticed that instead of flakes emitting from the started hole, there was powder, which was an immediate indication that something was wrong, therefore I stopped the press. Sure enough, I started drilling on the Cr. (Plano) lens. Panic, I do not have a replacement Plano lens for this spec.

Anyway I switched to the next eye and proceeded to drill, then continued drilling the other two remaining specs. After I installed and glued the required telescope in each of the three spec. and by this time the two drying lenses were ready for cleaning and installation. A sure sign of exhaustion, since this has never happened to me before. What to do? Should I prepare the three spectacles and explain my shortcomings, which would require them to have another lens edged to replace the mistakenly drilled lens?

This means that they will have to get a lab to edge a lens to fit this spec. which is done by computer, which traces the inside of the frame and forward to the edging machine with a Cr lens in place which cut away the waste portion resulting in a fitted lens for installation in the spec. There would be a time problem, since first, I will have to mail the package back to the Co. then them to the Lab for edging, then back to them. <Whew< a costly (Time and price) preposition. In order to save face, on my part, I decided to try to rectify my shortcoming, (not mistake).

I decided to take the risk. I searched my stock for a Cr (Plano) lens closest to the size of the damaged one and with clamps, I sized them and traced the smaller to the larger, and then placed a grinding stone on my drill press and proceeded to shave bit by bit, and after several attempts I was able to match the dimensions and contour of the damaged lens, to that of the replacement. I was finally able to fit the manually edged lens to the frame, then I tightened the retaining screw of the frame and it was a perfect fit. Mind over computer. This proves that with thought, mind and will, it was done and they were none the wiser. Three completed jobs sent to the Company as required, my invoice for three jobs will follow. Even though additional time and efforts were involved, I will absorb this, with the idea of "A lesson learned".

I have received another job for drilling lens today (Friday), which confirmed that the previous job was received, and the patient must have received their prescription, no complaint, therefore, it is to be considered a job well done. Whew. This time I immediately removed the lens to be blackened, and proceeded to mark and drill the remaining lens, and surely it was the right lens this time. After drilling and inserting this lens and the blacken lens in the frame, which was dry at this point, the spectacle was cleaned and packed for shipment, only this time I was a bit tired from some early repairs to a basement door which had to be adjusted for proper closing, for security purpose. If I decide to rest a bit, it would be near to closing time (6:00 pm.) I will have to ship this job early tomorrow (Saturday) at another U.P.S office which is open. The usual office which is closer to me (less than 3 miles round trip, I checked this out) is closed on Saturdays.

There seems to be a coincidence that these jobs seems to come on a Friday. If I do not get to complete them on Fridays early enough to make the U.P.S. office in time prior closing, In order to make timely shipments, I must travel over 4 times the distance (one way) in a much travelled route, to the other office, it occurs to me that perhaps I should charge a little extra for the additional travel distance & time, this makes sense to me, so I will start with the next invoice, to test the waters (so to speak). This is justifiable, after all I did not charge for the extra time and additional material sustained on the previous Jobs. The next time that I have to travel to the other U.P.S. store, I will track the distance and travel time in order to verify the additional charge, just in case there is a question by the Co.

The past occasion mentioned before, at the funeral celebration of the life of Sonny, I met a few dear friends and was able to tell about my Book during conversations and I was able to make a presentation to the sister of Jean also a childhood friend, in honor of the occasion. And also another friend, Owen with whom I had a long conversation regarding my Facebook interaction, also about the "Good old times". I also sadly learned of the passing of a very good friend and school mate in Abel Bravo High School, Colon, by the name of Jerry. Owen graciously agreed to purchase a copy of my book (*What If? The question or a Statement*) I did not have these copies with me at the repast, but as usual, I had them in my car, He and I walked to the parked car and during our walk we talked, It was so refreshing to speak to someone who remembered those times we spent in our hometown (Colon). He mentioned a person who was the son of Mr. Clark the tailor in 6th street, I was so taken back since that was the Tailor I spoke of, where I apprenticed as a Tailor. It surely is a small world, especially the world we call Home (Colon), this brought back some memories. I respectfully asked him for a feed back after reading my book, he promised to pass information of the book on to another friend. That's who a friend is.

This Thursday I visited the church where Fr. Alleyne has been appointed as Rector for the "Church of the Advent", Westbury Long Island. The occasion was the celebration of Evensong and he requested the St Gabriel's Chancel choir to participate, I was only too happy to attend, the choristers who consented to attend, were been transported on the Church bus capacity 14, considering there were 13, I agreed to be part of the group, unfortunately, as the time went by, there was another person who agreed to attend, I ten agreed to withdraw and decided to drive myself, and not wanting to make this trip alone, mentioned it to Olivia, who was all too willing to accompany me, so this all worked out.

The duration of this trip is usually about an hour, but given the time of the day and conditions, it was much longer, especially when one is not familiar with the area, and has to rely on the G.P.S. We started out before 5:00 pm. And arrived somewhat after 6:30 pm. The idea was to be there early enough to acquaint ourselves with the choir formation and rehearsals warm up with the organ, etc. The service was scheduled to start at 7:00p.m. Notwithstanding, Fr. Alleyne was elated to meet us and he especially indicated that he was elated that both Olivia and myself were able to be present. I told him that the sentiment was indeed mutual.

The rest of the members, the Church bus and other cars, arrived at about the same time, we were able to meet with Fr. Alleyne and family who were on hand to greet us all. After a brief warmup we were ready to "get the show on the way" Evensong went quite well and a guest preacher who is a longtime acquaintance of the rector, and was well received by the congregation. On completion of the service, Fr. asked each of us to introduce ourselves, he also told of his working along with each of individually, on my introduction he mentioned the fact that in addition, I was the author of a book about the church, I immediately took this opportunity to go to my ever- present bag, and retrieves a copy and presented it to him, he asked me to sign it to the Warden and his wife, (Another book dispensed). It was his way of getting us acquainted with each other. We were invited to the hall below for some food, which was very nourishing, and fellowship, which lasted for a while, most of the others left after but we remained for a bit longer.

I was shown the structure of a massive pipe organ, with all the pipes and blower that supplied the air with all the connections to operate the organ, located in several rooms in the undercroft. This must have been quite an instrument, the only thing missing was the console. We wondered aloud, this must have created a great and holy noise unto the Lord, on seeing this, I reminisced to Fr. about the time back home in Colon, as a lad, the pipe organ (not as massive as this one) at Christ church, Colon, Panama. At a period in time a note was stuck in the organ which created quite an inconvenience when been played, and at one point, been a slim person, I was able to squeeze into an enclosed area among the pipes, and asked the organist to play notes near to the offensive one, and by him doing so I was able to see the actions of each piston, thus locating the one piston not opening and shutting while he was playing, this permitted me to pinpoint and correct the offensive one. In Fact, I actually solved the problem. Not to say that I repaired the organ (smile).

The name: "The church of the Advent", is quite unusual, I am sure it was named to represent the Christian's calendar to signify the period prior to "The coming of Christ" however, it is a very nice and distinctive looking church building, which made quite an impression on me, it reminded me of our good old Christ church By-the-sea Colon. It is situated on Advent St. and occupies a very large property, a separate parish house, and the rectory which is connected to the church building by a breezeway, it is very impressive. I mentioned to one of the members who was showing me around, that this church should be considered a historical monument, he assured me that in fact it was, I also learned that it was in existence 150 years.

This has been a very satisfying visit to this church, from our meeting with each member of the Alleyne's Family, we can ascertain that they are very happy and comfortable in this new environment and assignment, the children are happy with School and home, I Asked Mrs. Alleyne regarding her commuting from Long Island to work In New York City, she said that timewise, it is good except for the added transportation cost. (Smile) Rev. Alleyne is happy with his new endeavors, his only complaint is that the only sound he hears at nights is the incessant sound of crickets, (smile). I am happy to say that "All is well".

This is most appropriate since the Christian's Church is celebrating the period of Advent in preparation for the Celebration of the coming of the Christ Child. In a few weeks all of Christendom will be celebrating the festive feast of Christmas. This been the 2nd Sunday of advent, the Lesson was taken from the book of Isaiah 40:1-11. On hearing this lesson read, I got up from my place in the choir and approached the Organist and pointed out to him that I would like to sing the recitative "Comfort Ye My People" Part 1 of Handle's Messiah during this service, which would be very appropriate at this point. He went to convey my wishes to the rector in order to determine at which point in the service this would be accomplished.

Verses 1-3 reads as follows: "*Comfort ye, comfort ye my people, sayeth your God. Speak ye comfortably to Jerusalem, and cry unto her, that her warfare is accomplished, that her iniquity is pardoned...*" from the Authorized King James Version (The words on which the recitative is based). Since we had considered singing it at some point, no better time than the present. During the sermon, the organist and myself were able to go to the choir room to retrieve the scores, mine from my bag and his from files, and planned the sequence of event to sing during the administration of communion of the choir. We were able to make the presentation, and thankfully, I was in good voice. Praise God from whom all blessings flow.

During the notices, prior to ending of services, I also decided to address the congregation regarding the request by Fr. Alleyne, to have members of the Chancel Choir visit to participate in the service of evensong, also to convey well wishes on behalf of Fr. Alleyne and to notify them that the entire family members are quite happy and comfortable with their new assignment.

In order to explain my impromptu decision to perform this rendition, I must point out that it was always my desire to do so at this time, I have previously performed this with proper preparation and accompaniment. Following the #1- Overture which opens Part 1 of the Handel's Messiah The #2- Recitative for Tenor *"Comfort Ye My People"* is continued by #3- Air for Tenor *"Every Valley Shall be exalted"*. This is usually done together, however, due to the appropriateness and the season (Advent) also the lessons of the day, I was spurred to do it now.

We now look forward to the Christmas season, and preparations are been made by most of the church choirs I am familiar with, and one of the most popular musical work to be presented is the Handel's Messiah mentioned above. There was a time that I looked forward to be a part of a Choral ensemble in this endeavor. I will instead, take out my various recordings of this musical work, and other seasonal recordings, and sing along with the familiar ones. The past years I have spent Christmas in Pennsylvania at *Chez B* with the Family. At times we had a full house with upward to 24 persons including the children, on the morning it was always a pleasure to see them rip open their gifts, and the joy on their faces when the see what Santa had brought them.

As the years went by, there were less and less persons making the trip, since each of the children went to the homes of their respective families, in-laws and friends. Last year I decided to stage a personal strike, and decided not to put up my usual yuletide decorations and tree. We remained in town, and visited Rich's family for the day. Considering that the year before, only my sisters, Yasmina, Yolanda and brother Roger were present, and we had a pleasant and enjoyable time. The venue this year is *up in the air,* so far, a trip to Virginia (Samantha) or to Connecticut (Rich's in- laws) was proposed, but the long trip to either place during the Christmas season is cause for concern. The other alternative was to visit long Island (Sherena's in-law's home), which is local and will be considered. The three- way pull is quite an ordeal, the real deal would be when all parties converges on one local. As it used to be. This bring to mind the Movies/T.V shows about "*family reunions Madea*". Quite entertaining.

Sunday 23ʳᵈ· Services 9:30 am. Celebrated the fourth Sunday of advent. Was fairly well attended the only exception was that the schedule was a bit hectic for the attending pastor therefore there was a pause in the service to administer him some medical attention, In the meantime some hymns were sung. In order to fill the time, fortunately, we had some brass instruments accompanying the choir for the presentation of the Hallelujah Chorus from the Handel's messiah at the end of the service.

The Trumpeter played a solo selection of "O Holy night", during the early part of the service. Therefore during the pause of the service, I decided to approach him and asked him to accompany me doing this number, which is one of my favorites, in order to fill the time, as he was setting up his score to get started, fortunately or unfortunately, at that moment, the pastor recovered and was able to continue the service. Well it was an effort tried.

Monday 24th. 9:30 P.M. the midnight service commenced with a Lesson and carols prelude followed with Vigil of the nativity service 10:30 P.M. continuing into Christmas Morning.

On Christmas day Tuesday 25th, we drove over to the Lawson's in Elmont L.I. early afternoon and followed them to Pete sister's home in Freeport, L,I. Together with the rest of his sister's family and friends, there was quite a gathering of young folks, we had a sumptuous lunch, and there were board games played among them, I joined the men in the *Man cave* and enjoyed an evening of watching the ball games on television, and had lively conversations on a variety of topics, followed by dinner. We actually spent the day in good company and lots to eat.

This has been quite an active week as can be noted, with the various places to go and not to mention the early mornings before services and the evenings of rehearsals. Well, we did not spent the Christmas week at Chez B. but the week before, we did go and it was eventful, since there was the usual task of trying to get the televisions back in to connection, and it was not as was predicted the time before, since they assured me that upon returning, all we had to do was call and alert them of our return. Not so, since we had to go through the usual rigmarole of unplugging the units which I refused to do, since the units are built in and require me going in the back room to do this. On my urging they were able to get me in connection with a supervisor which walked me through the process in getting the required code in order to set each unit. I decided to write down the process, and hopefully, the next visit this can be avoided. I guess this was accomplished due to the fact that I threatened to cancel the service and go back to the previous service provider. I hope it does not get to this point the next time I visit Chez-b.

Beside the television fiasco this time, I also had another project to do, after removing the filters from the boiler blower, washing and cleaning then replacing them. By way of explanation, I do not use the normal/ usual paper filters, since the size necessary for this particular boiler is unusual and would require me ordering each time. I was able to find reusable sets which can be adjusted to fit. The manufacture does this in order to insure continued replacement.

That done, I had decided to minimize the necessity of purchasing bottled water and coping with disposal of the empty plastic bottles which required me transporting them back to Brooklyn, disposal is somewhat complicated at Chez-B, since we are not there during extended times, to require garbage disposal service, at times I am able to fill a garbage bag and, if lucky, I am able to discard the bag at a gas station or anywhere I spot an available trash bin.

The alternative: I purchased a cooler which dispenses hot or cold water with a 5 gallon replaceable glass jug which is replenished when necessary, all I have to be aware of is to be sure to turn off and unplug the unit each time before leaving. Where to locate this unit? It had to be placed near an electric outlet, not near a source of heat, after placing it in a suitable area, it occurs to me that I would need a place to store cups and other accoutrements, easily accessible.

To the utility room/workshop I went, to look around for material, I found a 4x4 plywood which was not all suitable, also a solid table top which I knew would come in handy at a time such as this. I Plugged in my rotary and table saws and went to work designing, measuring and eventually cutting, I also found a pair of tapered legs remaining from a previous project. After cutting the required material (Using the best part of the plywood) I had all the necessary tool to get this project assembled, only to realize that an essential tool was missing. The drill/driver which I always bring with me, except this time, I suppose since I had to load the unit in the truck, it was heavy and quite large, a young man passing by offered to help me. (There are always good people). I thanked him kindly. After loading this, I forgot to bring down the drill.

Speaking of good people, there are always good neighbors, I was able to borrow a drill from Bob. And then proceed to put this design together as well as possible, since I could not use part of the plywood, the unit is incomplete but not to worry, I will be sure to take the missing material with me on the next journey. I returned the drill to Bob on my way back to Brooklyn. As I write this, I have the piece of lumber to use as the shelf which I saved here while making some amendments to a cabined to accept a flat screen T.V. As it turned out, the removal of a shelf from this cabinet, will become the shelf for my water cooler stand.

On my next trip to Chez–B, I should be sure to place this lumber with the drill, along with the hinges which I have purchased, also additional lumber for the door to complete the unit, in a conspicuous place in order to have it all together when loading the truck for travel to Pennsylvania.

It is now January 1, 2019 HAPPY NEW YEAR. The weather was not conducive for travel to church tonight in order for us to celebrate the advent of the New Year. I was looking forward to attending, considering that the choir was scheduled to present a caroling prelude, also I was advised that the newly ordained priest, Mother Leandra was scheduled to be the presiding rector for this service, also I had a photograph of her recent ordination to give her.

It seems to me that Old year night is always the worst weather, I remember it was this night the year 1962 when I experienced the bitter cold for the first time. (Below 0) never to be forgotten.

Anyway, unlike previously missed midnight mass where I mentioned, that I listened to one of my favorite classical music composition by Ravel "Bolero", I have decided to write and in the meantime, I am watching channel 13 "Great Performances" mass choir and orchestra, some great singers, performing familiar musical works, among those presented was the orchestral score and singers in "west side story", and other musical performances with musicians such as yo-yo Ma. This lasted well into the early morning.

After breakfast, and nowhere to go and nothing else to do, I have decided to rearrange my dresser drawer and clothes closet in order, then discarding unused clothing, I came across a set of pajamas which the pants was damaged but the shirt was in great condition, I had to make a decision to discard the pants and save the shirt which could be used with any other pants. This would result in a mix match. Well now let's see, perhaps I could cut the legs, which I concluded to do. I retrieved for my portable sewing machine to set it up but, **no, no, no**. it won't work.

I decided to see what the problem was, I oiled the moving areas but still it was very sluggish, I opened it by removing the back, and while trying to operate it, noticed that the belt was rather loose, which indicated that it needed a replacement which was not possible at this time. There was not enough tension and while I was inspecting the machine I noticed that the motor was mounted by two screws in oval slots, Bingo, there is still a way to remediate this situation, I got a small wrench, screwdriver and by loosening the screws I was able to pry the motor away, thus engaging the belt, while holding it in this position I then proceeded to tighten each screw, upon doing this, the tension of the belt was increased. After securing all the screws, I oiled the internal moving parts then closed the back and I now have a working Sewing Machine and was able to sew the pants hems of my complete pajama fit for summer time with calf (I/o ankle) length pants.

On the matter of pajamas. One thing became obvious to me, in most cases I come across only Pajama tops, and wondered about this. My conclusion is, the tendency is to mostly wear the pants especially if the night is a bit warm, consequently the bottoms (pants) gets the most wear, therefore, the most aggressive washing is administered, this affects the elastic waist as well as the total garment. Instead of having several Pajamas tops with no pants, in the future this is the course I will be taking, repair the elastic waist by sewing in elastic, or making several waist tucks, or proceedings as indicated above, this way I can have a complete matched sets available for wear, looking good even while going to bed in style. Long pants in the winter time and short pants in the summer time (smile).

A good start for the New Year. Following this trend, I had bought some numbers from the N.Y lottery and upon checking, I had a (box) winning which paid $40.00, it has been a long time coming. Not much but it's something.

It was time to check my bills and found out that I had to make payments to Chase Bank, Citibank and AmEx. That's three payments, I got dressed and put on my coat, stuffed the envelopes in my jacket pocket, locked the door, went to my car and off to Chase bank, (first stop) Parked the car and on exiting the car I reached for the envelopes to retrieve the envelope for Chase, what is this? I only had one envelope, Panic sat in; back to the car to look around nothing, after checking all pockets even though I know that all three envelopes were supposedly placed in the Jacket pocket.

I got back into the car and headed back for home, on reaching, I parked the car, checked the route on the way back to the house, then climbed to the top stairs, whew, and there is an envelope on the floor of the top landing, so I started back downstairs toward the car but **wait. There were three envelopes**, this is only two, and I then looked around to see if perhaps the third envelope might have been blown away. After looking around, it was nowhere to be found, so back upstairs I went, and decided to open the door and as it opened, voila/ **there** was the third envelope on the floor. Boy, this is something else. An old saying, // *haste make waste*\\.

To resume: first stop, to Chase Bank, – second stop, to the post office, – third stop, to Citibank. Checks are written, bills are enveloped and delivered to their respective places, all is well and life goes on. Next week will start another round of bill payments and so it goes.

Sunday January 13, 2019 we were fortunate to have the returning bishop from Barbados on a visit, just in time to be the celebrant of services at St Gabriel's, especially since the bishop in residence is ill at Hospital and we are without a Pastor. Today there is one service at 9:30 A.M. after which the congregation retired to the Golden hall to conduct our Annual Parish meeting.

There was election for 1 warden, 3 vestry members who have served their required term. It was determined that due to the transition of a search for a replacement pastor, I was asked to nominate the outgoing warden in the essence of continuation. In doing so, I pointed out to the group that due to the present situation, and the fact that we are not presently with a pastor who, (if he were present), and had worked along with this warded during this period, would have exercised his option to re-appoint said warden.

During my tenor as a warden, when we were in the process building the new church and my efforts in working toward this end, the then pastor did in fact, re-appointed me to continue another term, towards this end. One of the parishioners objected to my statement and stated that "Mr. Buery is not the pastor", well I was incensed and immediately retorted that I did not intimate that I was the pastor, and he had with malice, misstated me, he then said that he was joking, I pointed out that this is a serious matter and not the time for jokes. There was another point made by the moderator that the rules had been changed, and the rector no longer appoint wardens, which in my estimation, prompted this comment by the parishioner, again I have been misstated and misunderstood, I certainly did not say or intimated this.

It certainly is an indication that those persons are relative new to this process, I had in my hand a copy of the "A Vestryman's Guide "to verify my statements. This practice has been in effect for the past three previous wardens, therefor, this is not new to this congregation (especially for those "old-timers" such as myself), in spite of the professed rules change. I do not deny that the wardens are elected by the congregation, what I said was, "the rector had the option to re-appoint the sitting Warden for the purpose of continuation". **(Having eyes, see ye not? And**

**having ears, hear ye not? And do ye not remember?) A quote
from ST. Mark: chapter 8: verse18**.)

Eventually, there were no other nomination from the floor for warden,
and the name of the sitting warden was unanimously re-appointed.
Again I say all is well that ends well. The rest of the open slots were
filled and after a heated and interesting meeting, which is a good sign,
which affirmed the interest and concerns of the congregation. We now
have a full working appointed persons and graciously look forward to
the future of St Gabriel's Episcopal Church.

In place of the sermon during the mass, one of the warden read a
(Farewell Discourse) submitted by Reverend Eddie Alleyne and family,
whose main theme was based on St. Paul's letter to The church of
Corinth. **Corinthians 13:11. .....** "Finally, brothers and sisters, good-
bye. Aim for perfection, listen to my appeal, be of one mind, live in
peace. And the God of love and peace will be with you". It was well
read and graciously received by the congregation. The entire letter was
printed as a part of the Annual Parish Report which will become a
keepsake for all.

I am quite aware of the anxiety felt by most, in regard to the feasibility
Study of the proposed building. Which was not openly addressed,
however, included in the "Annual Parish report", The (Building and
Grounds Report), read in part.

"Early in 2018, the Property Management Committee, with the
approval of the Vestry, conducted a feasibility study funded by a grant
from the Diocese of Long Island. The study suggested that the best way
to maximize the financial benefit to the church was to incorporate the
parking lot space and to extend the Parish House. A series of meetings
were held with the vestry and organizations within the church during
the year, conducted by Canon Andrew Durbige, the Diocesan Property
Manager, to examine that feasibility study. No decision has been made
on the way forward for this project. The goal is to explore other
options, including a new feasibility study, other income generating
options, and additional housing opportunities for seniors, veterans and
other groups within the community in keeping with our mission and

ministry….. "the committee members representing the church and those representing the Real Estate consultants were listed"

From this report, one can assume that the original plan which was contested by myself and other members of the parish, would be "put to bed". *Assume* is not a word I like to use for very obvious reasons. (Ass u me) for this point I hope the assumption is verifiable and a reality.

Next Sunday, again there will be one service starting at 9:30 A.M. the reason is to combine both congregations, which is coined as a "Parish Summit" The reason is a guide about the process of *Transition,* explaining the pursuit of a new rector for this parish. Hopefully we will still have the visiting bishop from las week to celebrate the mass, especially since the resident assisting bishop Allotey has been hospitalized for the past two weeks. Our prayers are that he will recover soon.

I had another wake up dream, perhaps before going to bed I heard on the tele that there will be celebration for the anniversary of Martin Luther King which is Monday 21 of January. I only mention this since perhaps this has influenced my thoughts. The dream as I remembered it, was that I was attending some sort of a showing, perhaps in a Theater, I was sitting in a section with some friends, and at one point the person on my left got up. Which leaves an empty space on my left. On my right there was a beautiful lady who appears to be white complexion, but seemed somewhat familiar. After a while, a gentleman came up for a seat therefore I decided to move to my right offering him the seat on my left, which gave me an excuse to get closer to the lady on my right (smart move won't you say?).

As time went by, I had the opportunity to start a conversation with her, and realized that she was someone I already knew, well here we are, me a dark complexion person in conversation with an apparent white lady, so it would seem, apparently, to the lady in the front row, who was a little concerned, and began speaking to the lady at my side, I could not help been curious about what she must have thought of this couple behind her, and wonder what she must be saying to my companion, which obviously was in a hushed voice.

As it turned out, the light complexioned lady was a very good friend, which I had not seen for a long time, we will call her (lady M.) At the end of the show, as I got up to leave, Lady M, who had come in to the show a little later and intended to remain to catch up on the show, which was a re-running show. She mentioned to me as I was leaving, that I could come to her place and mentioned the Apt 4A. I thanked her and continued toward the exit, as I was passing I saw another Lady friend. (Lady B). It was obviously a popular show since, as it appears, there were other of my friends there, I spent a little time talking to (Lady B), the said my goodbyes.

The building where (lady M) lives seems to be near the theater, where we were since as I approached the area, I saw (Lady M) standing in the doorway of apt 4A I wanted to go to the bathroom prior to approaching her, after doing so, as I neared the apt, I met a few more friends who were exiting her apt. and I greeted then as they exited. On entering, I noticed that there were a few chairs set up in a semi-circle. I said to her "it looks like you had company" I did not remember if there was a reply from her, I deduced that those exiting friends were there to view a close circuit T.V. show or something. My dream ended at this point since I actually awoke to go to the bath room.

*I had an appointment with the doctor:* Let's talk about health:

During the course of this narrative I have mentioned on various occasion, my disdain for dentists for reasons explained. This past week I visited the dentist and he continues to cajole me into a dental extraction, I assured him that I am comfortable with my molar, and I have been chewing my food without any problem. Their records show that I was not really scheduled for dental work, I asked why I was invited to visit his office, and anyway since I was there, he decided to ask his staff to ascertain if I was due for dental cleaning, since this is all that he could do at this time considering that I refused to have his aide take x-rays of the complete area of my mouth, only the affected area where the molar was. Only the cleaning was done and I was off to home.

Now back to my visit to the doctor, I was due for Lab works and a checkup especially to monitor my blood pressure. It is the practice when you arrive, a nurse takes your vital readings which consists of Weight, Height, then: Temperature (normal) - Pulse (normal) - Respiration (normal) - Oxygen Saturation (normal) then comes the Blood pressure, which reflects a slightly high reading. This always gives me cause of concern since this is precisely my reason for these visits. After we return to the waiting area until the Dr. is ready to see you. During this time I usually will read or do some crossword, anything including deep breathing, to relax.

During the examination. We will talk and I will inquire regarding the progress of my pressure if it within a controllable area? However, another pressure test is taken and in most cases, the result is less that the original. This has given me something to consider, and I have expressed this thought to the doctor, it seems that the traveling to the hospital is usually the cause for my high anxiety, (1) Driving from Brooklyn to upper Manhattan then parking. (2) Taking the train then a crosstown bus to the building. All this is reason for a high blood pressure reading during my first test, after my settling down and waiting to see the doctor, it gives me time to relax and calm down, hence the reduced reading the second time. This has been manifested many times during my visits.

Well for this visit today, we have the benefit of using the Access-a-ride, thus leaving the driving to others, which reduces my anxiety level tremendously. Considering that the first blood pressure administered by the nurse resulted in a reading a bit higher than normal, the actual 2nd reading which was administered in the exam room, the resulting reading surprised the doctor to the point that elicited a comment that I had the reading of a teenager. In spite of the fact that I am not medically trained, it seems logical that my personal conclusions are verified, don't you think?

Back to reality, we are expecting a snow storm. As indicated by the meteorologist report, consequently the "Parish Summit", a scheduled meeting after service in order to discuss the parish transition, was cancelled, since the thought that there would not be a full congregation in attendance.

Comes Sunday morning as we looked out to see this expected snow storm, there was only rain. Don't get me wrong I was not disappointed, to the contrary, we decided to attend service. I was happy that this decision was made since, many more parishioners were able to attend and Reverend Mother Leandra was the pastor in attendance, I was finally able to present her with a photograph I had taken at her consecration.

The city of New York was all geared up for this impending snow storm, roads pre salted and plows in place to avoid previous shortcomings, that's all in the past now and we are all ready to go on with our daily lives. It was my plan to visit Chez-b in order to get the place ready to go through this winter. I place a phone call to my neighbor there, to inquire about the driveway conditions, and he said that there was a cold spell and rain which resulted in accumulation of ice on the driveway. I would not try to go there at this time since, getting there might not be too hard, but trying to negotiate the inclined driveway would have been quite risky.

Thursday, since I did not go to Pennsylvania and not been able to continue with the project there, I have decided to take on a project here, can't seem to remain quiet and took on one of my aquarium which was in dire need of a cleaning, this is a monumental task and I have been putting it off for a long time, after removing all the stones and ornaments, took them to the bathroom in a basin and got my brushes to scrub them clean, also a scraper to clean the growth of all the internal glass panels. After this I replaced ½ the water. Also the filters in the pumps. (I told you this was a big job).

With fresh water, clean tank, new filters, newly scrubbed stones which are a collections of Caribbean visits, let me explain this. It is my custom to collect stones from the place travelled. It is now a pleasure to sit and watch the fishes swimming around a clear and clean aquarium tank, instead of been in the dark. While sitting and watching, I decided to turn on the component to listen to some music, and you would not believe this, it seems that the fishes are reacting to the music, this might sound strange to you as you read this.

This reminds me of a long time ago I had a gold fish which I actually won in a game at Cony Island Recreation Center, It grew very large and I would physically take it out of the water and into a container during tank cleaning time. At that time (in the 60's) I had only one ten gallon tank, this has been a hobby for me. I remember playing my music and I have actually recorded with my movie camera, this fish which seemed to be moving in accordance with the music and I have named that scene "The dancing fish" as I write this, I wish I could locate and view this movie tape to verify my tale. (Smile). I now have an additional 15 gallon tank, which I will have to put off cleaning at another time, this one is not as bad as the 10 gallon tank which was cleaned.

This hobby has its drawbacks, to name a few, when I was travelling I had to be sure to have a vacation block for each tank which slowly dissolved over time and released nourishment for the fish, also I had to be sure that the filters were new and the pumps were in working order to insure proper circulation of the water. I remember the time when we were going on an extended vacation and considering the size of my goldfish, a vacation block would not be the thing to use. Therefore I bought a full can of fish food, and asked a trusted friend who resided in the apartment adjourning to ours, after informing her of the feeding portions and times to feed the fish, to which she agreed, I was then satisfied that this was in good hands. You see, if the pet in question was a dog or a cat or even birds, I would take them to the pet hotel, (which exists for this very reason) but this was another situation, given the complexities that existed.

Off to vacation we went, and enjoyed the time spent confident that all was in order. After two weeks and returning home, the first thing that struck us as we opened the door to our apartment, was a vile odor which assaulted the nostrils, I immediately went to the fish tank and saw my beloved fish floating and bloated in the tank which was all clouded. With despair, I had to dispose of the remains and emptied the tank of all contents, washing everything and fumigating the apartment. I noticed the new can of food empty and thought, this is very strange, since this can contained enough food to last a month, at least.

I confronted the friend to offer her a present for taking care of my fish, but asked her **"what happened with my fish"?** Her explanation was, "I noticed that the fish was not eating so I fed it the contents of the can" I thanked her for her trouble, gave her the gift anyway. With much trepidation, my conclusion was that she did not want to be bothered to do this daily task, therefore decided to just pour it all in. I kept this thought to myself since she was a good friend of my wife and I did not want to be the reason for any hard feelings. I learned my lesson and thereafter, relied on the vacation blocks and plant vegetation in the tanks, also, I am aware of the fact that fish tend to eat the algae that grows on the glass, therefore I usually keep the back glass panel partially without scraping it, especially when travelling, this way even if the "block" does not suffice, at least there is some way to keep them nourished. ***"You can feed a fish to death, but it is harder to starve it to death"*** - words of wisdom-.

We also have birds so when we are travelling on vacation, we will either take the caged birds over to our daughter in L.I for the duration, or if not a long vacation, we will ask a friend to come over to the house at specified times, to change, water and feed them, and while there I have asked her to add a pinch of food to the tanks no matter what. I realize that this is taking a chance but for this present situation, this friend will be visiting the house anyway to feed and water the birds. If we are going to Chez-b for a week or weekend, we will take the cage with us where we have a stand on the premises, no problem, but as usual the fish tanks presents the usual situation and are then handled as indicated above. To minimize any unforeseeable problems, I have placed the tank illuminations on a timer circuit to come on specified times of the day and having the pumps on *constant* operation to ensure continued circulation of the water. ***Forewarned is to be forearmed.*** (Ditto)

It was my plan to spend the next few days at Chez-b in order to finalize the project started on my last visit and to make sure that all is well, especially because of the cold spell last week. A few years ago during our visit, on entering there is a routine to follow. Turn on the water pump and trip the determined circuits. That done, while resting in the dining area after the voyage, I suddenly heard running water and before I could react, \\ whoosh// and the light fixture cover fell followed by flowing water. I made a dash to the pump downstairs to turn off the supply. Then checked the affected area. Unluckily/Luckily, the damage was caused by a thirsty squirrel who managed to enter the ceiling through a loose fitting soffit (roof extension) / the rodent chewed the pipe (PVC) looking for water luckily I say, since I had turned off the water when leaving the last time there, so the water was not that much and actually fell on the tiled kitchen floor. I quickly placed a pot to catch the remaining trickle, and cleaned up the mess.

The next morning, I took the chewed elbow pipe and got a replacement along with the necessary glue, and I was able to re-install it, replace the cover, which thankfully was plastic, it came loose from the weight of the collected water, I only had a minor water damaged area to do some cosmetic repair to the ceiling. That was a blessing since it was exactly where the electrical junction box was located. It really paid off to follow this strict warning to homeowners, when leaving your home for any extended period of time, please turn off the water supply. Suffer the thought, if I did not follow this set rule.

In the beginning, what I did was to identify and number all the circuit levers, then I made a chart, identified all the areas to be tripped (off) when leaving, especially those to be left (on) such as the ones affecting the refrigerator, alarms, entry lights, security, phones etc. once done, I made a few copies for distribution to the kids (just in case they wanted to visit Chez-b, which was my desire) also to have one posted next to the fuse box. All well and done.

The routine consisted of, first: turn off the water, then flip the switches as indicated on this sheet. Well unfortunately, if this is not followed flawlessly, chaos will ensue which happened to me on a memorable occasion, it was during the Thanksgiving time when I had stocked the fridge with choice meats etc. for our return which was weeks later. The problem was immediately noted when entering the door and turning on the entrance light, a terrible stench assaulted my nasal organ, I quickly went upstairs to the kitchen from whence the unpleasant *aroma* emanated and led directly to the refrigerator, all the meat was affected. And had to be discarded, no amount of cleaning and disinfecting helped, therefore the refrigerator had to be replaced also. This was a very costly and emotional error on my part.

It is not that I have sensitive nasal organs, but the odor was really, really bad. The cause was due to the fact that I did not pay strict attention to my own chart, and I accidentally tripped (off) the refrigerator's circuit switch. Well, allow me to repeat the previous warning, **Forewarned is to be forearmed.** In order to not repeat this or any other mistakes **(warned)**, I have placed a strong/visual tape over the switches that should not be disturbed. So far, so good. Now I am (**Armed**).

I mentioned the loose soffit where the squirrel enters the roof area, I know this for a fact because at one point when on the deck, I looked up to see a section partially displaced, there are two options, (1), cut down the tree which is close to the house, which allow this rodent easy access, (2) which was the option I exercised. I called the builder to inform him of this loosely fitting soffit and that he should replace it the very next time he is in the area, which he eventually did. I wondered why this is not a rigid and stationary roof covering. He explained that this is according to building code. It seems to me that this is a misnomer. Instead of **soffit** it should be called **loose fit** because the very name indicate a **fit,** which it doesn't. Well that how it is. The builder replaced it with a wider material thus minimizing any shifting, since then I have not noticed any displacement. So far, so good.

It was my plan to be at Chez-b this week but there were meetings, doctor visits, Physical therapy and other reasons why the trip had to be cancelled. It seems that I am the only person anxious to go there. Trips are planned by others to go skiing in other parts of the country, and there are popular ski resorts right there in Pennsylvania a few minutes by car from there... Others go to areas right there, a few towns away, where they have a place to stay overnight and still attend to their pleasures and recreations in the area. It really makes me wonder if the idea of having this place was a good one. Chez-b was, and is my intention to share with family and friends, not only for my personal relaxation and recreation. It is also a place to continue in the family, not to be considered a burden or inconvenience. (This is my Rant).

There was another prediction of cold spell and snow squalls for Sunday, therefore the *Summit meeting* after the 11; 00 A.M was cancelled, and the prediction was not materialized. As a matter of fact, the rest of the Sunday afternoon was pleasant, therefore, the persons who attended services were happy they did so.

The Church Council's meeting was scheduled for Tuesday night, but the weather forecasters again predicted heavy snow and wind, therefor the chairman rightfully so, cancelled via e-mail. In replying to the message, I responded, giving the past experience, I wrote the following message "it is not likely that the predicted weather forecast would justify cancellation of the meeting, however I would be guided thereby." Wednesday morning, the day was gloriously pleasant, I got to my P.C and sent the following message to all copyreaders. "It is a glorious day, I looked out last night there was no snow, (I told you so) however, let us rejoice and be glad for the day our Lord has made. It seems that the meteorological prognosticators again cried WOLF" This time I imagine they were a little ahead of the timing, since later this afternoon there was a light dusting of snow. As the saying goes, "the weather is unpredictable".

This past week, as usual, was very hectic. On Friday 2/1/19 we attended a funeral service for the aunt of a very good friend of mine, who was part of our wedding party back in 1964. He travelled from California for the occasion therefore, I was happy to attend and it allowed me an opportunity to exchange some memories, also to offer him an autographed copy of my book *What if?*, especially since I was unable to get in touch with him at the time of publication.

At a point during the service, he delivered a prepared speech which he opened with the following statement "Usually when I stands before an audience, it's to sing, which I no longer do" then he continued on to thank all those persons who are in attendance to this (going home service) for his aunt, also those persons who attended to the deceased during the time of her convalescence. While he continued on to thank individual persons, I discretely got up and approached the organist to inquire if he had a hymnal book, he did not since apparently, he was a guest accompanist. I thanked him and asked if he could accompany me with the organ to the tune of "The Lord's prayer", to which he agreed.

At the conclusion of his speech I respectfully asked to say a few words on behalf of my family, which was granted. I introduced myself for the benefit of those few persons who did not know me. Please note that I said "few" it is a small "village" I then proceeded to express

my disappointment for him not singing since we all are aware of his
singing prowess *back in the day* when he was called "Mr.B" (the source
of is inspiration) which elicited a quite a favorable response from those
who knew this. He was quite a crooned then. I then advised those who
wished, could sing along while I sang *"The Lord's prayer* "Thankfully, I
was in good voice so I did the beat I could and the Organist joined in,
therefore we made a joyful noise unto the Lord. I secretly hoped that he
might have re-consider his stance, and grace us with a rendition of his
own. Not the case, since me maintained that he has retired from singing,

Sunday 2/3/19 after the 11; 00 am. Service, we finally had the parish
council meeting, and a progress report was presented by both wardens,
for record purposes I also embraced the opportunity to mention that
since there are 6 applicants for the position of rector for the church, I
have suggested that each of them be afforded a copy of the book *What
if?* Which would be a source of information as well as enlightenment
about the Church.

The primordial reason for writing the book is to record the origin,
process, and eventual construction of this new building, somewhat like
a manual and how it was done, consecrated as a place of worship known
as St Gabriel's Episcopal Church.

In the same light of a person seeking employment to an organization/
Company it behooves them to seek information about said company.
There was a bit of a push back by some, but I immediately pointed out
that this subject was brought up to the wardens and it has been approved
and acted on, therefore my reason for mentioning it at this point is, as
mentioned, for recording in the minutes of the council meeting.

Sunday 2/10/19, the Summit meeting. It started out with an overwhelming
attendance of congregants. After service, the members were asked to go
downstairs to the Golden Hall where the meeting was held. Usually
when there is a planned affair after service, half the members attend, not
this time, most of those attending service went downstairs, which was
an indication of the importance of this this process. A lunch was served,
considering the anticipated length of the meeting.

After all were fed and satisfied, the meeting was called to order with prayers by Bishop Allotey. Followed by a presentation by the Transition Consultant, of the Diocese of L.I. who was very thorough, leading off with the question **"Why are we here?"** – Each person had an outline of the various questions and procedure to be followed throughout the presentation. After this, small groups were formed, with the admonition that all questions were noted and organized for eventual presentation of their report to the gathering. This allowed all persons to voice their questions in a uniform manner.

A condensed form will be published on the church's web site for eventual consumption by all applicants, I should interject at this point, that along with copy of my book "What if? "The Snapshot" of St Gabriel's church, should be encompassing.

Each group had a representative address the gathered audience with their presentation, some were duplicated, hence to reason for condensation. There was a period of individual attraction and reason/ reflections for becoming members of this church, which were varied and quite interesting in each case. I will take this opportunity to mention Olivia's reflections. First she stated that her original religious allegiance was to the Roman Catholic Church, which is a co-incidence (I was baptized in the R.C. church) which she continued here in Brooklyn. She also pointed out that because of the fact that services there were rather short, approx. half hour, she would come over to meet and wait for me at St. Gabriel's church since her wonder was, why was our services so long? This elicited some laughter.

Continuing on her dissertation, she further mentioned that over time, she gravitated to the comradery and warmth felt here, therefore without any external prompting, she decided to join forces, so to speak, and along with other close friends, decided to attend (what could be considered confirmation classes conducted by Fr. Llewellyn) This led to the eventual reception into the Episcopal Church. She literally rolled up her sleeves and got very involved in the workings and operation in the form of, member of the executive committee, Vestry, Sunday School teacher, member of the weekly counting team to name a few.

As she continued to call names of persons whom she had taught in Sunday school and have gone on to great individual accomplishments. I realized that it was a touch- and -go situation, forgetting to mention persons who were actually there, I asked for the mike and decided to make a comment of my own thus relieving her.

My brief comment was, that on immigrating to this country, I had started attending worship at St. Phillips Church, Brooklyn, then while attending a wedding of our mutual friend in 1966 at St. Gabriel's church, which was a church building in the ground with a roof (literally) and I am still here 2019. I also was attracted to this little church which reminded me of the church we attended back in Colon Rep. of Panama, and was one of the original members of the Choir, and eventually became quite involved in the maintenance and eventual building of this new edifice.

Most of my accomplishments have been mentioned on other occasions, as well as outlined in other venues. A thought for my attraction to this church is remembered by the introductory lines of the Hymn, "There is a sweet, sweet spirit in this place, and I know that it's the spirit of the Lord"…

From reports of unanimous reactions, the Summit meeting was well organized, informative and executed. The next step planned, is a "neighborhood prayer walk" around the perimeter of the Church's location, for the purpose of meeting and talking to folks, and noting the changes/improvements which have taken place, effectively increasing our outreach efforts.

The primordial concern is, how long will this take? On previous instances, this could be a long process, we can only hope that, relating to the proper preparation, presentation and attraction, and other related situation, will dictate the length of time. In the meantime, we are blessed to have the presence of the assisting Bishop, and the availability of visiting clergy to keep us going on. ***To God be the glory.***

# Do You Remember?

The question we ask each other when meeting after a long time apart, then we go into the exchange of memories, this conversation tend to revive good times and can go on and on. This is one of the reasons that I embarked on the project of recording my memories for the sole purpose of keeping those memories alive. At least once it is written down, they can be passed along to those who follow us.

Years ago while I was employed with Bunge corporation in New York City, and used to travel to Panama on occasions on behalf of the Co., after meeting with customers and taken care of whatever business transaction which required my attention, I will take some time to visit my hometown Colon, to meet with some friends and cousins then have a look around the town to observe the changes since the time I lived there.

After a day's stay, I will catch the bus back to Panama City to visit with my sister. Most times my trip will include a weekend, therefore, on Sundays we would attend church services then go to dinner at the Post Exchange or other places, then back to the hotel to recover my bags. Usually I would get the Sunday evening flight back to New York in order to be on the job on Monday morning with the check covering cost of goods collected from the Panamanian Co. and report on the transactions.

I remembered the building I lived on (7th. Street). Also the building at 8th. St and Central Av. Where we had removed to. I witnessed a fire on that building while on the balcony while sewing, since I knew some people still living there, I ran across the street and helped some folks out of their room, and tried to go up the burning building, the fire had not gotten to the side where I used to live, I convinced the fireman that I knew the people living on this side, therefore I went up and was able to close the doors to my previous neighbors. I took this action since it was a common thing for persons going into rooms and "helping themselves" to what was not theirs. Fortunately, the fire did not get to this side, it was a large building.

I mention these two buildings at this time, to make the following observations. A) The 7th Street building known as Theater Building was eventually destroyed and replaced by a Mac Donald store. B) The 8th St. known as Albert's bar building, which was located on the ground floor. We eventually named this building *The Bridge*. We used to have "Night of fund" paid parties, to raise cash to fund our Christmas celebration. The bar has been replaced by a variety store named *Bonanza*. The present owners have taken over the entire 3 storied building for their residence and warehouse.

As explained to me by a friend during one of my visits to Colon, the reason this was done by the owner of the Bonanza store, is that they used to store their products in warehouses, but this created situation/ financial problems, such as space availability, transportation cost back and to the warehouses. By storing products in their own building, this resulted in prompt availability of replacement products, as well as storage cost. (Storage cost- verses- rental of available rooms) I suppose this was a cost effective solution.

Going back in time, I also remember the building at 4th. Street which I have referred to earlier in this narrative. Life at the Gordon's this is where we were placed as young children, while Mother used to visit us when off work. I have described this building in some details and the time spent there. I have not had the opportunity to actually see this building, but I know from passing by on the Central Ave side in transport when going to Christ Church, the times we were featured in concert. And far as we can tell this building is still standing.

As previously described, we could access the building from Central Ave. and it extends to the other street I think it's called Cash Street, where I mentioned at the time, this street used to be closed off the length of the city on Saturdays for skaters who came from the Canal Zone area and the rest of the city to show off their expertise on the skate.

It was during the time we lived there, at the age of 8 yrs. I remember the time of Japan's surrender, we used to sing in the park (4th and central Av. Colon rep. of Panama.), a tune to the words "wo-wo-wo-wo Japan surrender, na-ni-na-ni ho you (WA)" --, Japan surrender". While repeating it over and over, we will hold hands and jump around in a circle. It was September 2, 1945 (aboard the USS Missouri)

In contact with a friend, I was informed that the situation which occurred with the 8th street building, a Co. took over the building in 4th street and established office space on the top floor. I am not sure what the nature of the business transacted was, but he used to work for them and he has quite a story to tell. For the purpose of telling his story, I will tell it under the title of

## "Oh I wish I controlled a fly on the wall, or a bug in the line" (this is the story mentioned earlier in this narration)

On one of my encounters with my friend Berto I asked him about the building and he proceeded to tell me of his travel from the interior and was looking for a job. Through a mutual friend, he was given an address in Colon, on arrival, he looked up the place and met a girl by the name of Carmela who he knew during school in the interior, but she was a grade ahead of him and had travelled to Colon a couple years before. She introduced him to the owner and was able to secure employment there.

It appears that the balcony area was converted to the office space, and the back rooms (where we used to live) were converted into some sort of dormitory therefore, they each had separate rooms. I think the owner lived on the other side of the building, I asked him what was the rest of the building used for, he did not specify exactly. I wonder if, like the building at 8th street it might have been rented or for other unspecified use. For the sake of this story, it was not related, therefore I let that question go unanswered.

By trying to get some inkling as to the nature of this business, I can remember that at some point while I was working for Commander Steamship Co. in N.Y, I received a call from Panama by one of his friends, asking me to inquire about the necessary documentation required in order to export Shrimp/fish to the U.S. and a possible contact. I was able to tell him according to my knowledge that the required documents were: Bill of lading (set) – several copies of a packing list, Certificate of Origen- necessary food and drug certification, and they will need a Custom broker to transact the local paper work. And whatever documents required by the Panamanian Gov. in order to export this product.

The rest was up to them to secure the transport, cartage etc. and port of entry where the receivers will accept the product for local distribution/ consumption. I did not hear anything further and perhaps this may be the outcome from that call.

From subsequent conversations with Berto, I asked what his duties were and how things were handled. He said he did regular office work and whatever else was necessary, (office clerk). After the work day, he will take some time to meet with friends and at some times, he would meet Carma (the short version of Carmela) at the local restaurant for supper, I slyly said to him, you mead a dinner date? He smiled, but no comments.

This is his story about *the Fly on the wall* as I previously mentioned. "It seemed that one night I was awaken by a persistent whispering coming from the front office, she was speaking on the phone and kept repeating (*but Pietro, then a pause then again Pietro--- Pietro*) followed by a long pause then she whispered again (*this thing has to stop—this thing has to stop*) the one sided conversation continued for a while this is where I wished I had control of the *Fly*, (or a bug on the line, in this instance) in order to hear what *this thing* was about, also the gist of the total conversation" This prompted me to wonder if this one sided conversation had anything to do with the ornamental fly which sat on the file box on her desk,(he had mentioned previously), or was there some kind of clandestine relationship going on between them. Not my business.

Perhaps I should tell about this box, I'm not sure if it was previously mentioned. Carmen used to receive a box about the size of *kardex* files approx. 3x5 "(brand name for index cards) used for desk files. It was wrapped in brown paper but never opened, and she used to have this miniature colored glass fly so realistic looking, sitting on this box. At one time when she was not present, he sneaked up and flicked the fly off the box and it somehow seemed to leave a trail as it fell. The next time he saw the Fly it was again placed on the box. He wondered aloud, could it be some sort of intelligence gathering tool?

Berto continued to tell his story by recalling an instance where, the person who delivered the file box from time to time, met her in the office, and they were coming down the balcony towards the back to take the stairs, "I was just come up the stairs and saw them, so I decided to pull back in order to avoid been seen. One evening when Carma and I were having dinner, a phone call was receiver by her, and after she returned to the table, I couldn't resist the urge to ask her what that call was about. She hesitated, then said it was about an appointment with the hair dresser. Huh I thought, but left that alone."

"After some time had passed after the one sided conversation, considering that our meetings were less frequent, I got the courage one evening while dining, to ask her who is Peter? I guess I caught her by surprise with this question since she did not reply right away, the she asked who? I repeated "Peter" Oh you mean Pietro, he is my financial advisor. That ended the conversation between us." Our supper *dates* became less frequent, due to all kind of appointments."

IT would have been so great to have been able to photograph this building for the purpose of display at this point, the last time that I visited Panama, and travelled to Colon in order to board vessel when we went on the cruise, as usual I always had my camera.

Speaking of Camera, this is a great time to speak about my interest in photography. My life as a Photographer and its vicissitudes. In those days, I was a wedding photographer for two studious: Liberty Arts and Vogue Studio. There were times especially during the weekends, where the studio would assign me to weddings, I was given a work order with name, address with all required information also a supply of films. After the shoot. I would take the exposed rolls along with unused films. And collect a stipend for the weeks work.

This was a great way to supplement my income, also an opportunity to meet people of varied backgrounds, also an occasion to visit various places, Banquet halls, churches, and venues for photos, this was also helpful for me when doing my own personal weddings. The relation with Liberty Arts studio, which also operated their own Processing lab, permitted me the access to have my own prints made, also roll films for my personal use at a professional price. A contact source for photographic equipment, Cameras, repairs, information, this helped me in the advancement of my craft.

In as much as this was an enjoyable pursuit, at times it was long and some evenings tiresome. Starting time, then travelling to the prospective bride's home, then to the church, followed by a trip back to the studio for formal group shots, or to a venue for outdoor shot, then to the reception hall, in most cases, the bridal party would provide a plate of food for the photographer, which was quite welcomed and deserved, considering I had an early start.

As a wedding photographer. I will cite some scenarios, in order to shed some light thereon.

Scenario 1: One day as I returned to the studio and was standing outside, I observed a lovely young girl with an equally lovely lady, which I assumed to be her mother, seated on a nearby bench in a very lively conversation, at one point, the lady stood up and assumed the pose of what seemed to me, as that of an archer, I could not hear the conversation, but it appeared as if she was showing the girl the proper was to handle the Bow and arrow.

The following week, after returning the past weekend's work to the studio, I noticed a car at the front and passenger's door was open, eventually, I was called to the car and realized it was the same lady, and her daughter (I think), as I approached, the lady started asking me some questions about something she was told by the girl, I had no idea of what I might have said and at what occasion, Since the questions were made in an inquiring, (not menacing) manner, I realized that this will take some time getting to this, th3erefore I entered the car, and asked the driver to take us on a drive, while we talked.

As it appeared to me, the young girl was a prospective bride and the Mother was, inquiring regarding the procedure for contracting a photographer, the girl might have been part of a previous wedding I might have covered, and she pointed me out to her mother. I hope this is the case, however I decided to introduce her to the owner of the studio, I thought this was the best way, and not to handle it as a personal contact. I do not know them. Hopefully a wedding contract was struck with the studio and perhaps down the line, I might have been assigned this job, or not.

Scenario 2: On a very busy weekend, several weddings were booked, and it seemed that most of them were scheduled for Formal wedding group at the studio, consequently, its first come first served. This is where things get hectic, since each respective wedding party is rushed to the studio followed by ensuing photographer in his car. The race is on. This particular evening did no go well, since it appears that the Limo. Driver was going too fast and the photog. Had a hard time keeping up, and he was pissed. And proceeded to puncture the limo's tire. This was bad.

Scenario 3: The bride was late, I got to her house first, after waiting for a while she came home from the hairdresser, she had to take a bath, and in the meantime I had set up my camera and decided to tidy up part of her bedroom, in order to have an area suitable for the photos. She came out wrapped in a towel, looking for her underclothes, I presented them to her since I knew where they were. She got dressed but was unable to get those covered button in the tiny loops that ran from the waist right up to the bodice, I was able to help her since she had her nails done. This was a delicate and uncomfortable maneuver on my part, while doing this, in order to ease the tension I said to her in jest, "I suppose the reason these buttons were so many and hard to get done, was to make it difficult when time to undo them". This elicited a smile from her and a definite easing of tension.

This situation: compared to a *patient* in the doctors clinic-- or a *subject* in the photographer's studio. I got the required photos putting on the finishing touch, by this time her maid of honor had arrived at the home, and we were off to the church.

Scenario 4: This was a memorable situation, since in entailed a white bride. I arrived at the home and was greeted at the door by the father of the bride who ushered me to the bedroom where his daughter was. She closed the door while we were getting her ready and setting up the dresser by removing unnecessary clutter for photos, which required me using her looking in the mirror while photographing her. We did not want reflections from anyone else, hence the reason for closing the door. After the photos and getting ready to leave, she gathering her things, and me armed with my camera, proceeded to open the door, which was not happening.

We both tried repeatedly, to open the door to no avail. (Talk about rising tension?) She was getting flustered and called out to her father to **get us out of here**. He was trying on his side, it appears that this was a newly installed door. I realized the *danger* of this situation, and asked the father to get a flat tool to pass under the door since there was a space. He was able to push a flat chisel under and I was then able to remove the pins from the hinges, removing the entire door.

During this ordeal, word had gotten to the church where the services were to be held, that the **bride was locked in the bedroom with the photographer**. I wonder if the actual gravity of the situation was really conveyed, (a black photographer) I guess this was not the case, since I was greeted with smiles at the church, and to make the situation more comfortable for me, The Mother of the bride asked me to dance with her at the reception.

Scenario 5: This wedding was quit another situation. All appearances were that it would be easy since it was to be at one venue, (Services and reception) I did not have to go to the home of the bride, therefore I met them there. Easy. Not the case, since the guests were arriving, Bride and most of the bridal party were present. The groom was not present, since some relative insisted that he pick them up. We all had to wait because of the insensitivity of a few. The pastor could not wait. Another pastor had to be recruited to perform the ceremony. What started out easy, became long and trying.

Scenario 6: This situation was a bit different from the previous one but also reflected some insensitiveness'. The process went well, I met the bride at her home, all went well, the ceremony went well, except I had to contend with anxious persons with their cameras trying to take photos, I cautioned them that as the official Photographer, I should get the first shot, also it was best that they should take advantage of my expertise and let me have the first shot and they would have a carefully crafted (posed) photo. This seemed to make sense to most of them, therefore the interferences were minimized. At the reception, I wanted to have all in order therefore I arraigned the bridal table bride/groom in the center, flanked by the maid of honor/bride's maid and best man/groom's men on either side. Then the bride's/ groom's families on respective side tables. Can you picture this? It all presented a great setting for Photographing.

There was some disagreement and confusion coming from the table of the bride's family and the bride was in tears, this was too good to be true. As I approached the bride to inquire why she was crying? She said that her mother insisted that she be seated on the bride's table, if this happens, then the groom's parents would want the same, there goes my careful set up.

The bride was pleased the way I had set everything up, but she was confronted by, and had to deal with her mother. I had to take this situation in hand, especially since this would not be the way the studio would like the photos. It was photographically incorrect. In order to console the Bride, I told her to place the blame on me, and this is the required settings for photos, after I had taken the photos, they could sit wherever they wanted. The mother was convinced and comforted, the bride was able to smile for the camera. All was well that ended well.

Scenario 7: This was, as far as I can remember, the worst situation I faced as a Wedding Photographer. It was a recommended wedding and I was not familiar with the participants, however I met the Bride and Groom at the venue where the ceremony and reception were to be held, after the ceremony, I asked the couple to assemble the group in order to set them up for group phots, The groom refused to be photographed with a certain young lady in the group. This presented quite a problem between the bride and groom who almost ended up in a confrontation. Whatever his reasons were for this refusal, I do not, nor did I care. I had to take some photos, therefore, I decided to take photos of the bride and Groom separately, and the ladies and gentlemen in a combination of photos. I wonder if this union lasted much after that day.

So there you have it, there were some great times, and experiences as well as trying times. In order to end this portion of my narrative on an upbeat.

I remember a situation where I had to go quite a distance in Long island to cover a wedding, after arriving at the direction where the bride lived, she was surprised to see me, I introduced myself and mentioned that I was assigned to this wedding, She retorted that she no longer required my services. This took me for a loop, since I had travelled this distance to no avail. I showed her the work order given me by the studio, from her reaction, I surmised that she could not meet the expense required.

The procedure at the time of contract, a deposit is required in order to cover the expense of film also the stipend for the photographer, followed by another deposit in order to retain the services, which in this case was not forthcoming, and the studio had asked me to collect this portion. She was unable to meet this cost, and the assembled bride maids offered to put up the amount. The Father objected, obviously due to pride. There was some disappointment displayed by these ladies. Well here I was after such a long drive, set to return empty handed (so to speak) I suggested to the gathered ladies, so beautifully dressed for this pending wedding, that I will shoot a roll of film (20 photos) recording their lovely dresses for the day, and that at any time later, when finances allows, they could order prints from the studio. I felt a personal reward that I had at least done this, which must have made their day in some way.

Another memorable instance was the Saturday morning on the way to the Bronx, which presented quite a problem finding locations, I always insisted that the studio provide me with detailed traffic details, G.P.S was not available, so one had to have a knowledge of the destination. After much driving around, I saw the street name I was looking for, but was unable to get across, by asking questions and some detours, I finally got on the street listed in the work order.

As I drove down the street I saw in the near distance, a bride fully dressed along with some other folks waiving, thankfully, as I approached the group, the bride asked me if I was the other photog. I asked her what she meant by other? She said "a call was made to the Photo studio requesting another photog". I indicated that I was the one assigned to this wedding. Well I was not so dejected, knowing that I was not alone in this predicament. At least I made it. After profusely apologizing for the lateness, she was understanding and stated that she was aware that the location was difficult to find, that is why they were in the street on the lookout, and we all had a good laugh. This relieved me some, since I always tried to be on time for all my gigs. I did my very best to compensate for this shortcoming.

Reflecting on scenario #7, where I expressed my wonderment regarding the duration of the wedding commitment in question. I cannot help but to recall the year 2014 when we (me and my wife of course), celebrated our 50th wedding anniversary. I was asked by an acquaintance, what is the secret? I had to give this some thought. The first thing came to mind was, "I always kept in mind the marital vows. (**To have and hold until death do us part**) but in a realistic point of view, I always knew when to back out of an argument (and there were some)".The year is now 2019 which if my math is correct, will be our 55th year and counting, as long as we can keep out of bickering.

In retrospect, perhaps that couple should have be guided by a failsafe plan, when selecting the participants in their wedding party (when possible). For the Best man, a brother or member of immediate family. For maid of honor, Likewise, the sister of the bride or a very dear friend who is the closest to been one, then the rest of the wedding party to be made up of family or relatives, This way the close friends of the pair cannot feel slighted in any way, since the wedding party would be a Family Affair. Their friends would remain **their friends, who are a very precious commodity for as long as they keep them.**

This third week in March has been a trying one, since unfortunately, I lost my total writings and all efforts to recover them were futile. This has happened earlier in the month but at that time I was able to back up on an external portable hard drive. With the help of Mr. Chance to whom I extend my thanks. I decided to transfer this to my P.C and have spent this weekend remembering and re-writing approximately three pages that were added to the lost information. I am at a point where thankfully, this has been accomplished to some extent. This Saturday evening, I decided to listen to some exiting Jazz music on F.M. radio 89.9 - 100 year anniversary of pianist Lenny Tristan (born 1919) with his unusual jazz style of feuding with the guitar and the bass. Very exhilarating music. This seems to help me get back into line. I remember while writing my book *What if?* There was a period where I spent listening to jazz 88. With the same outcome. **To each his own**.

As a freelance photographer, I have had the opportunity to be the photographer for several occasion, covering Debutant balls, where during the course of the preparation I will take photos of each debutant as well as related participants in the production of the Journals, this was a challenging venture since these photos spans a period of time, shooting the photos, selecting, printing and presenting for final approval, and eventual printing of programs for the evening, also covering the actual Ball, these photos are usually used for the Journal of the following years production. This was a very rewarding and satisfying relationship with the group known as the Dedicators Inc. who sponsored these periodical affairs to generate a scholarships fund.

There were also other occasions that I served in this capacity, for Social clubs, Churches and individual persons in addition to weddings, such as anniversaries, concerts, graduations, reunions, honor achievements, Family gatherings, to name a few. It is always a great feeling, when during my walk in life, to be reminded of the time I took such and such photos.

To relate memorable instances: I was named the official photographer for the national Black Athletes Hall of Fame, held during the course of over a week in Caesar's Palace in Las Vegas Nevada U.S.A. in the company of some notable entertainers: Aretha Franklyn who performed for the ceremony. Mr. James Brown who in addition to performing, was the replacement for Bill Cosby, as the Master of ceremonies, along with other performers. Some of the Athletes who were honored and inducted, were, O.J Simpson, Roy Campanula, Jim Kelly, Gayle Sayers, Elgin Baylor, Henry Armstrong, Willie White, Pop Lloyd of the Harlem Globe Trotters and others. I was able to sit and confer with some of them.

Another memorable occasion was in 1976 I was part of the production and Photographer for the Miss Black America of New York State. This allowed me to spend quite some weeks accompanying them during the eliminations also the final group of 25 lovely ladies 0n various activities such as tours of Harlem, museums, points of interest around New York city/State and vicinities, highlighted by an evening where these ladies were driven by limousines to enjoy an exciting evening at the Broadway hit musical "Me and Bessie" performance by Linda Hopkins. After the show Linda Hopkins and cast, personally acknowledge and greeted the ladies. This was my cue, as the Photographer, I ran on stage in order to photographically record this occasion, I was barred from going on stage, but I insisted that I had a job to do, which created some uncomfortable moments, at which point, Linda Hopkins herself heard the commotion and realized my predicament, therefore she voiced her displeasure with the guards and said to me audibly, *"take your pictures honey"* this brought the house down with laughter and applauds and I was very happy, and went about taking my photos and have the record of this occasion.

I was also the photographer of record for the ensuing pageant held in a New York City venue, seated at the table with my family was Dionne Warwick. The master of ceremonies was G. Keith Alexander, among the performers; Chuck Jackson, Crown Height Affair and others.

My personal darkroom at home surely served me well, since I had to develop the rolls of film, and printed contact sheets of the photos for final selections, to be printed for this production journal. This was quite an experience and I have retained a copy of the printed booklet with my picture as part of production as well as Official Photographer for the Pageant.

In the year 1978 during the dates of July 3-28 – I was allotted ¾ the exhibition floor of the Brooklyn Public Library- Grand Army Plaza to display - MY PHOTOGRAPHS "AS I SEE IT"- quit a collection of my photos were on display and I even had an offer to buy some prints, but I did not plan on this. At least I was flattered to know that there were some prints qualified for sale. Thanks to the contact of Natalia Davis. For my book signing, I was able to include some of these photos along with others, in order to add some diversions for the guests, while awaiting their turns to have their copy of the book signed.

Today I was happy to receive a phone call from my friend Wilfred, who has returned from Panama after spending 7 months and 1 day, as he so succinctly stated. We exchanged thoughts and previous conversations held while he was in Panama. I mentioned that I was told that the Washing Hotel was demolished, much to my disappointment, consider that this place should have been retained and be considered a national monument. Good news, he said that the Hotel is been refurbished not demolished. I was very happy to hear this, it is always a good thing to verify news such as this. I have mentioned earlier in this narrative, thankfully, this information has been rectified.

I also expressed my thanks for the information regarding the demolition of the 4th. Street residence in Colon, where the story regarding *"The fly on the wall "*was developed. He confirmed this, it appears that the area has been targeted for some renovation in the future. This store can be found earlier in this narrative.

Rupert also expressed his delight regarding the many renovation of our beloved country of birth Panama. I agree with him since I too have been privileged to see this during my trip there earlier in the year, as I alluded to when telling of our experiences on the tour in parts of South America and Colon.

This past week I have been the recipient of a Phone scam perpetuated by some unsavory persons victimizing senior citizens. I will try to outline this with the hope of alerting anyone who may read this. It all started out with the frantic phone call from a female who, when I picked up the phone proceeded to speak in a hurried voice saying "Grandpa, I ask you please, please keep this what I am about to tell you strictly between us, promise?" Well she got my attention, therefore I decided to go along with this to see where it was going. I asked "where are you?" She replied that she was at the precinct but she wants to tell me what happened. Ok, I said.

"Grandpa, you see, I was at a party and I had a beer and (cough) then I accepted a ride with a guy, but he was *wasted* (cough) but we got into an accident and the police (cough) took a breathalyzer and found me to be a little over the alcohol contents limit, (all through this narrative, I realize that this is no one I know, but continued to listen) so I mentioned to the police that I was taking some cough medicine, so this may be the cause of the high alcohol contents." I interrupted this narrative to ask where exactly is she calling from, she said "at the police precinct, and she has been issued a D.W.I. and that the car was totaled and the rental agent wants $16.000.00 but the other girl with her has pledged to pay $8.000.00 and could I offer to pay the balance, which she promises to pay me back".

I mentioned that I will have to discuss this, and I proceeded to ask her some questions, she became agitated and said that they are waiting to use the phone, but a lawyer will call me with the details. After she hung up, I knew this was rare, since, my grands, have not used the term *wasted* to describe drunk, let alone to sample beer, and accept a ride or even drive a vehicle.

Shortly after I received a call and the person who said that he is the lawyer for Your Granddaughter, to whom you spoke about 10 minutes ago, and she told you of the existing problem, and are you the person to handle the payment? I said I will have to discuss this with my wife. He further stated that she was issued a D.W.I. because of the high alcohol contents from the analysis (which was a bit different) I pointed out that, as she stated, she was taking a cough medicine, which might have a bearing on the outcome, he agreed and said he believe her but the rental agent, will agree to drop the demand if they are reimbursed with the 16, thousand dollars. I mentioned to him that I cannot make a decision without my wife, he agreed and said it's a good thing to speak to both of you, I said unfortunately she is not presently here.

He stated that he has to attend to some pending case, but will call back in about 2 hours. I asked his name, he said it was Richard Cohen, (Hint) I said my name is also Richard, therefore Richard I will await your call. In the meantime I called Olivia to tell her to come home before 2:00 Pm, since there is a problem with our Granddaughter, this is to insure here timely return. At about 1:30 Lawyer Richard called, I told him my wife has not returned as yet but she is due shortly.

When Olivia returned home I started to tell her the story, she immediately said she will not keep this from the mother, and I will call her. I insisted that she don't, considering that I wanted to discuss this between us to verify that this has the tone of a major scam, I wanted to voice my findings and in doing this, we could both verify a scam, which we agreed. Before going any further, to be absolutely certain of our decision, I asked for the phone Number of our Granddaughter and made the call, when she answered, and from the brief conversation with her regarding her schedule for the day and a little chit-chat. I was totally confident of our conclusions. There was no reason to call the parents to upset them, especially since we had decided it was a scam.

With this in mind, I did not want this to go any further, therefore when the Lier (oopps) I mean Lawyer called to ask if my wife had returned, I could not let it go any further. I asked him outright, "WHAT IS THE NAME OF MY GRANDDAUGHTER? ---CLICK--- He hung up and so ends the plot.

## CONCLUSIONS:

Firstly: I am reasonably able to identify voice inflections and tonality of my family members. The next thing I am sure of is, that in order to rent a car, there is insurance posting as a precaution.

Secondly: I am aware of the fact that my granddaughters do not possess driver's licenses and driving a vehicle is not presently one of their abilities,

To further draw my attention, was the fact that the percentage of alcohol contents stated, were different between the Female and the man posing as a lawyer. Also the urgency to call back. When I asked his name, it took him by surprise and coincidentally he must have known my name since somehow he got my phone number, also "Cohen" as a lawyer's name was presently in the news. I must point out that they have gone to lengths to develop this scam.

Once we had concluded that this was indeed a scam, I did not want him going over this tall tale for the benefit of Olivia, and no telling what her reaction would be, hence my reason to cut him short.

This has not been the first time been submitted to this sort of thing. Earlier in the year, this time the caller was a male. "Hi Grandpa" I asked who are you? "This is your favorite grandson" my response was, "I do not have a favorite grandson" then I hung up the phone.

It is a sad, sad, sad, thing that there are persons who set out to hurt/target unsuspecting and vulnerable people, of their possessions. We should all be aware of this and be very careful when these cases occur, listen and make notes, also do not volunteer any information.

After returning from church services, which as usual, was quite late in the afternoon, therefore all the parking in the near area of my house was taken. I decided to look for parking on the proper side of the street in order to avoid early rising on Monday to comply with alternate side of the parking rule. I found parking down the end of my street, therefore on Monday I did not have to worry about the car, I mention this since Olivia parks her car in the driveway of the house, what was our garage, have been converted into additional living area (den/darkroom).

Haven mentioned this, on Tuesday I definitely had to get my Jeep and bring it in front of the house, to get available parking in sight. As I approached the car, I noticed two gentlemen standing on the sidewalk adjacent to the car, as I entered and unlocked the security bar, I kept my eye on them while starting the car and preparing to back up in order to merge into the main road, in doing this I also noted that there was a late model car parked behind me, therefor I was very careful while backing in order not to hit this car, which I supposed was owned by one of those gentlemen. Suddenly I sensed a banging on my car, my attention was drawn to the origin and in panic, I stopped the car and dread the thought of having bumped the car behind me.

As I exited my car, I noticed that one fellow was still standing on the sidewalk but the other was in the area behind my car, but my immediate attention was to investigate if and where I had hit the car behind me, after noting that my car was still about 6 inches from this car, it was then that I realized that it was he who had pounded my car and he was ranting and ranging that I was about to crush him since he was standing between the cars, this increased my panic at the thought that I might have hurt a person, I assessed the situation and wondered why was he there, seeing that I was backing up. I held my tongue and instead, apologized, stating that I was viewing the approach of my car by looking through my side view mirror, and not noticed him stepping between cars. I also wanted to say to him that it was foolish of him to do this, but refrained from saying this, seeing that it was two of them and only one of me. I therefore adopted the status of the pennant one, and again say I am sorry, and went back into my car and took off, thankfully, the latter was not the situation, with a sigh of relief **WHAT IF? *The question*.**

DE-JA-VU

Today April 15, 2019 at 1.44 pm. I called my sister Yvonne who lives in San Antonio, Texas, to touch base with her to talk about this & that, including the present political fiasco which is always a topic of conversation these days. While speaking, she happened to mention that Notre dame was on fire, what// Do you mean London? No she replied, Paris. At that same time the image appeared on my television screen, 6;50 pm. Paris time, which I was not really viewing at the time, but as I looked and saw the devastating fire that engulfed the steeple, I said to her that I do not think it will withstand the fire and will eventually fall. We spoke for a while then said our goodbyes, soon after, I witnessed the steeple falling, and this evoked a similar sentiment when I witnessed the world trade towers fall.

I can now truly state, that I know exactly where I was at the time of each of these two catastrophic occurrences, it was a DE-JA-VU. Moment.

As for the present, just to verbalize and see it in writing, it was 4/15/2019 sitting on my couch at 1987 Linden Blvd. Brooklyn N.Y. at home, talking to my sister Yvonne I witnessed the massive fire that engulfed the Cathedral of Norte Dame and the intense fire which caused the steeple to fall.

On September 2011 while spending a couple weeks at the Carriage house hotel, Las Vegas Nevada, on the precise day while awaiting to go downstairs to the lobby for breakfast, I was watching Television and saw one of the world trade center tower in N.Y. in flames, and I called out to Olivia, to say that I think there is a movie on television about New York, immediately I saw a plane heading straight for the second tower and exploded in the side of the building. It became obvious, I called out again to say this is happening for real, she came out to the sitting room and we both stood there and watched in awe, as the towers fell.

After this happened, we both went downstairs to breakfast, we were approached by those who knew us as regular customers, extended their condolences. That day, the bright and dancing lights of all the establishments, were turned off in Las Vegas, replaced by red/whit/blue and symbolic lights. The city was in mourning, so to speak.

We have spent some time in Rome and visited some of the important sights, but were not able to join a group who was going to Paris for the day, which I would have enjoyed, and would have had the opportunity to photograph and visit the Eifel tower and most assuredly, Notre Dame Cathedral. Hopefully someday, God's willing, I will have the opportunity to photographically record the new and improved Notre Dame Cathedral.

May 2, 2019 is my birthday. I spent the day getting things together for our yearly Red Top dance, I had previously purchased the libations, Beers, soft drinks and other things, which were loaded into my Jeep had to take them to the Golden hall for storage in anticipation of the celebration scheduled for tomorrow. After returning home all tuckered out, I had supper and after digestion, went to bed for much need rest.

Friday, May 3rd the (D) dance day, after loading the truck with other things we had to be at the church by 5:00 p.m. after the Senior Center folks are out, in order to get the hall ready by setting up the tables and decorating the hall. I had to unload the truck and take the first set out of storage, then I had to set up the serving area (Bar) place all the drinks into ice for cooling, had a bite to eat, then just before 9.00 P.M, I Changed into my Red top shirt and set up in anticipation of the early arrivals. I had to do double duty, since the assistant which we had contacted to help in the bar had not arrived, neither was the person who will dispense the tickets for the Bar. It was rough going for a while.

My assistant arrived and in her usual efficient manner, filled right in and got things going, then the other member arrived and got thing off just in time as the traffic started to increase. We had a rather smooth operation going for a while, until some of the folks began to get a little out of hand, by asking for all kind of brands, which they are accustomed to when frequenting an actual Bar establishment. I had to point out that this is a fund raiser sponsored by the group of Panamanians (15 ladies, only about ½ are active, and 1 man, me) as our contribution to assist in the operation of the parish.

This is our 31st year of sponsoring this dance, and in the beginning, the clientele was matured and fairly responsible consequently our dances were without problems. As the years go on the younger set who have grown to maturity, are more belligerent and poses quite a behavioral situation.

By explanation of the history of this Red Top dance. It was principally held at a hall on Eastern Parkway, we were required to hire 2 security guards, and obtain a liquor license for each occasion. After the Church building was erected with our expressed desire, to insure a legal hall, which increased the original cost of the building. Each nationality formed their respective groups and sponsored their separate event in order to contribute towards the upkeep of the parish. Considering the fact that our (Panamanians) dance has always been orderly and enjoyed by all who attend, There are some who have attended from the beginning to this day. It became unnecessary to have guards, especially since our venue is now held in the Golden Hall of our Church building.

A smorgasbord is provided free of charge each year. The food is donated by each member of the group. The funds are generated from entrance fee and the sale of libations (beer and sodas). The profits are turned over to the church as our contribution towards its maintenance.

There are some folks who bring their own "Brown Bag" which drastically reduces the intake from sales this might have generated, in order to compensate for this loss, we ask those persons to purchase a "Set-up" (consisting of sodas, bowl of ice and 6 cups) and a nominal charge for extra ice. This has now become a source of contention to some, even though they have deprived us from this additional income, they are adamant and insistent in avoiding this minimal charge, by all means. At any other place they frequent, this demand is not made.

This has been the source of displeasure, and even the use of foul language and threat of bodily harm, also verbal insinuations and accusations of watering down beer, which is insidious. My name is spelled (B-U-E-R-Y) not (b-r-e-w-e-r-y) therefore I am not associated with brewing or manufacturing beer. Each case purchased, was sealed and individual bottles labeled and capped by the manufacturer/ distributor, all with the logo *(Light)*. I have noticed that most major brands of beer are now producing in addition, the *(light)* version of their products, which might be an indication that there is a definite need for a less harsh product.

I might have unwittingly done them a service by minimizing the damage done to their stomachs, by purchasing the *(light)* version of this product. It is no secret that there are many persons who have succumbed to illness, as a result, due to the deterioration of their stomachs.

This incident occurred just prior to the D.J. calling me to bless the food, which under normal circumstances I would have been happy to do, but I was still offended and not at ease to do so at that time. The thought of a prayer in my mind was as follows, I would have started by singing a tune to the verse from the bible, "Behold how good and joyful a thing it is *brethren*, to dwell together in unity, together **in unity**," followed by "*Our Father* in heaven, please Bless this food, Bless those who provided it and we who will partake of it, that it might be a source of nourishment to our bodies as well as our souls, this we ask, through our lord and savior, *your* son, *Jesus Christ,* Amen." Closing with the saying *Peace and Love,* (Paz y Amor). In retrospect, I did not ask to bless the drinks, considering that the lighter strain of the beer would have been better that the stronger one. **Easier on the stomach.**

From this experience, I have expressed my doubt weather I will be willing to be a part of the Red Top dance for another year, God's willing. It was a very long and strenuous day, loading time at home, then to the venue location from 5:00 pm to 5:00 am(next morning), for my mind and body, not mentioning the day before (My Birthday), and to attend church services on Sunday morning. 2 days later, I am still feeling the effects.

Members of the Panamanian group met in the conference room at the church, to prepare the financial report of the dance. In spite of the drawback which occurred, we are proud of the fact that this coming Sunday may 12, 2019, we will be making a presentation to the treasurer of the church, representing our contribution towards its financial upkeep in keeping of our yearly efforts.

Mention of the words *financial report* above, it brings to mind a situation which occurred some time ago when I was warden of the Vestry. In going through my records looking for some information for the present vestry, I found an exchange of e-mails which coincidentally, had to do with the church's finances dating back to the year 2013. It all started with the Minutes of the specially called vestry meeting held on Friday, March 8, 2013 which listed those present and those who had issued excuses for their absence, which included the then secretary. I mention this since it had a baring of what transpired, and resulted in the reason for me bringing this incident up at this time.

One of the members present was appointed by the chairperson, and she graciously consented to perform the duties of the secretary for the meeting. On the next scheduled meeting march 19, 2019, as part of the agenda, the *minutes* (Prepared by the substitute secretary) was read, after which the next item was for- *any corrections/amendments- Among* other response, I Ask about the following paragraph, which I will mention in part, at this point.

"...A discussion on the prospect of beginning the next audit of the Church financials followed. It was agreed that...."

The word *financials* struck a chord with me therefore, I asked that this should be corrected and be replaced with the words "**church finances**" I was immediately interrupted by a few persons who indicated that I did not know what I was talking about, and a lively discussion ensued which lasted over 15 minutes.

The next evening, I sent an E-mail to the actual secretary which read as follows:

"Hi -------

Regarding minute's correction.

Firstly. It is truly amazing that an item which takes 5 seconds to correct, has brought about a discussion of over 10 minutes. It is no wonder that meetings lasts so long, time is spent on semantics I/O facts. It explains why the English language is so complicated, people tend to use words that evokes these discussions. ...

Secondly, it was out of order for those persons to interrupt me while I was speaking, all I am asking is that the minutes be corrected with the proper word for the records. It is no reflection on you, especially since you did not write this Minute in question. Would you consider writing the corrected minutes for my records since I tend to save them? E-mail it to me, no need to make copies. Thanks for your consideration. R.B."

I then proceeded to send an e-mail to all the copyreaders of a previous message, informing us of the subsequent scheduled vestry meeting, which reads as follows.

"Greetings all:

Regarding amendment to minutes read last night, I checked with all the dictionaries in my possession, and grammar articles, and there was no reflection on this word *Financials.* What they all indicate is that the word **financial** (adjective) having to do with finances. It modifies a noun. In this case the noun is **report.** Financial reports. A further point of grammar, you do not pluralize an adjective."

To further indicate the extent of insult by the substitute secretary. She replied to me writing,

"Richard you might not need a dictionary for this one… an accounting class might solve the problem…."

My response was. "…… your reply was very offensive to me. I am a graduate accountant and have been conferred a diploma which reads (Bachiller en comercio) and I have worked for over 22 years on Wall Street, and I have no problem. English is my second language, therefore when in doubt, I go to the source."

All I have to say at this moment 6 years later, is that there are words which are improperly used, and are eventually adapted to common use, I do have a word that might not be in the dictionary,

But here it is, ***bastardization*** of the English language. I.e. One of the definitions of the basic word. = (American Heritage Dictionary) 2. Something of irregular, inferior, of dubious origin. Truly applicable in this instance.

We received an invitation for the institution of the Rev. Eddie Alleyne as the fifth rector of the Episcopal Church o0f the Advent. Saturday, May 18th 2019. This is the church that he has been accepted as rector, after he left St. Gabriel's church, which we graciously accepted and attended. It was a well-coordinated and planned ceremony, attended by an overwhelming number of St. Gabriel's church, as an indication of the esteem held for our former rector and his family.

In addition to the membership of the Parish of Church of the Advent, also those of St Gabriel's, there were quite a number of clergy and the diocesan bishop, also rector and members of neighboring parishes, the church was packed to capacity with well-wishers. I was asked, by Fr.

Alleyne to be part of the augmented choir in order to enhance the music for the ceremony, I was happy to be part of this momentous occasion.

After the Ceremonial religious services, all persons were invited to relocate to a large tent erected on the grounds, for entertainment and catered food, which was welcomed and enjoyed, by all, culminating a long and well spent day and drive home.

In spite of all the enjoyment, I experienced a bit of a setback, when entering my vehicle to prepare for the drive back, I noticed some damage to the rear tail light and fender. I cannot determine when this damaged occurred, since where the car was parked at the time, there was no visual evidence, since I was standing next there when the next car parked beside mine. I can only assume that this might have occurred prior to embarking on the trip since I did make a short stop in a mall near home, and at that point the car next to mine must have caused it and left the scene, since it was not there when I returned to my vehicle. In my anxiety to get going for this anticipated celebration, I must not have noticed the damage.

In anticipation, it occurred to me that this occasion would be a great opportunity for me to be able to sell some of my books. With this in mind, in addition to the constant companion of my tote bag, which usually have about 6 copies of my book, I packed a hand bag which has the capacity of 4 copies and it would not be as conspicuous and heavy as the tote bag, which would remain in the car if needed.

Armed with this hand bag and my Camera, same size bag, along with my choir vestment, I entered the church and wade way to the altar in order to join the others for a quick rehearsal of the music to be used. The scheduled starting time was 5: 00 P.M, we arrived about 4:00 which allowed for this warm up period. As it turned out. I did not use my vestments especially since it is a red robe with a white top. And the others were wearing total white vestment, therefore I used on of theirs.

The usual configuration of choristers is, (facing the Altar) Tenors sit in the row behind Sopranos on the Epistle side (right side) and Bases behind Altos on the Gospel side (left side). After sitting for a while with another chorister, I asked him what voice he was. He said "bass" after assessing the situation, I realized that we were only 4 male singers, so I made an arbiter decision that we should all sit in the same pew (bench) there is a reason I mention this, which will be further explained.

As we prepared to leave, I decided to go get the car, which was a bit of a walk, and the ladies (I did not previously mentioned that we also gave a ride to the celebration) as I was saying (excuse) writing, the ladies had their last minute details to take care of, therefore I walked the distance to retrieve the car, this is when I noted the damage. The bishop of the diocese and the newly instituted pries were standing right there, when I announced the damage, The bishop quipped, "Make the parish pay for the damage" The priest quipped "mage the diocese pay for the damage". Passing the *buck* so to speak. All good-naturedly. In order to undo this situation, I declared to both of them that, this might have occurred when I made this early stop in the mall (Brooklyn) and I might have not noticed it. Removing the *buck* from the fray.

I got into the vehicle and drove to the tent area to recover the *damsels in distress*. Now placing all my belongings in place to make room for the other lady, I made the startling discovery that I only had my vestment and Camera bag. Where is my cap and other bag of books? (I wonder) it is at this moment that I deduced that in changing seating, I must have left the bag and cap at the previous seated location, since all I had was my camera, it is a good thing that I had occasion to take a few photos of the ritual. Then went over to the rectory, (Priest's residence) which is attached by a breeze-way to the church, I rang the doorbell and asked the young lady who answered, if she could alert someone of my predicament. She said the church was locked and would leave word. (Now is has become obvious why I mentioned the seating arraignment).

Fr. Alleyne was speaking to the ladies when I got back to the tent, therefore I mentioned the missing items, he was willing to go open the church, since he now has the keys that were turned over to him as part of the institution ritual during the ceremony. At that point I did not want to inconvenience him since his company was in demand everyone and their brother/sister wanted to speak with him. He agreed that in the morning he will look into the situation. We thanked him and said our goodbyes.

On Sunday morning I called early before 8:00 A.M to remind him before his first service. There was no answer therefore we left a text (wonderful new technology). Describing what and where the missing items were left.

My original plan did not materialize, I was hoping that during the service, He might have said something which would give me a lead to offer my book to the present congregation. He has been promoting the book on past occasions while at St Gabriel's and would offer it to newcomers and visitors as a means to acquaint themselves of the Church. I kept listening for an opening during his discourse in thanking all who were there, allowing me to jump into action. I did not want to rain on his parade, so I kept my cool. (A lost opportunity). The reason I was presumptuous to think he would do this at this time, is because on the previous visit we made to the church of the Advent, he mentioned the book and asked if I had a copy, and as usual I did, and offered it to him for his warden. You can then realize and appreciate why I would think this could have happened.

Prior to us leaving home to attend the 11:00 a.m. I received a call from FR. Alleyne to say that he was able to recover the items and will try to get them to me somehow. I decided then and said to him Thanks and he should remove the 4 books in the case and keep them for sale to his parishioners and only return the eyeglass which was in the case, the case and my cap. He agreed to try to sell the books on my behalf, and return the other items. In this case, all would not have been a loss. **From every disappointment, a good.**

One of the things Fr. Alleyne asked me if I had one of the program, he wanted to show me something, I told him I had one in the car, well he reminded me about what I used to say "if you want to justify where we are, it was imperative to know from whence we came" I wanted to show you that I have considered this in formulating the Program cover, I said, "yes" I did in fact, noticed the cover. It highlighted the following points: at the top of a church steeple reads, (look to the future) then on the left side (Remember the Past 1910) and on the right side (Celebrate the present 2019). I was very pleased to know that after all was said and done, my thoughts had made an impression with him. The year 1910 was the year before the First rector. The Reverend Richard Pope (1991-1941 a total of 30 years)

Second: The Reverend Frederic Underwood (1941-1965 total 24 years)

Third: The Reverend Herbert Beardsley (1965-1995 total 30 years)

Fourth: The Reverend Jeffrey Krantz (1996-2015 total 19 years)

Fifth: The Reverend Eddie Alleyne (2018- Present). The void bet. 2115-2118 (3years) perhaps were filled with supply priests.

I am happy and thankful to say, that the missing items were returned to me including the 4 copies of my book, no sale, I guess.

# Spring is here"

The very thought of the approach of spring means that your attention is turned to the outdoors, in order to enjoy this outdoor living, a quick look around suddenly there is this and there is that to do, where do I begin? First the air conditioner cover has to be removed, We have an in the wall type out front, after removing the cover, suddenly you noticed that the unit requires cleaning, after doing this I have decided to remove all the accumulated gook, then I look around for some paint, I found a can left over from the outdoor tubular metal chair which I repaired and re-positioned on a wooden stand. This is a yellow rust-oleum paint which looks good and attractive on the casing also the removed cover. I also cleaned and repainted the outdoor benches on the front attached porch. I received some offhanded compliment from a neighbor, who asked me if I repaired the benches, I responded that I repainted them, he asked this, since from where he was, they looked like new wood. (Transformed from the weathered wood look) I supposed the yellow color gave this impression. The porch now has a new look along with the painted metal railings.

In view that the home next door has been renewed and finally there is a new neighbor, in order to *keep up with the Jones syndrome* I have purchased a can of black rust-oleum paint and have painted all the iron fences and railings in the front, then next I had to prune the bushes in front and back yard and left the cuttings to dry out, this way to reduce the bulk and weight. A funny thing happened, while painting the stair landing in the back, the paint can turned over and spilled what was left in the can. In order not to let it go to waste, I decided to spread it all over the landing and be sure to leva a path unpainted where I would be permitted to step on in order to enter the room. I proceeded to paint alternate steps. Now I can climb the unpainted steps and reach the landing to enter the house. After a few days and the paint is dry, I can paint those unpainted parts and be sure to identify the dry steps by placing markers (brush, cans etc.) Now I can enter and exit the house without trailing paint into the house.

Next I had to clear the drains in front and back. I have found a way to delay the accumulation of dirt and leaves from clogging these drains by using a pair of tires, which I have painted to blend with the walls and have cut holes in the undersides, this way rain water can pour out and not accumulate inside, crating breeding ground for insects. From time to time I remove the tires and clean away the accumulated dirt around them. In the back I have placed a used storm window with the mesh, elevated over the drain opening, water is allowed not the trash, as little as possible. Phew, now I will have to deal with the Trees that shed during this time, and I will have to leave a push broom out front to keep this to the minimum.

There seem to be a jealousy going on between the indoors and outdoors, I mentioned this since, after the massive work weeks that just transpired, I was told (Honey do) there seems to be a settling of water in front of the refrigerator, I fetched the mop and after a few swipes, it kept coming, on careful inspection, I realized that the compressor is not operational and the ice is melting from the ice maker, this is the source of the leak so I turned it off and changed the filter, and tried vacuuming the coils from the bottom (front).

This is serious, we had to call the professional. It seemed that the blower fan was frozen. The fellow came and did his thing, I asked him to replace the internal light bulb which was inoperable, I have tried to get to it In the past, unsuccessfully, he had a hard time finding it also, but I insisted that there is a bulb in there somewhere since it used to be lighted, we removed the shelves and \voila/ we found the culprit, and he was able to go to his truck and fetch a new bulb. Between the both of them, they were able to move the unit and get to the back for a thorough cleaning. Our worst fear was squelched, in his words "you now have a unit that is good for a few more years".

I mentioned the leak but what I neglected to mention was the damage done to the floor laminate which was installed a couple years ago. A few of the seams resulted in welts where the water had seeped. This required some brain thrust on my part, so the place I do my best thinking, is trying to go to sleep at nights but instead, as I lay half-awake wondering what to do. Then it occurred to me that when ironing my clothes, I use the iron to flatten out the seams in clothes, why not give the iron a try? The next morning I got dressed and went to the hardware store to purchase a tube of clear silicone. On my return home, I got the clothes Iron and plugged it in to heat.

I used the iron on a strip of hand towel and pressed the seams to dry them out wherever possible, this reduced the welts to a certain extent. When this is done and the seams are dried and cool, I cleaned the areas, then ran a ribbon of silicone in each of the offending seams. It does not look professional but it works, and the welts are not as noticeable as before. A mat in front of the fridge serves as a camouflage. The nicer the mat the better the job of hiding, my next thought is to get some diluted polyurethane and spread it over a small area at first to observe the results. The idea of this action, is to render the entire kitchen floor impermeable. I do not think there is going to be any kudos from the flooring company. Though stuff.

My plan was to make a trip to Chez-B Monday 5/20/19 – Saturday 5/25/19. Due to some reason I had to start on Tuesday, therefore on Monday, I decided to visit the A,T&T store in the mall in order to have them connect with Dish network to have the system activated by Tuesday, after spending a few hours In the office, I was advised that all will be well on our arrival. The first thing I did on arrival at Chez-b was to go to the main television set and turned it on. Wonderful// It worked. This was too good to be true. What we did not mention was that on our last visit February 11-14, the living room set was not working and it was finally decided that the Mini box needed to be replaced.

It was agreed that they will send the replacement to our address in Brooklyn and we would be sure to bring it to Penn on our next visit. We never heard from them. Well here we are Tuesday May 21, 2019 before opening the door, what do I see on the floor? The package soaking wet. Delivered 4 months ago. It's a good thing that the item was shipped in a plastic bag, therefore undamaged. A lack of communication won't you say? So here we go again the same old period of frustration with Dish Network.

We called them and after numerous conversations with different persons, we were able to have them assign a person to visit the premise on Wednesday, to fix this situation. As I said previously, this has become a habit to spend the day of arrival each time we visit with this company. I was able to connect the replacement, however, on obtaining the required code to get the set connected, no luck, therefor I had to be without the set in the Living room for that day.

Wednesday the technician came and took care of the problem, including replacement of batteries in the remote, which fortunately, I happened to have in my possession. Everything is in working order for the rest of the week, I made sure of this before he left by turning on all 4 of the sets and had them on for the rest of the day, with one exception, at one point, the unit in my office, went off while I was watching, and a note appeared on the screen (*signal lost due to inactivity*) I asked the tech. about this, he said that is the way the Co. Saves power.

My contention is, if the Co. is aware of the inactivity of a T.V. unit and can suspend service. They should be aware that there is no use of television signals during the months I am not using the sets, therefore they should not charge me for use of full service. I think this is a justifiable conclusion on my part, don't you think? I have addressed this point to representatives during my conversations, and asked that there should be some allowances made in this regards.

Hopefully, there will be some adjustments in this coming month's bill, since the person I spoke with last, agreed that this is possible. Until next time.

On another subject. During our stay, I was checking out my new mobile phone sitting around the dining table, and suddenly both our phones sounded an emergency tornado warning alarm, advising that we should take cover in the lower part of the home. It was a good thing we had the television in service, and were viewing it at that time. We tuned in to a local channel and watched the development and progress path of the tornedo. We were close to the stairway to the basement, therefore I took the stand where the birds were hanging and brought it near the door, just in case we had to go downstairs. I did not mention that at times when we are going to Chez-b for a prolonged time, we will take the bird cage with us. Fortunately, while watching the progress on the T.V, we were advised that it was moving past our location, so there was no need to- *run for cover*.

Based on the above situation, I suppose it justifies our having the use of television service while at Chez-b. I was honestly considering suspending or replacing the service due to the constant frustration with the satellite service provider. As a matter-of-fact, I have decide to visit the local A.T&T store, and have again voice my opinion and frustration to the mgr., and he has agreed to schedule an appointment with a service rep to visit Chez-b on my next trip on 6/19/19 in order to replace all existing boxes (4) with the prospect of obtaining a reduced monthly charge and supposedly, better service. **We will see how that goes.**

For the records, we could not start on Monday since there was doctor's appointment, so we started on Tuesday, 21st. You already know how our arrival on Tuesday went with the television fiasco. The next three days were spent with me finishing some projects started on previous visits, we had to leave one day sooner, Friday 25th. It was our intention to visit the Garnes family on the way home, but due to a late start and the traffic congestion this was not feasible. Our arrival time would be dark when reaching Brooklyn. We had an early morning start for a pending bus trip on Saturday 25th.

Fortunately, the bus boarding local was near our home, just down the road so we were able to get there close to departure time. I say fortunately since on arrival and I was about to park the car in the conveniently available parking lot after letting Olivia off, we forgot something very important home (cash) so I had to return home to fetch some (Naturally), since we were destined to make a trip to Connecticut Mohegan Sun Casino.

This would have been a great opportunity to have some of my books to dispense among friends. There were two busses, but I was aware that this would have been a hard sell considering that most of the folks were watching their cash for the Casino, also a few of them already have copies of my book. As a matter of fact, I was in the company of two couples who had the book and I was honored to be able to get some feedback from Tony and wife who actually read the book. That was a good feeling.

The trip was long but enjoyable and I am happy to say that close to departure time 8:00 P.M., my machine (Slot) began to reward me therefore, I came away with a few dollars more than I had taken. **Good trip- Good Company and good balance. (Financial)**

Monday 5/27th is Memorial Day was a good time to recover from the past hectic weekend, is allowed me to plan for the next trip to Pennsylvania, with this in mind, I again visited the AT&T store in order to discuss a change in the Television service at Chez-b and with the cooperation of the store manager, I was able to come to an agreement to have an appointment with a technician to have all the mini boxes changed and an adjustment in the service.

**Hold the press///.** I mentioned earlier in this narrative, that an appointment was scheduled for a service rep visit to chez-b during a planned visit 6/19th. Well it seems that this will not happen, since my wife has other obligations during that week. I guess a cancellation is in order.

During the course of this week I have received an on- line request for my attention regarding a particular situation, in view of constant recurring practice where plans to visit are been cancelled due to one or another personal responsibility, this presents a predicament.

Well at this point, I have decided to forward the message to her on- line account which reads as follows. "Since I cannot make any decisions as a Husband, I leave you to take care of this as my commanding Wife"… Remember the calypso? {*"Oh my commanding wife, you want to destroy my life…"*}. This make me wonder if this visit will materialize at this time.

Hopefully, things will work out, the age of technology is marvelous, I say this for the following reasons.

I have been contacted via e-mail, by AT&T, requesting confirmation of pending appointment for the visit of the technician this coming Wednesday, as it turned out, the plan is for us to visit Chez-b on Tuesday, which, Gods willing, will work out fine, so I confirmed. This will enable me to disconnect all the boxes to the televisions in preparation for his arrival. We will see how this works out.

This past weekend has been hectic, to say the least. Friday night, we attended a lovely 75th birthday celebration for a good friend who is also a member of the Panamanian group at St. Gabriel's church. Fortunately, my sister Yvonne was in town, and was able to attend, considering that the honoree is a childhood friend from Colon, Panama (our Hometown.) It was well attended by a number of mutual friends therefore as usual, I travelled with the same bag which was returned to me (unsold) after forgetting them along with my cap at the institution of our former priest at Church of the Advent. I told this story earlier in this narrative, Remember?, anyway, I mention this to say that I was able to sell a copy of my book. This leaves 3 more copies in the bag. One-by-one.

There is a reason for my mentioning this at this time, since, to go alone with my narrative regarding this week-end. This morning, (Saturday) we attended a dance recital of Sydney our Granddaughter, in Mineola L.I. speaking of technology, My G.P.S started out giving me wrong directions, it's a good thing that I had some idea of the intended route. After some re-directions on my part, I was able to get on the right course, which only caused some delay, at least we were able to get there just after the opening presentation, knowing that we were late, I did not want to waste time seeking parking, so I just left the car in the middle of a parking area, and was in the auditorium in time before her group presentation. It was an enjoyable program, and I must say that Sydney aced her performance, we were all impressed and I admired the progress she has made in her dance. As soon as the actual program was over, I hightailed it back to the back to the parking lot to move my car which as mentioned was blocking all, then I returned to the auditorium for the ending preliminaries (handing out awards etc.) **All is well, for now.**

After leaving, we coordinated a trip to a favorite restaurant to enjoy lunch, there were three cars involved in this caravan, therefore instead of getting a pen to write directions, and my daughter Sherena notified me that this is the age of technology, then she proceeded to text me the direction, in the event we get separated by traffic congestions. (See what I mean?)

In order to avoid my past transgressions, I decide to link the two handbags, one with my Camera along with the other containing the remaining three books. There is no forgetting either one.

After a sumptuous lunch a enjoying a family reunion, we all departed to our separate ways. On my way along the road I reflected how well this all went and with the car window partially open, I felt the breeze and suddenly was aware that my head was a bit cool, and realized that I was not wearing my cap so I asked Olivia to look in the back seat to check if my cap was there along with the bags, she was not able to ascertain its presence, I remembered at one point during the lunch, Sherina notified me that my cap was on the floor, so I picked it up and placed it on my knees, (not wanting to wear a cap at the dinner table.)

I became obvious that I did not remember putting it back on as we left, I suppose since the weather was quite nice, it was not missed. I asked her to call Sherina to check with the restaurant, since they might have been closer, well she was not so I told her of my situation. On reaching home, we called the restaurant to tell them that I had left my cap there, which I described and the area we were seated, the person there said they did not see the cap. Here we go again. I guess this time the cap is lost, since Sherena also called and was told the same thing. I asked to call again to tell them that the cap might be under the table, but the call was not immediately made.

After some time had passed, I received a call from my daughter to say that she had the cap, it appears that since she was in the vicinity, she had returned and was able to retrieve it. Great guns, my Father's day gift, she will have it to give me tomorrow Sunday, considering we are scheduled to meet for Dinner. **All is definitely well now.**

This weekend was not without consequences. On Friday I danced a bit, as it turned out, among the persons at the table where I was seated, I was the only able man to dance with, when there was a danceable tune, I asked Olivia to dance but she was having a tough time with her feet, so I suggested she just drag them in lieu of any fancy steps. We sat the next few pieces out and I realized that there were other ladies sitting idle, therefore I did the gentlemanly thing of sharing a dance with a couple of them. My knees were not at their best. You understand what I mean.

We reached home about 3:00 am. And my knees were beginning to feel the efforts made that evening, so I got the Balsam cream and proceeded to apply it to both of them, then paced a sheet of paper towels on each knee and cover them with a copper infused brace, the reason for the paper was to prevent the cream been absorbed by the brace. With those in place, I wore them all day Saturday. They were back in shape and on returning home, I finally remove them, so far they are bearable.

The next problem was, after been slightly wet from the previous night shindig, walking to my car about 20ft from the entrance to get into my car, then without my cap, I began to feel a tingling in my throat which indicated that a bit of a cold was coming on. So I applied (what I call) MY PERSONAL BODY- MED PRINCIPLE. I did what I had to do and was able to gain control of the impending head and chest cold.

My sister Yvonne and partner were in town from San Antonio, Texas, so we invited them to Church on Sunday. I embraced the opportunity to invite them to join us on the trip to Chez-b on Tuesday. In order to save departure time they spent the Monday with us, which allowed me to get an early start. Unfortunately not as early as originally planned. We got started a bit after noon and encountered quite a rainstorm midway into the trip and a longer travel time and what I feared most, was that it was dark and visibility was impaired, anyway we made it in safely which was important.

After unpacking the truck during constant rain, which did not help my cold any, and after going through the regular routine of turning on the water pump and turning on all the necessary switches then settling down, I did the next best thing by turning on the Televisions and miracles of miracles they worked, so we were able to avoid the usual discomfort getting a signal, and view the weather and other programs. It was a good thing since my sister and company did not have to witness my reaction with the Dish network provider due to the usual lack of T.V.

We were up late exchanging thoughts and experiences etc. It was my intention to follow orders given me by the T.V. Provider to disconnect all the boxes (4) before going to bed since the technician was scheduled for 8:00am. Instead it was very late and we all retires to our separate rooms until morning. I awoke early and decided to disconnect the boxes, but it occurred to me that this was a bit senseless to me, when the tech comes, he might want to check the signals prior to him changing them. So I decided to disconnect only 3 boxes and leaving the main box connected.

Soon after, I received a call from the tech informing me that he was on his way, I indicated that I was up and ready for his arrival. After entering, the first thing he asked for, was the location of the main unit since he wanted to check the incoming signal. So I was not wrong in my assumption, I told him that I was instructed to disconnect them all, he said I did the right thing, since it would have been a long process to get started. After going through the system and replacing all the boxes, and checking the reception of each set, we made sure that all were in good working order.

He further advised me that during the course of the evening the boxes will re-boot which is a normal thing. There was some inconsistence in viewing the living room set so I attributed it to his advice of re-booting.

During the day, I noticed that the set in the living room was not properly synchronized, (sound with action) I made a note to tell them, since the tech. said I would be hearing from the home office regarding his performance, which was not forthcoming. This inconsistence continued during the evening, therefore I decided to check each box, and sure enough, there were some loose connections which I tightened, The problem seemed to be corrected, hopefully, the next visit there I hope all will be well, and I can count on been relaxed and not frustrated.

I had to bring the 4 boxes with me to Brooklyn, and was advised to take them to any UPS Store, and they will take care of receiving, documenting and shipping to Direct TV. Which was done.

My next project was to reinstall the internet, since it was our hope that now the television is working, let's have the internet installed, I called the Telephone Co. Frontier, to make the necessary arrangements, the person with whom I was speaking, was not familiar with the name of the town from where I was calling, Sugarloaf Heights. He asked me to spell (Sugar loaf) I said "sweet sugar" this kind of conversation continued with this person, I was beginning to sense the raising of my frustration so I asked to speak with someone in authority. When I was connected, I asked about the flier sent me with the special package for installation of the internet, he was not aware of it'

The conversation went on and he was not even aware of the county or location, I pointed out to him that if he is a representative of Frontier, all he had to do was to verify my phone number which is in their phonebook, he eventually determined that I was in Drums Pa., Eventually he made an appointment for Thursday at 1:00 p.m.

I waited until after 1:00 p.m. to verify considering the hard time experienced the evening before. The person answering told me that there was no spot available for internet installation, well this got me riled up and said "if I did not call, were you going to let me know this?"

I asked to speak to a supervisor in order to rectify this situation after asking a few more questions about the location, I replied to him, "how are you going to help me with the installation of the internet and you are not cognizant to the fact that there was no slot available" This encounter got so much out of hand that I asked him to cancel my number especially since we hardly ever use the land line phone. I thanked him to delete and discontinue the phone. After this fiasco, we decided to drive into the town of Hazelton for some shopping and sightseeing.

My original plan was to be at Chez-B until Saturday, but due to previous commitment, plans were altered, therefore Friday morning

I got up early and started to get things ready by loading the car and preparing to get the house ready for closing, by checking all switches, water connections and thermostat, I wanted to on the road early since we planned to make a stop on the way, by permitting Yvonne the opportunity to visit the Garnes family. Before starting, I stopped at the top of the driveway to retrieve any letters from the mail box, fortunately there were two, I mention this now since coincidentally, one letter was an offer for free installation of internet. This causes me to wonder if this mail was deposited in the box earlier in the week and in retrospect I might have been dealing with this company regarding installation of internet instead of the unpleasant experience with the Frontier telephone co. **Just a thought**.

We made great time travelling on Route 80 East, up to the Delaware water gap, which is the border crossing into New Jersey State. At this point, we encountered tremendous traffic delay, which obviously resulted in a longer travel time. (At least this weather was not the culprit this time). The family was happy when we eventually got there and we enjoyed our abbreviated time together.

After some rest the earlier part of Saturday. It's a good thing the bus ride scheduled for Atlantic city was cancelled, since this would have been much too much, with church service on Sunday, then on Monday we attended a rooftop graduation party at Erick's home, for Peony, the elder daughter of Yolette (Yvonne's granddaughter) which was one of the reason for leaving Pennsylvania on Friday. It was a splendid party and a happy reunion of Family and friends.

Justifiably so. Can you imagine? After a week at Chez-B then returning to attend a Bus Ride (cancelled) then Sunday at church followed by Monday *upon the roof* (pun intended). Still Young at heart.

Sunday 6/30/19 after church service, I had to attend the Parish council meeting, especially since I was appointed as Chaplin for the group. In preparation, I had f few typed lines which in essence were those I wanted to express for the closing prayer. For open prayer, I sang the words to a familiar prayer, "Behold how good a thing it is brethren, to dwell together in unity, together in unity" the I followed with "may the words of our mouth and the thoughts of our heart, be acceptable in thy sight Oh Lord our God" paraphrased from a passage from the bible.

The meeting was then called to order and the reading of the minutes followed. I mention this because I was having thoughts of a recent finding among my record, where co-incidentally. The situation existed at that point, where I came across a set of minutes, from the year 2013, the secretary was not present and a member was selected to fill in the void, certain situation occurred which resulted in some unpleasantness, which I elated earlier in this narrative. In this instance, after the minutes were read, the next item on the agenda was, *Matters Arising from the minutes*. I asked to address a matter with witch I was concerned, in regards to a video which I had produced during the construction of our new church building, which I titled *From Demolition to Construction*.

This was the same point brought forward from the previous month's meeting which was because the person in the vestry handling this, mentioned that the title should read From "Demolition to Re-construction", at which point I respectfully objected. I feel that the word re-construct did not apply which implies a makeover, considering that the original structure was completely demolished and was in a different and smaller place. We actually constructed a whole new and much larger building in a different place, therefore, as the producer of the video, I would rather the title be as I had stipulated.

Now as I began to speak and asked about the Video and progress in application for adaption for viewing on the Church's monitors, before I even got my thoughts out, I was loudly interrupted by the same person voicing opinion on previous occasion,(a developing pattern) at this point I completely lost my cool and was annoyed, to say the least, by this lack of decorum, and the reason for inaction, this has gone on for quite some time, and I indicated that if the video was unworkable for the intended purpose, I would be happy if it was returned to me since, to me it was a labor of love and devotion. In lieu of going to my job each day, (the source of my income) I attended and recorded each phase of said demolition and construction.

During this display of disruption, there was a new addition to the council, and the lady voiced her shock and disappointment, I apologized for my reaction and assured her that was not my *way*, but this is a regular recurrence from certain persons, which triggered the outburst at this point, and it was a sign of frustration on my part, but I sort of anticipated this and was prepared with a prayer, and showed it to her hopefully to soften the situation. Then I pointed out that the minutes of a meeting is the record of the business transacted and decisions made. Any accurate record will serve to clarify any situation in the future, which has been the case in many instances. We cannot rely on memory of what has been said, the written word is there for reference and record.

On many occasions I have been asked to verify certain situations, which by checking records of past minutes, I am able to supply accurate information. Accurate and corrected minutes should be a permanent record of each meeting. I would like to make a point, in the respect to corrections and observations made during (*Matters arising from the minutes*) these changes should be accurately stated and added to existing minutes. For good order sake, corrections should be read and all persons should record these to their personal copy of the minutes, especially the official copy for permanent records of the organization (group). If this is not done, then there is **no** record of what actually transpired in said meeting.

At the end of the meeting I read the prayer with emphasis on key words, first by repeating the opening verse "Behold how good a thing it is brethren to dwell together in unity, together in unity"

**Closing Prayer**:

"Lord of day and night, of beginnings and endings, as we prepare to conclude this meeting, we once again lift up our hearts to You, the Divine Source of ALL Life. We thank you for the gifts that have been present within this act of service to the Church and community.

For the gifts of **fellowship** and **understanding**, of **mutual respect** and **shared vision,** we are grateful.

For the gifts of perseverance and insight into the common concerns we share, for these and all other graces, we are thankful. As you have blessed our coming together, now bless our departure and journeys homeward.

May **your** blessing be upon us, in the name of the Father, Son and Holy Spirit Amen.

The latest development at the church. The bell in the New Church building, was purchased from schulmerich Carillons 1990 but I kept the electronics at home safe and secured until it was ready to be installed in the completed building.1991. Case in point. I am able to provide this information because of the accurate files retained in my possession.

Some weeks ago I was notified the bell was not working, so I looked up my files and was able to pass the information on to the warden in order to get in touch with the supplier, to secure a copy of the operating manual, since the original cannot be located. Coincidentally, Fr Alleyne had called me earlier, for this same information regarding a set of bells at the church where is has been recently assigned in Long Island. The past week while I was away, I received a call from him, asking for the information again, since the person he assigned the task of looking after his set, has misplaced it.

I was not at the Brooklyn home and was not able to provide the info. But since I had passed this info to the warded at St.Gabriel's church, I called and asked her to forward the information on to him.

It has been a couple weeks since my return, and I have not heard anything further about the receipt of the manual, therefore I asked about it, and was told that the person assigned, had not reported any progress. There seems to be a pattern here, passing on the buck. Monday July 1st. I went back to my files, looked up the telephone number and called about the bell, after providing the necessary information, I learned that this company no longer handles this type of bells, therefor I asked who dose? The result is that this product was sold to another company. "Who are they?" After my insistence and explanation regarding my inquiry, the person with whom I spoke, promised to call the new co. and pass on the contact for them to call me. I asked the company's name and who will be calling me? After a while, I decided to look that company up on line, Verdin Co. located in Reading Cincinnati, Ohio. I acquired the e-mail address, and proceeded to contact them directly, and supplied the necessary data regarding the purchase from Schulmerich. Which resulted in a subsequent phone call, and we entertained a very rewarding conversation. I received an e-mail with phone numbers and name of contact person, which was eventually passed on to Fr. Alleyne, now he is up to date for contacting this Company for his consideration.

As it turned out, the fee for a service call with no guarantees, is $600.00 and because of the age of the unit (about 25 years).might result in the purchase of a new system. We then decide that I will go to the venue and photograph the unit and copy to her, which might help in the search of their archives in order to locate a copy of a replacement manual.

Giving the prospect of a major investment, I decided to have a look at the unit, and in doing so, I finally was able to get the bell ringing, now I will have to monitor the performance to verify that the programs: tolling, swinging, mass call and the Angelus are functioning. At the very least, I was able to save a service call. I have called Louise to inform her of the progress made, and promise to keep in touch.

Good news, I was able to e- mail the photograph of the electronic unit as well as a copy of the original contract, of which Louise (contact person) acknowledge receipt, and replied that the research department is assiduously searching for a copy of the related manual, in the meantime I have *been* several times to the church in order to verify that the bell is ringing automatically, I have not personally experienced this since on occasions I have checked the unit and noticed that the bell switch was in the off position, which gives me cause to wonder if someone has been turning it off, so even though I was told on several occasions that the bell did ring, until I can personally experience this, I will continue to monitor it and then confirm to the contact person at Verdin Co. Notwithstanding I hope the manual is located in order that we would be able to adjust the Bell programs to respond in a timely manner.

Before continuing this narrative, let me first state that this morning at the 9:30 am service, I actually heard the bell ring at a time which would have been timed for the mass call. I can honestly and factually state to the Verdin Co. that things are apparently working out, and all I actually need is the Manual, in order to program the actual time for ringing. I will send Louise an e-mail to this effect.

My sister Yvonne and Ernie (who lives in San Antonio, Texas), spent the past 5 weeks in New York and she was able to accomplish quite a bit, visiting friends and family, for Graduations, Dance recitals, Doctor's visits, and most of all she was able to attend Sunday services at St.Gabriel's church, where she was able re-connect with childhood friends and fellow parishioner with whom she was acquainted. We embraced the opportunity to have them accompany us to Chez-b the previous week's visit. Back home in Brooklyn, this past Sunday July 7th. While in the company of the Panamanian group in fellowship after service, a close friend referred to Yvonne's pending *birthdate*, since she was scheduled to return to San Antonio during the next week, I prompted the singing of the Happy Birthday song, both *traditional* and in Spanish, much to the delight of others in the hall, most of the parishioners are fascinated by us speaking Spanish and are constantly trying to adopt the language, Even during services during the passing *of the peace*. They will utter the phrase in Spanish, good influences.

On Tuesday I called Yvonne at night to wish her a pre- birthday wish and inform her if no other plans were made by her children, we will be coming to see her on Wednesday 7/10th. Which is her actual birthday anniversary. As it turned out, some of the other siblings and children had the same thought in mind, and what was scheduled for a short visit, turned out to be a whole day's visit. It was decided that we go to a local Panamanian restaurant but waited for the arrival of Erick (Son) at whose penthouse they resided. On his arrival, the group (14 strong), departed.

Olivia and I as well as Yvonne and Ernie had lunch on Sunday after service, and were impressed with this relatively new Panamanian owned restaurant, and I had met the father in-law at our recent Red Top Dance in May 3rd related to previously in this narrative, therefore he welcomed us. I mentioned to the owner when leaving, that we would be back. Coincidentally, here we were, this time 14 people 3 days later, undoubtedly they were happy on our return with 10 additional persons. It is good to be good.

The final outcome was not well, since, at bedtime, others were not comfortable with some of the food, Yolanda had a negative reaction to something she ate, and brought it all up. It is doubtful that there will be a return to that place. Edgar was able to transport Yolanda back home to New Jersey on the following day. Yasmina and Janitzia Arrived home to Boston safely. On Friday Yvonne and Ernie had a pleasant and safe trip back to San Antonio. By the Grace of God, everyone is back in their respective place.

Friday after a long and exiting day, I spent the time painting the reverse side of a sign which I had previously prepared by using a discarded satellite dish, by removing the original logo and used Charcoal black paint, and asked Edgar (the artist) to paint my logo (CHEZ-B -348) which I was able to pick up and bring home, I used a flat black paint and copy the same information. This will be mounted as a property marker for the house in Pennsylvania, it will be visible to travelers coming and going along the road.

This was not physically taxing in any way, but somehow while settling down for bed I must have somehow, strained a muscle, since I began experiencing some pain in my left back just below the waist line and just above the rump bump, my way in describing the actual location. Another way would be to say where one would *akimbo off*. You get the picture. Remember the childhood song? "There's a brown girl in the ring"(*Will you show me akimbo, show me akimbo, la,la,la, la, la…*), anyway sleeping was restless. All day Saturday I resorted to my practice of trying to rest and recover which has served me on a previous occasion. It became quite obvious to Olivia so she called the children.

Samantha the doctor, called and asked me for the symptoms, after responding, she also asked about the threshold of experienced pain, 1 to 10, I said "about 6" her preliminary conclusion was that it appears likely to be *stones* but she asked me "how was your fluid intake," In order to be as accurate as possible, I thought for a brief moment and realized that I actually had not drank water after breakfast, she admonished me and said to be sure to drink lots of water, to which I agreed. I further inquired from her "is it possible that the condition of *stones* should have manifested in some way by a slightly previous presence?" which was not the case, since the pain actually occurred while I was turning in bed in order to reach a spittoon, considering that I was developing a slight cough".

The final analysis was for me to keep drinking lots of water and to monitor any easing of the pain, if not, an appointment should be made to visit the doctor. This is sound advice, which I have followed, and was happy to mention to her on subsequent calls, that the pain has subsided, and today, contrary to my reaction, I have actually told Olivia that there has been a reduction in the pain, and I will be monitoring this quite closely. Excuse me while I go to have a full glass of water with my pill. It was very endearing to hear from my children and siblings who have responded to the call, I will convey the progress to them.

Allow me to describe what I call (My Personal Rest & Recuperation Practice) "P-R&R-P ". As I lay in bed I try to accommodate myself as much as possible, to give you an idea what I mean by this, try to imagine a puppy or a kitten as it wiggles up and finally settles down for a nap. After I am relatively comfortable, I place my open palm on a section of my body, as close as I can, then concentrate on the sound of the window air conditioner, as it changes from "fan" to "Cool", I do this in order not to be distracted from any other sound, while remaining completely still.

This goes on for as long as I am no longer aware of the changes in sound, which is an indication that I am actually drifting off to slumber. At some point, I am experiencing an internal gurgling in my internal system, which as a child in primary school, I asked the teacher what was this called? *"Movimiento Peristaltico"* **peristalsis movement,** anyhow, while this internal action is going on, I begin to feel a gradual easing of the akimbo pain. It is my naïve assumption that the water is traveling through my system and eventually reaches the area of my bladder to accomplish its mission.

The next day as I went shopping for materials I decided to take a walking stick Just in case there is a need for support. On Sunday even though I had the stick in the car, I was able to do without it. This is some sign of improvement, monitoring will continue.

Let me ask you this question, "What is: Forever and Always a Mystery Intended, in this Life of Yours?" think for a while before going on, to see if you can provide the correct answer. The answer will be provided as I go along.

========

Answer to the question: By using the capital letters in the sentence provided, the word would be revealed, which is what guides and determines me.

As promised, today (Wed.) the pain has been reduced and I can detect a slight soreness, which is a reminder of what it was like. I have conveyed this information to all who have asked. Thanks be to God.

Great news, I just received news via e-mail from the bell co. perhaps as a result of the photograph and copy of the original contract, (which as usual, I kept in my personal files) I e-mailed them, identified the model 36-367 of the bell, and they forwarded me the operating instructions which I immediately downloaded for my records, and proceeded to forward same to the Wardens of the church, which hopefully, will be secured safely and available for future reference. My response and thanks were immediate, to the research person and the office manager Louise for their efforts on behalf of our church. I will personally check the instructions to adjust the programs of the bell.

I received a package via UPS from the Optical office with two jobs, consisting of eyeglasses where I drill the lens OD (right) or OS (left) as required, to be drilled, and loupes (specified strength) to be installed, in this case one lens had to be Blacked out, so I prepared that lens and sprayed it black and set it up for drying while completing the 2 drillings, by this time the blacked lens is ready to be installed in the spectacle. The finished jobs are cleaned and packed for shipping, I prepare the invoice and shipping document.

Thursday, I was feeling no pain therefore on rising from bed, knowing that I have to move my vehicle to comply with alternate side parking restriction, after a quick breakfast I gathered the package and shipping documents in order to get going in time. Alternate side parking is to allow the city street cleaning truck to do its job between 11:00 am to 12:30 after noon. I mention this as explanation for those who were not cognizant to this. Fact.

After delivering the package to the UPS shipping store, which is rather near, (less than two miles), instead of going back home to find alternate parking for de duration (12:30), I decided to make a run to the Church, and arrived before 12:00 noon just time to actually and personally hear the church's bell ring on the dot. I know this since I went into the area where the electronic console is located, and checked the clock.

Now my next wish is to be there at about 6:00 pm.to actually hear the *Angelus,* which would definitely confirm the good working order of the applied programs in the system, in the meantime. As promised, I will send an e-mail to the Verdin Co updating them accordingly.

While there, I went into the office to ascertain that my e-mail was received by the custodian also the administrator, and to verify that the attachment was downloaded and printed. To my dismay, on checking the message on their desktop there was no attachment. I promised that on my return home, I will re-send the message. On sending the message I also included my desktop as a copy-reader, then I checked my message it was confirmed that the attachment was not sent. I did the next best thing, I sent another message reading "I will produce copies of my printed document for each of them".

I printed the *bell operating instruction* and added it to my "briefcase" the bag which I always take with me. On Sunday, I will take it to the office and have a number of copies printed, to be distributed among them for safe keeping, "me with mine, they with theirs" then I can truly say, "*All is well that ends well*". Mission accomplished. Just in case you have not arrived at the answer to the question asked a couple of pages before. It FAMILY. A precious commodity in our lives.

# Trip to Chez-B

7/31/19-8/4/19

Before starting, it is only fair to relate the tale of how we got into this trip. It was some time ago I was left with a satellite dish from a previous system which I had to cancel due to constant reception problems, it had to do with the actual location of the satellite and I had to cut down several trees which did not solve the problems. I had to change to another satellite network who installed their satellite dish therefore I was the proud owner of a discarded dish.

As the saying goes "someone's trash is usually another's treasure", therefore with this in mind I saved the dish in a corner of the deck. I occurred to me that this dish could be the perfect slate for a sign to replace the 5"x2' board sign at the top of the driveway with the logo "Chez-B" and address identifying the entrance to the property. It has served me well but it was fading and somewhat rustic in appearance

The previous trip there we had my sister Yvonne and Ernie as guests, and since on return to Brooklyn I will drop them off at her son's home where I will leave the dish for the expert artistic sign painting by Edgar. I dismantled the mounting connections and stripped the existing logo of the satellite co. and sanded it to the bare metal and prepared the surface with Charcoal black paint. And a drawing on paper outlining the proposed idea, the final design is in his hands.

The final outcome was unanimously approved by all. After a few days, I took it home in anticipation of my next visit, but during the time it occurred to me that if this sign is placed on the road at the entrance of the driveway, it should be viewed going and coming down the road, the logical thing to do is to recreate the same Logo on the back, so I went to work and coated the back with the charcoal paint, but since I am not as gifted with the artist's brush, I used a chalk outline the best of my ability, and when satisfied, proceeded to paint the design.

Not bad, if I do say so myself, I check around for a post to fit the dimension of the mounting bracket, while perusing my backyard in Brooklyn I found a 7' pipe saved from a previous fence, (my treasure) which was a tiny bit thinner, not to worry, I will find a way to make it work.

In the interim, I was pleasantly surprised with a communique from Hugh in Costa Rica, inquiring as to the health of our boyhood friend Roy, to which I responded, "Not too good". He indicated his desire to make the trip to visit him in the Hospital depending on accommodation, to which I readily agreed, and offered to pick him up at the airport, on completion of his travel plans.

On Thursday 25th, I picked Hugh (Winfield) up at La Guardia Airport, which resulted in a traffic nightmare due to existing construction and renovation of that facility which is no geared to the facilitation/navigation of travelers etc. to access this area (to say the least). After several calls back and forth and with intermediaries, he was assured that I will find him, and the type color of vehicle to look for. Happily after a slight delay, there he was calling to me as I neared the pick-up area.

On Friday, we surprised Roy in the hospital we (Olivia, Hugh and myself) had a pleasant visit, despite the sad circumstances. On Saturday we attended the St Gabriel's church Street Fair. On Sunday we attended Church services, where he met some folks who knew him, and heard about him from Myrtle Bryant (R.I.P.) during fellowship, I was reminded and recounted the story of how we found our present home.

In those days, when he attended ST. Gabriel's church, he used to stay at Myrtle home and I offered to take him there after service. We got into the car and I told him to direct me as we progressed. This took

me into the vicinity of East New York, which was not familiar to me
been a new driver. After reaching Bristol Av., his destination, I asked
him the direction to get back to familiar road, he said to me "follow
that bus in front of us" I thanked him and took off in pursuit of the bus,
well at the following street light I got the red light and the bus didn't.
The scenario now is that I had to stop and the bus did not have to stop
therefore went on its merry way.

The light is now Green and I had to go. Where? That's the question, I
continued driving for a few blocks and reaching a street which appears
to be navigable, I made a Right turn and on reaching the corner, I
noticed that the street was Linden Blvd. *aHa,* I know this street, as a
safe and careful driver, I stopped to check for oncoming traffic in the
service road, as I looked to the left, I saw a For Sale sign on this small
but attractive house. I parked the car, did I mention that this was a 1964
Ford Falcon? After parking the car I proceeded to the balcony where
the sign was posted, and remove it and rang the doorbell, An Italian
Lady answered and I gave her the sign and said "I will be back", I went
home to 1216 St. John's place where we were presently living, and asked
Olivia to get dressed, we went back to the little place 1987 Linden Blvd,
and the rest is history up to now.

Continuing on my narrative, after fellowship at the church, Winfield
and I went to look for the residence of Jacinta, Myrtle's daughter.
Again **de ja vu** a number of years ago, both of us together seeking an
address, only this time neither of us knew where we were going, and
this time we are travelling based on directions given by a friend of a
friend. After getting to the end of the road, it became obvious that we
were travelling in the opposite direction. We eventually retraced *our
path taken*, and found the address and this time a happy reunion, and
a lovely time spent with Jacinta and Daughter. We reminisced about
times spent at St. Gabriel's and about her youthful days, much to the
delight of Her Daughter.

Olivia and I were very happy to have spent the time with Winfield and
offered a stay at the very home he had some connection as evidenced
by the narrative told above. On Tuesday 30th I drove Winfield to JFK
Airport (a less complex and shorter trip) this was 7 days spent in good

company, while here in Brooklyn N.Y. unfortunately too short a time since the very next day Wednesday 31st we were off to Chez-B and would have been delighted to have him accompany us there.

We were on the way at about 12 noon for our trip to Pennsylvania, the traffic got congested as we approached the George Washington Bridge but eased up a bit after crossing. We continues a t a steady pace until reaching the Delaware Water Gap which is the dividing line between New Jersey and Penn. We encountered torrential rain for a few miles, after which all was dry. The wonders of nature, I suppose the condensation of water from the Delaware River must have contributed to this rain (Hmmmm) in the area.

One of the main reason for this trip was to install the sign with the 7' pipe (another item saved) which was loaded in the car. I remover the previously mentioned marker I repainted it and redid the logo in red/ black, which I mounted on the top of the stairs of the building. Then came the remounting of the mounting connection to the dish, then I had to insert the pole which as mentioned, was a bit smaller, by using some metal strips (saved from a previous project) I was able to obtain a secure fit to the mounting apparatus.

There is some distance to the top of the driveway, in order to ease my burden, I loaded everything along with some cement and bricks, stored in the shed also required tools, onto the car then drove up. First I built a platform with the bricks with the cement and pieces of stone to fill in the gaps then I secured the sign, after working my tail off, I stepped back saw a completed job. I got into the car a rode a bit down the roar, made a u turn and headed back up to observe and confirm the visibility of the sign, then photographed my handiwork with my camera, due to the marvel of modern communication, I also photographed the sign with my cell phone (had to say this) in order to text the photo to my sister Yvonne, who is now back in San Antonio, TX, considering that she was here at the inception of the idea, and its befitting that she see the sign in its intended place.

Sunday after breakfast, there is a certain routine to get the place in order to lock up, such as turning off the water supply and filter, flipping off the required electrical switches, checking the thermostat settings, checking all the doors, windows etc. I have made a chart and posted it at the switch box, in order to leave things right.

This procedure is very important since there is no telling when we will be returning. There are a few examples if this routine is not stringently followed it will lead to catastrophic results. 1) I accidentally flipped the switch for the refrigerator (prior to Thanksgiving) which was the next visit. As I opened the door downstairs, upon entering, I was greeted with a foul odor, on following the scent which lead me upstairs to the kitchen area, where it was strongest, all the stored ham etc., was completely rotted. There was no other recourse but to discard the food and refrigerator. There was no way to get rid of the residual odor. That was a very costly error.

2) Luckily **I did** turn off the water supply in this instance, after settling down after bringing all the baggage upstairs, I heard a trickling of water coming from the kitchen ceiling light, before getting up to investigate the source, the light fixture suddenly erupted and fell, spewing water(not much), after cleaning the floor and getting a step ladder to see the damage, I noticed a pipe elbow was completely chewed into (the work of a wayward squirrel) as a result of the weight of the water that had accumulated in the pipes when I had turned on the water supply on entering, I quickly went back downstairs and turned it off. Imagine the catastrophic result of a flood if I had not turn it off on departing on the previous visit? The fix was not that bad, since I was able to get a PVC elbow from the hardware store to replace the damaged water pipe (me the plumber) and repairing and painting the surrounding ceiling tile, (me the builder) The light fixture's cover is made of plastic therefore it did not break, thus easily replaced. A lesson learned "Always turn off the water when leaving".

As I was saying, after *lock up,* then an earlier than usual starting time of *hitting the road,* we made a stop at the Garnes at South Orange N.J., for a visit, some vittles and pleasant chatter, we reached home in Brooklyn about 10.00 PM, Now faced with unloading the Jeep and taking everything up, it was time to hit the sack for a much needed rest.

A couple pages ago in my narrative, when relating the circumstances in our purchasing this home in Brooklyn, it occurred to me that this coming December2019, it will be 52 years since effecting the purchase of this 6year old building, so this *old house* is now 58 years **young** and we are still here by the *"grace of our Lord & Savior Jesus Christ"*.

I also noted for the first time (I think) in the pages referred to, the words "path taken" I wonder if you noted this. After writing the first book "What if? The Question or a Statement" my intent is to continue that narrative in depth, therefore the original idea of a title was of this present book was "What if? Expanded "which in fact, is the intent, but considering the gist of the first few lines where I mentioned that if you wonder how I got to this point, it is imperative to know from whence I came, so logically in order for me to arrive at any given location, it was necessary for me to have *taken a path*. With this in mind, my first trip was to travel to these United States which was previously mentioned, but for the purpose of continuity, I arrive these shores on December15 1962 and after 5 year, we purchased and still occupy, our home at 1987 Linden Blvd. Dec. 1967. As I write this, it adds up to 52 years in this place we call home, and counting.

I have travelled many paths during my lifetime to date, some of which cannot be remembered without some in depth research, but some I can remember, where as a family, have travelled. It began with the purchase of a previously owned 1964 ford Falcon. Note that I did no say **used** since it was a fairly new car when it was acquired, and the price was right. And suited our needs

I was able to make ends meet, by having an additional part time job, in order to meet the immediate deposit of a second mortgage on the home and when that was paid off, I was back to normal employment. This is where the ford came into play. We all got on board for trips first to Orlando Florida, and were among the first set of timeshare holders, this way we were required to fulfill our desire to travel yearly. After several trips to Florida and surroundings, several states of this country, Canada. We made use of the exchange options which allowed us including our children, to travel to Hawaii and other islands, Mexico, Las Vegas, sightseeing the areas of interest in that part of the country, New Orleans also Alaska and Vancouver,

As our travels expanded, I was able to make that possible. One special way was by me preparing my yearly taxes, I was able to write off the travel cost of Olivia, who was a teacher in the public school system, teaching English as a second language, and social studies. By travelling to Spanish speaking countries of the world where she was exposed to the culture and lingo of these countries which enhanced her ability in serving those children. At those times an allowance was accepted and encouraged by the Internal Revenue Service. In actuality this served us and New York equally, by providing quality education through the school system. Tax refunds helped to defray expenses. To name a few countries, Panama, Puerto Rico, Spain, Santo. Domingo etc.

When this was no longer possible, due to the idiosyncrasy of the I.R.S who dropped this allowance, it did not deter our travel experiences since we have travelled to Italy, France, The principality of Monaco, London (big ben), to name a few, using our Time share, in some instances, and some tours.

**Greece** where there was a special desire for me to visit, a place referred to in biblical history, I rented a car and drove from Athens, (where we lodged for a couple weeks), to Corinth passing over the Canal of Corinth, which was of interest to me since this was a sea level canal unlike that of Panama (from whence I hailed), which is a "locked" transiting from a higher body of water to a lower level. We were able to actually see some of the historical and biblical sights such as the Temple of the Olympian Zeus Parthenon, the Acropolis, The theater of Herod Atticus where there has been actual modern concerts recorded "yanni live at the acropolis". Temple of Apollo, the church from where the apostle Paul addressed his letter to the Corinthians, the Agora, The fortification of Acrocorinth. The temple of Athena Niki, the Caryatides where the temples of Athena and Poseidon were built, and much more interesting sites.

**Rome:** where we visited the seat of the Catholic religion *The Vatican* visiting the Museums and other places of interest, most of al, the Sistine chapel whish was fascinating especially the renown paintings/ frescos of Michelangelo ceiling, Again the warning no photographs, but as that goes, I could not have travelled to such a place and not exercise my desires to do just that, which I did. (Both still and some movies with a small inconspicuous movie camera), when I was approached, I apologized, and put away the cameras, however, I now have the photos for my personal appreciation and memorabilia. The *Trevi Fountain, the Pantheon, and the Colosseum.* We visited other places of interest. One evening, we visited a popular restaurant and most interesting, there was a piano entertainer/ singer, and I could not resist the urge to ask him to accompany me to the Aria "Tourna a Sorrento" to the delight of the numerous customers, I can truly and honestly say that I have performed musically, in Europe (Rome)

**Madrid:** with all its Plaza and famous buildings, the home of the Spanish language and one of the Prado museum, is one of world's most greatest galleries, I was allowed to photograph some of the great paintings including the both Maja by Goya The nude and the Clothed Maja (1797 & 1798) I asked and was told that there were objections expressed by someone (don't remember who) because of where it was displayed at the time, he painted on clothes. I must have made an impression on the guards since they asked the viewers to step away for a while, permitting me to get my shots. I have the photos to ascertain this fact. It was quite an experience.

**Toledo:** We visited some of the artisans at work with pottery and gold plating and designing. And the numerous and impressive cathedrals. At one I was not allowed to photograph the interior, I asked and explained that I would be nonintrusive, this person suggested that I should go up the upper level (quite high) but there was someone who prevented me, I decided to back into some of the niches in the wall, at some point I was able to sneak a couple shots. I was sad to have encountered this there was no way where any harm could be caused by their actions. European countries. I got my photos for personal memories and satisfaction they were causing more problems restricting me, than I was by tiptoeing around taking photos, much quieter than a mouse.

**Florence:** We walked around the Palazzo Vecchio and most of the statues are of nude males including a copy of Michelangelo's David. In the National Museum there are famous sculptures and paintings among which was *Birth of Venus.* I just happen to have a set of 8x12 copies which includes this particular reproduction (part of a pair) and I made a frame to hang this in one of the bathrooms in Penn. I also saw several unfinished sculptures by Michelangelo in a room. We were told of the relocation of the statue *David,* which was been damaged over time, by droppings by birds and other predators, and it was removed to a new site where we actually saw this statue been cleaned by a lady with Q-tips over the years, there was a scaffold around it from where she worked. Again, I was forbidden to photograph it, I could not honestly resist the temptation to sneak a shot of the real McCoy.

**London:** We have visited on two occasions, I should mention at this time that some of our trips were in the company of close friends and families. On one of these visits to London, we lodged at the resort --Walton hall. Walton Welles Bourne. Warwickshire, England ///////////

As outlined in my previous book, the group which I was a part of, "The Roy Prescod Chorale", travelled every other year to several Caribbean Island, Panama, Costa Rica, where we offered/performed concerts, as fundraiser for various organizations and Churches. As our sponsors, they provided us lodging, food and sightseeing. As a group, we took care of our transportation, funded by financial returns from our yearly local concerts, performed in local venues, covering religious, Classical, Contemporary/Modern music featuring local artists with full orchestra.

There is a story and experiences acquired in each of our travels, and the memories are with us for as long as we can remember, this is the reason I have recorded some experiences which, as I have previously mentioned somewhere in this narrative, The written words and photographs will last as long as the venue exist.

Monday August 26ᵗʰ 2019

We are booked for Jet Blue flight 1338 from JFK 8:12 AM to Martha's Vinyard.9:25 AM under 1hour15minutes. A very short flying time. Considering the fact that I could not leave my car parked on the street since we will be away from Monday to Thursday. 4 days. Because of alternate side parking, iii decided to leave my car at the church on Sunday after service, then get a ride back home by Xenia who passes by our home her way home. This worked perfectly.

WE booked ground transportation via Access-a-ride to the airport for a 6:00 AM pick-up. It's actually a longer ground ride for the shortest air flight. (Go figure) Prior to this day, I had made arrangements for boarding pass and seating, we decided to travel light thus, only a carryon bag. In order to avoid baggage check in. Apparently, we are set on arrival at the airport, to proceed directly to the gate for boarding time, so it seems. Well surprise, surprise. At this early time, the airport was jam packed, I rationalized that there is an explanation for this, which, in my analogy, is because on these short flights, most people want to arrive at their respective destination early in order to enjoy a full day. Factually so. It's a good thing we got there in time to spare, I Checked for the boarding gate but there was a long line in order to get there, but luckily, we had to acquire a wheel chair for Olivia which allowed us to by-pass much of the line, and to get elevator to the boarding area, also to be the first on board, so there were some advantages, however, it was too good to be true, since after going through customs, my bag was detained, and had to be checked.

The TSA agent found a very small tool which was a treasured gift from my granddaughter Sydney, which had the necessary tools I used to repair eyeglasses and small repairs, I pointed out to the agent that it is a rather small tool, but she maintains that it had a small blade, (which honestly, could not even cut into butter). She intimated that I could keep it if I checked the bag in which would cost me time and baggage fee of $30.00\. Not an option, I conceded it to her, I am aware that she was doing her assigned job, but with a comment that "the TSA does not enforce background check for possessors of weapons of war, but this tiny toy is such a problem". I reclosed my bag and off to the gate. While waiting for the boarding time, I decided to get my spectacles to read and unfortunately, one of the lens fell out. This is where the confiscated tool could help me to secure it, with some caution and know how, I was able to replace the lens. I had an idea, in a case such as this, perhaps, some mailing paraphernalia could come into play, and the item be mailed back home at your expense, instead of them keeping the items. *"What do you think?"*.

This was a very short flight, As the pilot announced the progress, he mentioned that the aircraft has now attained an altitude of 10,000 ft. and was now leveling off, before we knew it, the stewardess had to hurry the distributing the "sumptuous" lunch consisting of a package of cookies and a cup of water, since the next word from the pilot was to prepare for landing. It almost seemed to me that the plane travelled in an arc and upon reaching its apex, it began to descend for landing. I am not complaining, since the flight was smooth, except for the seating arrangements.

Please follow me on this. Each row consist of 2 seats on either side of the aisle **(A-B-/-C-D)** our assigned row was #3 The booking agent is aware of the fact that we are travelling together, however. We were assigned seats 3A and #3D (window seats) each way. Considering the fact that we are the first on the plane, for reasons explained before, I sat in seat **3A** and Olivia in seat **3B** instead of **3D** in order to be side by side (logically) I figured that this matter could be easily solved. As the passengers began coming on, I was asked by a young lady to relinquish my seat since she wanted to be at the side of her companion, I realized that this could be an uncomfortable situation, fortunately, the person in seat **3C** agreed to take the seat in row **4D**. Problem solved, she sat in **3C** beside her companion in **3D** without any ill feeling among us. The same situation existed on the return flight, the gentleman realized that we were a couple and decided to take the next seat, especially since there were many unoccupied seats. I trust this was not too confusing to you.

We arrived at the gate earlier than expected, since Rich was unaware that we were there until he saw persons exiting the building. We had our bags therefore there was no delay to board his car and we were off the town, making a stop for actually eating a reasonable breakfast, know what I mean? Breakfast consisted of 2 eggs scrambled with bacon and a large cup of coffee. After this, we were on our way to the residence, which was a rather quaint and comfortable house, located at 26 Somerset in Oak Bluff section. After meeting the boys and Deborah, we settled for a short while and it was decided that we go to lunch at *Sharkeys diner*, a small but a bit crowded place, we had a 15 minutes wait to be seated. Sherena, Pete, Jordan and Sydney arrived shortly after, so now we have the compliment of family together. All 10 of us. The 4 persons mentioned, Olivia and myself, Rich and Deborah Ellis and Ethan. I think I have mentioned all.

It was a bit cool so it was a good thing that I had a light jacket to keep me comfortable. We were seated next to a large plate glass window and at one point while waiting to be served, I had a strange sensation, since I notices quite a few persons as they passed the area, delayed their stride to peer at us, I wonder if they were curious about us since there were no evidence in the area of many of "*us*" I Smile inwardly at the thought. Mind you, this area is known to be frequented by the notable.

Generally, most persons were friendly, pleasant and greeted us as our path crossed, I guess they could never be sure who we might be, (Hint/Hint). I had a ½ rack of ribs with fries which amounted to a lot of vittles, and could not eat it all,(considering that not long ago I had the breakfast previously mentioned) so I did the next best thing, A doggie bag to take back to the house for later.

This place is rather unique, most of the houses are, what we would call *Ginger bread houses*, and compared to what we see in magazines as Doll houses, many of them in vivid colors and very pleasant to behold, some of these places, remind me of our visit to Alaska, and Vancouver where I actually saw and photographed a true Ginger bread house. It's no wonder that folks continually return to spend Summer time in Martha's Vineyard. I wondered about the origin of the name of this place, and supposed it was a place proliferated by grape vines (hence, vineyard) once owned by a person named Martha.

Tuesday, 8/27/19:

Deb. Suggested that I take a short walk down to the waterfront, so off I went with my trusted camera, and I enjoyed the experience of seeing and photographing the row of houses along the shoreline, also the numerous seagulls as they did their maneuvers going after nourishments, also the water traffic of ferry and other types of water vessels as they plied the waterway. It is truly amazing that there is so much activity this early morning, with the folks walking the shore line and vehicular traffic up and down the street.

After a while, I returned to the house, and later, we boarded the two cars, and went to town for lunch, then we were off to the beach, I supposed that this should be a short ride since we were near the shoreline but this was not the case, since we travelled quite a bit, and I realized that this island was not small,. After about ½ hour travelling paved and bush road, we finally reached an area, where a $25.00 fee for each car and I am not sure if there was a per capita charge as well. But the parking was rather crude, to say the least, but the vehicles were in a secured area,

After debarking and taking the chairs and other things, we had to walk at least, what appeared to be the length of a city block over a grave / grassy road, luckily Olivia remained at the house with Deborah. I jokingly voiced a comment during the travel that, "one has to really want to get to this beach after going through this" I trust this was received in a light manner as it was intended. After reaching a space and settling down with chairs blankets and tents, there were many folks there, and I can understand the reason for the popularity of this area. Allow me to describe it. The actual Atlantic Ocean was separated by a ridge, thus creating in an inlet, what seemed to be a Lagoon, which was conducive to wading and enjoying a pool like situation, since this body of water is stagnant, it is a bit colder than the ocean. If one is more adventurous and wishes, they could walk over the narrow ridge and immerses into the ocean with waves and all. It amounts to a unique situation.

At this point, I reached for my camera to record the scene, but it was not where I placed in what I thought, to be a protected area, but it was not there, after searching frantically, I found it in the back of the tent covering where we were seated. That is not where I had placed it. Sadly when I tried to use it, I realized that it was saturated with water, which rendered it useless. So no camera, what's more tragically, I had discovered my trustworthy movie camera was not operable since after all my using it during my many travels, there was a legend stating "insufficient space" No movie camera and now, no still camera. Talk about a *fish out of water?* This is my present sentiments. Now I am left with my phone to use as a camera.

I will check the manual for this movie camera to see it there is a way to restore space, in the meantime, I have checked my still camera and the best scenario at this point, is I can see the recorded flash drive through the viewfinder, but the actual camera mechanism is inoperable, I will try to take it to a camera repair place to see what, if anything, can be done in order to restore its usefulness.

Let's get off the subject of my camera, now at least I have the camera capabilities of my Cell phone. Moving along, we all got ready for an evening out for dinner. As previously mentioned we are a total of 10 persons to feed. With this in mind, Rich called a restaurant to book a reservation for dinner, and he was told that they were not able to reserve seating for all in one setting, but could provide 2 set of 5ea. He then called again and identified himself, we loaded into the two cars on a ½ hour trip to the Seaside restaurant which was on the southern end of Martha's Vineyard.

It was a pleasant evening, therefore as we arrived, quite a number of persons were milling around the area and there was a spectacular sunset view, which immediately caused me some concern for the loss of the use of my camera, Rich was the lead car therefore he approached the entrance and was met by an attendant, and was directed to 2 reserved parking spaces, That's class. He parked in one and Sherena' car parked in the other, we were then ushered into the venue and directed to a table set for all ten of us, now this is class. What a difference a well-placed call made to the right person. This restaurant was fully attended and the clientele seemed, shall we say, select. All things considered, the area, and the distance of the local.

Our spirits were heightened by the venue, the family unit, the food was good and plentiful, and the service was great. As the evening progressed, so did the sun sink into the horizon, some of us were able to get some photos of this scenario, I was able to get some record on my Phone. I truly missed my camera, since I would have been readily able to print copies from the flash drive, a task which is beyond the capabilities from the phone. Despite the shortcomings, we all enjoyed our evening out, I am sure I speak for all. We had a good drive back to the house, on arrival we all played some board games, some of which I was not able to participate in, since the topic was not familiar to me. (Hip-Hop & Rap) so instead, I wrote some notes from which this narrative was taken. These activities lasted well into the evening.

The next morning, after a light breakfast in the house, the children and their parents went to the Arcade where they played games and won some prizes, then Olivia joined them as (a spectator), at the park where they play touch football, the old folk (namely myself) remained at the house, I used this time of solitude to get my things together and started packing for our return trip. After a time, Pete came to pick up a kite and encouraged me to join the flanks at the park which is within walking distance (1 block) He unraveled the string for Sydney, since I am quite familiar with kites as mentioned in the narratives of my previous book, I schooled them in the practice of flying a kite (smile) Sydney stayed with it for a short time, since she was more interested in joining the group for the rough and tumble rigors of touch football, which she enjoyed been a part of. I used my Phone to take short videos of the game.

On Thursday morning the 29th. Considering that our flight was scheduled for the 4:54 P.M. Rich suggested we take a short walk to Martha's Vineyard Camp Meeting Association which is located in the same area Oak Bluff. It was a very rewarding visit to the area and eventually the museum. with my phone (camera) I was able to record some of the sites and learned a bit about the area, which was founded by a Methodist priests the year 1835 the area was a sheep farm, they started as a tent city and bit- by bit and with difficulty of getting the canvass to build the tents, they started putting up wood structures which ultimately developed into the present 2 storied houses some of which are now winterized and occupied year round.

Rich asked about the underground rail road, which the curator mentioned, and was unsure of their actual existence since there was no cellar etc. I interjected at this point that the term was merely a way to say illegal trafficking, which elicited a laugh from the gathering. I seized the opportunity to ask about my concern regarding the naming of this Island, she said that the original thought was about the founder's mother in law, but from further research, the thought was about his 8 year old daughter named Martha who was lost at sea between cuttingham and James town, and what was the sheep farm which grew wild grapes all over the place was named in her honor. (Martha's Vineyard) I thanked her for answering my question and the information, the gathered folks expressed their gratitude that I asked the question, otherwise they would not have known. So my thoughts were not so farfetched, after all.

I was not sure that the curator was comfortable with the questions about the underground R.R. from Rich and myself, (2Black men) among the rest of folks present, therefore I approached her and explained who Rich is, by mentioning that he was Deputy Mayor with Mayor De Blasio of N.Y.C. who spearheaded the (Pre-k for all) program in New York City. She thanked me for the information, and another person among those present was happy to know this, since she also worked in the Program and struck up a conversation with him, it's truly a small world.

This was a wonderful experience, the visit to the village no better way to end our visit to this enchanted place known as Martha's Vineyard Camp meeting Association. A Religious Community since 1835. And the visit to the museum, we were delighted by the wealth of information she provided.

We headed back to the house and attended to final packing and said our goodbyes, Rich took us back to the airport and on arrival, we were informed that the flight was delayed, the allowed us to have lunch the menu was quite good, so I ordered a Burger and fries, The attendant was very friendly and she advised us to share the order since it was quite a lot for one person, which we did, and thanked her for the info. Thankfully we had our fill, especially since that will be all the food for now, as you already know, there is not much provided on the return trip, however I must say that the stewardess did give me an extra pack of cookies (shhh)

Things went quite well on boarding, we had to await a wheeled chair for Olivia also the attendant offered to check our carryon luggage (no charge) this was quite helpful since there is a bit of a walk to the plane, and inclined walkway up to the door for boarding. Well we had the same situation regarding seating, the same configuration as mentioned before, with one exception, while we were seated, this gentleman approached us to claim his seat, but realizing we were together, said he will take another seat. No fuss. There were plenty seats to choose from. What a difference a day make.

On arrival at JFK airport (NY), we took a taxi home, since it was early in the day, Olivia drove me in her car to the church, and I got the keys and took my car back home that worked out very well. After reaching home, I had some time for reflections, after spending 4 days on that island, the realization came to me that this was a bitter-sweet homecoming, since while at Martha's Vineyard, I received a phone call informing me of the passing of my boyhood friend Roy, which was not completely a surprise, since the very week before, we visited him at the hospital, and realized that the long Illness was taking its toll, therefore the retrospective thought was that His maker had relieved him from this prolonged suffering and he had finally gone home.= to rest in peace.

The most likely situation was for us to spend a week on the vacation, therefore Saturday would have been our return day. There is usually a reasons for things happening as they do, case in point, our return was on Thursday, and the *"Going home service"*, was scheduled for Saturday. I would have been devastated had I miss this service.

I received some calls from persons who knew that I was a close friend of Roy, therefore wanted to verify this early notice, indicating that it did not allow for compiling deserved plans for their participation. I therefore confirmed the timing and indicated that I was also taken by surprise.

All thing considered, we attended the *"Going home service"*, and I was happy to be part of the choir for the service including some former members of the Roy Prescod Chorale, and together we performed one of his favorite anthem "TOTAL PRAISE" words and music by

Richard Smallwood, which we sang with all our hearts. Although not planned, I was moved to deliver a brief reflection of some time spent in our hometown Colon, and the fact that me & my siblings lived on the same building 8th and Central avenue, ending this brief talk with soliciting an applaud from the congregation in honor of Roy's long and fruitful life, now on his way home to his Lord and maker, TO JOIN THE CELESTAL CHOIR.

Continuing on **path I have travelled**, at this point I am obliged to mention the place I have travelled the most, which is *Chez*-B As a matter of fact, this past week we were there from Monday 23rd and returned on Thursday 26th. Which was shortened, since we had a court appointment on Friday 27th.to contest a summons issued on Wednesday August 28th by the sanitation department for garbage in the garage area a month ago. Please note, we returned from our trip from Martha's Vineyard to New York on Thursday August 29th, therefore from Monday August 26th, to Thursday August 29th we were not in Brooklyn, NY. I will follow up on this appointment after telling you of our trip to Chez-B.

On Monday, we left Brooklyn about midday and had a pleasant voyage, we arrived rather early in the evening, which allowed me time to unpack the Jeep during daylight and get things started, such as getting the water and house filters going, then flipping the switches getting the electricity on, then the usual problems with the television, which required some conversation with AT&T who now owns Direct dish network. I noticed that there was some apparent leaks in the main floor bathroom with discoloration on the wall and ceiling and presence of what seems to be an influx of moths. After checking the mechanical room, I had some plastic with which I was able to seal the bathroom window.

Early on Tuesday, I cleared the area in the ceiling and filled it with joint compound, and spent the rest of the day repainting the walls with a special; waterproof bathroom paint. Will get some moth balls just in case. That done, then comes the clean-up job. It all looks good, if I say so myself.

On Wednesday morning after sitting in the walk-in closet, I looked around and realized that that room was never painted after the original prime paint, I noted some evidence of wear, since I had some of the mentioned paint left, I jump into action and began removing the contents of the room (Not much) and got the step ladder and paint and paraphernalia, and got to work painting, now I can really say that the whole interior has been repainted. Except for a thought which I have entertained, which is to investigate if there is a plausible way (half panel or paint) for me to add some insulation to the basement floor, which is a few degrees cooler since part is underground, this would minimize my use of the wood burning stove during the winter time.

Thursday morning I started to get things ready for our return trip, then the ache of the pass three days began to be manifested, so a little rest was in order and we got started to leave about 5:00 pm, there was still some daylight, and we were well on the way out of the Poconos area and across the Delaware Water Gap into New Jersey, where the roads are somewhat brighter and manageable driving, arriving home about 9:30 pm.

After 3 and ½ days of strenuous working, I had to be up by 6:00 am (quite early), to be on time for the 8:00 am appointment with the AOTH *Office of Administrative Trials and Hearings.* Hearing division. We got there over an hour earlier, not because of over anxiety (smile) we got there with Access-a-ride. We spent this time at IHOP with added breakfast fortification (Know what I mean?) After filling out the necessary forms and waiting for the call, we followed the official to her office where we were advised of the formality, of the absence of *the offending* officer, and do we, or don't we require council?) After swearing that we agree to go ahead *as is,* and the truth.

Several questions were asked by the official, and to hear our defense, Olivia chose to be heard first, after her assessment of the situation, stressing the point that the infraction as reported, was while we were out of the country, therefore any garbage there, would have been caused by passersby and we certainly would have been unable to clean it up. I pointed out that according to the summons, the alleged trash was at our Garage, and the fact that, our automobile was parked in the driveway, enclosed by a 7ft high wrought iron fence resting on the floor and by a locked gate, consequently the terminology should have been stated as, "been on the sidewalk in front of our driveway", it was further stated that after living at that place for 52 years, and not having this problem, that traffic has been increased due to the fronting of a much used and rather huge playing field, the presence of schools on either end of the streets bordering our residence, and the increased amount of fast-food concessions. And as Olivia stated, persons have been seen to drop their wrappings, bags of residues as they pass by, which I have personally seen.

I have been present many times, and have swept the garbage wrappers etc. from sidewalk into the gutter as the mechanical sweeper passes, in order that it be collected. I have also presented the official with copy of our travel Itinery and boarding passes, in order to verify the period of our travel as proof that we were indeed out of town at the time of the alleged infraction. We have been presented with a document, indication what happens next. Informing us that within 30 days, we will be contacted within a period of 30 days, regarding the outcome of the hearing. Thank you have been exchanged, and now we await the verdict.

Unfortunately, we have received a notice from AOTH regarding the summons from the department of Sanitation, we were declared guilty and therefore requested the payment of the fine in the amount 0f $100.00. We have contacted our Council rep. who have been in touch with the AOTH rep. on our behalf. It was determined that we are obliged to pay the fine prior to filing a claim. So here we are, $100.00 out of our pockets into the City's coffers. My plan is to take some photos of the area, to be presented as further evidence/defense at the time of hearings. I will follow up on results.

It has been a few weeks now, regretfully, we received a letter from AOTH, denying the claim so this is not over since somehow, the check has not been received by them therefore our claim had been denied. We now have two options, submit to do community service in lieu of further penalty, or make a payment of another $100 in order to re-file a claim, ask the bank to issue a stop payment which requires a fee, or hope that the first mailed check will materialize and a refund issued. We have opted to refile a claim by making the payment in person, this way we will have an actual receipt and (hope against hope) **Trash can be expensive and wearisome**.

In the meantime, here is something for you woodworkers. Some time ago we had to re-do our kitchen floor which was done in ceramic tile some years ago and after much traffic, some of the tiles were cracked and instead of constantly replacing broken tiles, we decided to have it done professionally in laminate which was a lot less maintenance on my part. Also cost effective. We orders an extra set, just in case.

As time goes by, I wondered what I will do with it besides having it around taking up space. After repairing the bedroom ceiling earlier this year, (mentioned in this narrative) the drapes was in need of cleaning / replacement, Olivia mentioned that perhaps a solid valance could replace the fabric one that had to be removed due to this repair. Considering the fact that I had installed a wood valance over the patio doors drapes in *Chez-B,* why not? After some thoughts, the difference is that those are free standing due to the cathedral ceiling. This situation will require hanging from the 8ft. ceiling therefore a track will have to be attached to the ceiling in order to mount this valance.

While looking around for suitable material, while cleaning what used to be my Den and now a utility room, where I do my Optical work (Drilling lenses to install telescope etc. for an Optical Co.) I came across the package of additional laminates. Upon inspection, I determined this is the answer, since each is 5 inches X 4 ft. and the width of the room is 10ft, therefore two together are 8ft. plus an additional cut 2 ft., will do the trick. I started out by joining two of them with a brace on the back with glue and left for curing. Ok today Friday, I decided to get started. After placing the track on the ceiling, clearing the area and getting up the ladder, it became quite obvious to me that this require another pair of hands to hold one end while trying to secure the other to the track.

Well, upon realizing that this was not going to work, what to do? After a pause and reflection. I certainly could handle a 4ft. length alone, so down to the Den to fetch another 2 lengths, I was able to attach the first, then the other by joining it while attaching to track, great/ great, now I have an 8ft area mounted and now all I had to do was to measure the remaining apace to be sure of the next cut. After that was done, I mounted the remaining piece, then joined the pieces with back attachments. I can now clean-up and restore everything, stand back, and admire my handy-work.

Before going on, I will visit the lumber supply store to buy 10ft cove molding and adhesive to add for a classic finish. I had previously installed cove moldings in the kitchen and it occurred to me that perhaps there is some left over, and as mentioned before, *"waste not want not)"*- I decided to have a look around and there in a corner of the Den, was an 8ft. strip which I readily installed, therefore, all I have to find is a piece of scrap to match, in order to complete this job. Just to be clear, I have taken a photo with my "camera", I mean my phone, to be sure to have an exact match.

After finding the part, I was able to finish the installation and repair the flaws with a tube of 'fast dry acrylic latex caulk', this presents an apparent professional finish. I then got the drapes and installed all the hanging hooks then hung them on the traverse rod, \\Voila// we now have the finished product. Now I have a pleasing wall to look at when the drapes are closed. I can now proceed on to my next project, whatever that might be.

Thing have a way of happening, my Daughter Samantha called from Virginia to ask what were my plans for the next weekend. There was no special plan in mind, so I asked why? As she explained, it seems that Noah (her younger son) is part of a school related project, among 4th graders where they select a partner to build a working rat trap miniature race car, and there is the material to be worked from along with printed plans, and she would like me to travel to VA to help. There was some concerns where I could make a difference, before making a commitment, I asked her to e-mail the plans in order to have an idea what it was all about.

Upon receipt and looking the plans over, I agreed to make the trip, especially since she usually mention that Noah is always involved in making and doing things, which reminds her of myself, so how could I refuse the offer? It was necessary to take some tools, a jigsaw, cordless drill, a rotary cutting tool, and other accessories, which was neatly packed in my luggage. Along with a few articles of clothing. This was not a problem since the voyage was via Train. The meeting with his partner was scheduled for Friday evening at the school auditorium, therefore I decided to travel by Amtrak early afternoon Thursday, in order to be in VA at a convenient time for pick-up at Union Station Washington.

In order to get to Penn Station in New York City, I contacted a car service for 1:00 p.m. enough time to get the 3:00 p.m. As mentioned, I was packed and ready earlier in the week, so no problem. With my bag and camera etc. At the door, we received a call from the driver, he was quite early, therefore as I looked out, I saw a car as he described, parked in front of the house so I said may goodbyes and went to the car, The driver got out, met me at the gate and took my bag, saying "allow me It's my job" This was unlike other drivers, Pleasantly so, after placing the bag (I kept my camera) He asked me if it was Ok to for him to stand there and have a cigarette. As mentioned, he was early, therefore I agreed and said "It's ok with me instead of smoking in the car" I also commented that cigarettes was not good for him anyway, he agreed.

Apparently, he was previously smoking in the car, since there was a lingering smoke odor, I sat in the back with the door open to air it out, while he stood outside and had his smoke. We had guest in the house (Yolanda and her Cousin) I supposed they were wondering why we were still parked there, so Yolanda came down to find out what was the problem, I explained the situation that all was well. After *driver* finished his smoke, we got on the way and he pointed out that she was very protective of me, I smiled and said "she was a good friend and was worried" *Driver* "she is a good person".

The driver was very talkative and a pleasant person, he mentioned that it was his first time driving for this car service. He continued to talk all the way, and had polite conversations, I found him so amiable and he mentioned that he was from Pakistan (I think) He went on to say he thought that it was pleasant to talk to me and I reciprocated. He went on to tell me of several experiences. Allow me to tell this story which I suppose, he related comparatively.

"**Driver:** One early morning I picked up a customer and as he enter the car, I said to him "Good morning how are you?

**Customer**: It's too early in the morning to have a conversation.

**Driver**: "sorry." So I kept quiet for the rest of time, after a while the customer started to say something to me but I interrupted him to say, "Aren't you aware that you should not speak to a driver while he is driving? So do not talk to me."

This was his way to get even with this person. He continued to tell of other encounters, other stories he related, were entertaining and demonstrated a certain sense of humor. At some point, a car traveling behind continued to beep their horn, so the driver said to me that it makes him happy since that car cannot pass him so let him keep beeping. I mentioned, that is a very good attitude to maintain, he responded that it keeps him healthy, by not getting upset, which will make him sick.

As we neared the destination, the traffic started to back up, he then asked my age, I hesitated to respond and wondered why he asked, finally I told him 82 years, he was astonished and said I did not look any way near that, he mentioned that compared to some people he has met and of younger age, looks older, I thanked him and said perhaps it is due to the origin, food, mode of living which affect the aging process. He asked my nationality, I was born In Colon Republic of Panama. This is when he told me of his origin. This prompted another story of, and I told him of the place I live and path I have traveled.

We maintained mutual respect, and that I do respect persons who respect me, commended him for his good nature and openness, regardless of ones place of origin etc.

**Driver:** "I want to say a prayer for you, you must repeat after me word for word" I agreed and as he uttered each phrase in his language, I repeated as well as I could. I asked after he was finished to tell me what the prayer was? And he said "I prayed for your health, family, a good and long life". I thanked him and said "I wish you the same ".

As we arrived at 8th Av 31st. Street, the traffic stopped due to a large truck trying to make a turn and it was rather close to boarding time 3:00pm., the driver said "since I might have to make a turn, I will pop the trunk and you could get the luggage and make the short walk in order to the entrance", just as he was about to do this the truck moved and he was able to continue on to the entrance, but as fate will have it, the traffic cop signaled that he should move on to the end of the other block,33rd Street, that's bad news for me which means I would have to walk back a block. Prayer works, the traffic was halted by a red light, so right in the middle of the street, he popped the trunk, I got out quickly retrieved my luggage and made it to the sidewalk before the light changed. Good save driver/.

As I entered the station, I checked the gate for train #173 but it was not posted, I asked one of the red cap person to tell me the gate number, with the intention to position myself nearby since the hall was full of travelers, and time was fleeting, he did not know the number since it will be posted 15 minutes before, a bit of panic started to set in, I decided to position myself near a gate which looked suspect, I was near the rope separating what would be the entrance, kept my eye on the board, but I suddenly heard one of the attendants mentioned the gate number prior to it been posted, I was right there on the outside and would have to go around to form a long line, luckily there was an opening and I was able to slip right in front of a goodly gentleman who understood the situation since I was beside him but outside of the rope, so he just stepped aside to let me in. There exist evidence of good people most time, I got on to the train ahead of the onslaught, a good seat in front of the car, settled down and enjoyed a great ride to Washington. PHEW.

Usually, when I travel with Olivia, she requires Red Cap service, and they are aware of the gate number prior to posting on sign board, they take the short cut to the trains, getting us on board prior to the onslaught of riders, hence my reason for asking the Red cap person. This time I was on my own, but as noted in my case, I was able to circumvent and still get on board ahead of the crowd.

On arrival at union station Washington D.C., the train was a bit delayed so when Sam called to check my location, I was still on the train so she had to go around the waiting pick-up area, because the vehicles are required to load up and keep moving. At the time of her return in place, I was off the train and out front, so I was able to walk back to where she was in line, all loaded, off we went to Smooth drive Mclean Va. Sam had to go pick up Noah from an after school program. I settled down and had a snack. Later I telephoned my sister Yvonne in San Antonio Texas. She mentioned that the funeral service for the congress man Elisha Cummings was been televised, considering I was alone in the house, I turned on the T.V. and turned into the station just in time to hear the introduction of next speaker who was no other person but the former President Barack Obama. I was so happy to at last, hear a wonderful oration honoring the decease. This was so enlightening considering the daily Rant and Rave, tweets and other chatter fed by the media. To voice a quote "A Blast from the Past".

After watching the rest of the transmission of the funeral service, I continued watching the television programs and became aware that the Washington Baseball fans were riding high since their team, The Nationals were on the way of winning a World Series against the Houston Astros, this has been long coming since it has been 86 years since a world series has been played in Washington D.C. How ironic? I just watched the funeral service for the Honorable E. Cummings 68 years since his birth. (-86 years---68 years)- To set the records straight. The Nationals attained the title: *2019 **World Series champs**.* by mentioning this, I was asked if I believe in numerology.

Friday is the reason for me been there, so after School on Friday, we went to pick up Noah and continued on to the meeting place where the groups met their partners, each in separate parts of the hall. We had to move our table near to the wall in order to locate a source of electricity to plug in our tools. First we each got our plans after making a decision, Noah and partner had to cut up the parts, that is where I came in, since they were working with power tools, I guided them by setting things up and helping with the cuts, they dealt with the assembling and gluing of parts and other things until the evening was over.

On Saturday, there was some refining required, between Noah and myself, we did this and made the final assembly, leaving his partner to finish up the final point. There was a need to cut the metal axel, after they decided on the lengths. I had to cut this since the Rotary cutting tool was a bit much for them to handle. With that done, the wheels were installed by Noah and we got the unit rolling, the Rat trap installed, after a trial run, all was packed for the input for his partner for the final project at another time and presentation, I will be anxious to learn of the final outcome.

Sunday the next big occurrence in Washington is a monumental Marathon and a lot of roads./ streets will be closed and the individual schedule of Sam and Charles presented a dilemma affecting Booking my return voyage, inasmuch as my original plan was to attend church service in VA and depart after, which was not feasible. Early morning departure prior to the Marathon street closing was the deciding point. The trip was booked for 7:00 am which required Charles and I to leave at about 6:00am. I kept waking up at 4:00 to 5:00am and I was ready to leave prior to 6:00am. Not much sleep time.

The train was behind schedule, since we arrived at Penn Station after 11:00am. After finding my way around the station, I headed for the #3 subway train that travels to East New York and my stop been Pennsylvania station (Bklyn.) At this point I must make the distinction (for you who are not aware) I was travelling from Penn. Station N.Y. to Penn Station Brooklyn. All said and intended, this was not the case, since at the time I called home to alert Olivia of my early arrival, she was already off to church with the thought that she would meet me at the station in Brooklyn in the afternoon.

Surprise/Surprise, as I got to the subway train station the # 3 train was not running, but upon inquiry, I was told that I would have to take the #R train, which I was not familiar with. After a while on this train, I asked where I could connect with the train to Brooklyn, since this was not a path for me, A station attendant told me to connect at the Barclay Station (Atlantic Ave,) I then I would connect to the #4 train which was running on the #3 line I know that this is so confusing to all of you as you read this, anyway, I followed orders and finally I began to note familiar stations so I was on the way, but wait,/ the fun begins. As it came up to elevation above ground I see is pouring rain, luckily

I had packed a small umbrella which I retrieved when reaching the Penn. Station.

I hoped for a bus, or Cab to take me 5to6 block to my home. Which was not to be, so instead of standing there getting soaked, I decided to take the back streets where I could be walking under balcony at some points, but the wind was wreaking havoc with my tiny umbrella. I had a plastic bag which I was able to tie over my cap, which was not a match for the wind, so upon reaching another block, I entered a store and asked for a shopping bag, which was a little bigger and helped. Step by step I finally made it home, Oh what a good feeling to be under cover, getting out of the wet clothes etc. I will be sure to replace the umbrella (a bigger one) and a poncho which I had in another bag in my luggage. Thankfully, my camera (new one) was snugly in its carrying case, and I will be sure to include a plastic bag for future consideration.

So I missed Sunday church service, packed in my luggage, was clothes for church worship in VA as the saying goes, **"Man appoints, plans disappoints"**. During the week I was away, a package from the Optical Co was among my mail, therefore I decided to get working on the job, I drilled the lens and installed the Lupe as required, when this was completed, I packed it and prepared the invoice. On Monday morning, I shipped the package via UPS, especially since it is my custom to turn around the jobs as soon as possible, and did not want to delay this one.

It is time to pick up my special bag which is always packed, after doing some chores, we were ready to load the Jeep, and off we went to spend 4 days at *Chez-b*. This time on our arrival, there was no problem with the Television, after the usual searching for satellite connection, it operated normally thereafter. The rest of the evening was spent examining the work done on my previous visit, the rooms painted passed my inspection(smile), after some final cleaning, all was well.

The following days were spent clearing the fallen leaves, gutter clearing and exterior clean up. The next problem to be confronted, is the presence of a couple trees which are menacingly leaning towards the house, and appears to be dead, I have consulted a neighbor about the possibility of contacting a contractor cut them down before any catastrophic accident. I await the estimate///.

Here is some good news, remember the sanitation fine mentioned before, where we had to pay another $100.00? well today, we got a mail informing us that the original payment $100.00 fine was located, and we will have to go there to pick up the refund, things are about to get better. We had to return to the AOTH office to present copies of cancelled checks obtained from the bank to verify and justify the duplicate payment. Now we are playing the waiting game for them to eventually refund $100.00, also the date for the hearing to decide on the outcome of the appeal. Now we can only hope that everything will be cancelled.

From 1966 I have been an active and involved member of St. Gabriel's Episcopal Church, Brooklyn, There has been many occasions where I hope my presence have made a difference working in this vineyard, doing what I was allowed to by the grace of the lord. The Consecration of the new building, I was awarded the Bishop's cross in the form of a medal and certificate, a copy included as follows.

## Certificate: Bishop's cross

RICHARD E. BUERY, SR.

A FATIHFUL AND LOYAL MEMBER OF ST. GABRIEL'S CHURCH, BROOKLYN, FOR MANY YEARS.

YOU WERE ONE OF THE FOUNDING MEMBERS OF THE CHURCH CHOIR. AS A MEMBER OF THE EXECUTIVE COMMITTEE, YOU FURTHERED THE WORK OF THE CHURCH BY ASSISTING THE ACOLYTES AND HELPING TO DIRECT THE SUNDAY SCHOOL AND YOUTH GROUP. YOU ALSO HELPED TO ERECT STALLS FOR THE YEARLY INTERNATIONAL DAY CELEBRATION.

WHEN ST. GABRIEL'S BECAME A PARISH, YOU SERVED ON THE VESTRY AND PRESENTLY SERVE AS SENIOR WARDEN.

YOU HAVE ASSISTED IN THE PLANNING, RAISING OF FUNDS AND THE ACTUAL BUILDING OF THE NEW CHURCH, WHERE YOU SERVED AS LIAISON WITH THE CONTRACTOR, ENGINEER, ARCHITECT, AND SUB-CONTRACTORS IN GETTING THE JOB DONE.

IN RECOGNITION OF YOUR DEVOTED SERVICE, WE BESTOW UPON YOU THE BISHOP'S CROSS FOR DISTINGUISHED PAROCHIAL SERVICE IN THE DIOCESE OF LONG ISLAND.

BISHOP OF LONG ISLAND

March 1, 1992

**A vote of thanks to all with whom my life was shared.**

During the course of this manuscript, I have mentioned, and personally thanked those persons from whom I solicited their feedback/ comments, on reading the book *What if?*, for fear of omitting some, I will mention a few who have highlighted some of my personal thoughts.

**Samantha**: (my daughter) who edited the introduction of this project.

**My Family and siblings**: for their support and encouragements.

**Euclid Jordan**: Who have expressed some flattering comments, recorded in this project.

**Rico Campbell**: who have stroked my ego, pointing out that if I have written a book, then I am an Author, evidenced by record in the Library of congress.

**Silvia Lavalas**: Who posted an overview of the book "What If?" with the publisher, (who forwarded it to me), Also recorded in this project.

**Hugh Winfield**: whose comments and "his take" mirrored my thoughts for the writing of this next book. Also recorded in this project.

**Yvonne Walcott**: (sister) for catching me up with the memories of our youth, and helped to enhance this project.

**Rupert Cross**: with whom I entertained lengthy conversations, "probing" the wealth of his memory, (which jogged my own), of the era and area of our own little world. Colon, Rep. of Panama.

# Richard Evraud Buery

The son of Richard M. Buery and Winifred J. Buery born in Colon Republic of Panama. His formal education started at Christ Church Academy, then transferred to the Public schools Pablo Arosemena, continuing on to Colegio Abel Bravo, he graduated with a (Bachelor in Commerce) with special interest in Mechanical Drawing, and musical Education. He enrolled in the school choir also the drum and bugle core.

He attended Church services at Christ Church By-the-sea Episcopal Church, Colon Republic of Panama, where he served as an acolyte and was eventually drafted by the reverend (who was also the Choir director), as the youngest member in the senior choir as a Tenor, and became quite active in the church's life. He continued his singing pursuit and joined various vocal ensembles, quartet as leading tenor, and other mixed musical groups. His musical interest led him to be part of "The Harmonizers" a quartet that became recognized as the best in town.

After graduating from school, he was employed by the U.S.Caribbean Command Post Exchange at Ft Kobe, Canal Zone as a sales clerk, and occasionally helped in the Photography section. He received a letter of commendation for excellent service. From the Major, QMC. On leaving.

His interest in Photography, led him to enroll in a correspondence course the School of Modern Photography. He joined International Photo Co. as a stock control clerk/Paymaster and part-time salesperson where he worked until December 15, 1962 when he traveled to the U.S.A. and pursued his passion, Photography, working as a wedding photographer with 2 Photo studious on weekends, as well as affiliation as official photographer for the Black Athletes Hall of Fame held that year in Las Vegas, NV. Also Miss Black America.

He was employed with Commanded Steamship Co. as a Bookkeeper, then Bunge Corp. as a Commodity Traffic Mgr. and retired after 23 years.

He met and married Olivia in 1964 and was blessed with 3 wonderful children, who presented us with 8 sources of joy (grandchildren).

He continued musical endeavors with, Choral groups, choirs and very involved With St Gabriel's Episcopal Church Brooklyn., New York. As an author he wrote a book *"What if? The question or a Statement"* which expresses the experiences sustained "from demolition to construction" of the new church.

This statue is made of glass strips assembled in the form of a running man, which was a gift from the people of Athens to the city, commemorating the origin of the marathon in Athens.

TEMPLE OF APOLLO    CORINTH

THE HEROD ATTICUS THEATER